What Readers Are Saying About
Seven Databases in Seven Weeks, Second Edition

Choosing a database is perhaps one of the most important architectural decisions a developer can make. *Seven Databases in Seven Weeks* provides a fantastic tour of different technologies and makes it easy to add each to your engineering toolbox.

➤ **Dave Parfitt**
Senior Site Reliability Engineer, Mozilla

By comparing each database technology to a tool you'd find in any workshop, the authors of *Seven Databases in Seven Weeks* provide a practical and well-balanced survey of a very diverse and highly varied datastore landscape. Anyone looking to get a handle on the database options available to them as a data platform should read this book and consider the trade-offs presented for each option.

➤ **Matthew Oldham**
Director of Data Architecture, Graphium Health

Reading this book felt like some of my best pair-programming experiences. It showed me how to get started, kept me engaged, and encouraged me to experiment on my own.

➤ **Jesse Hallett**
Open Source Mentor

This book will really give you an overview of what's out there so you can choose the best tool for the job.

➤ **Jesse Anderson**
Managing Director, Big Data Institute

Seven Databases in Seven Weeks, Second Edition

A Guide to Modern Databases and the NoSQL Movement

Luc Perkins
with Eric Redmond
and Jim R. Wilson

The Pragmatic Bookshelf

Raleigh, North Carolina

Many of the designations used by manufacturers and sellers to distinguish their products are claimed as trademarks. Where those designations appear in this book, and The Pragmatic Programmers, LLC was aware of a trademark claim, the designations have been printed in initial capital letters or in all capitals. The Pragmatic Starter Kit, The Pragmatic Programmer, Pragmatic Programming, Pragmatic Bookshelf, PragProg and the linking *g* device are trademarks of The Pragmatic Programmers, LLC.

Every precaution was taken in the preparation of this book. However, the publisher assumes no responsibility for errors or omissions, or for damages that may result from the use of information (including program listings) contained herein.

Our Pragmatic books, screencasts, and audio books can help you and your team create better software and have more fun. Visit us at *https://pragprog.com*.

The team that produced this book includes:

Publisher: Andy Hunt
VP of Operations: Janet Furlow
Managing Editor: Brian MacDonald
Supervising Editor: Jacquelyn Carter
Series Editor: Bruce A. Tate
Copy Editor: Nancy Rapoport
Indexing: Potomac Indexing, LLC
Layout: Gilson Graphics

For sales, volume licensing, and support, please contact *support@pragprog.com*.

For international rights, please contact *rights@pragprog.com*.

ISBN-13: 978-1-68050-253-4

Book version: P1.0—April 2018

Contents

Acknowledgments

A book with the size and scope of this one is never the work of just the authors, even if there are three of them. It requires the effort of many very smart people with superhuman eyes spotting as many mistakes as possible and providing valuable insights into the details of these technologies.

We'd like to thank, in no particular order, all of the folks who provided their time and expertise:

Dave Parfitt	Jerry Sievert	Jesse Hallett
Matthew Oldham	Ben Rady	Nick Capito
Jesse Anderson	Sean Moubry	

Finally, thanks to Bruce Tate for his experience and guidance.

We'd also like to sincerely thank the entire team at the Pragmatic Bookshelf. Thanks for entertaining this audacious project and seeing us through it. We're especially grateful to our editor, Jackie Carter. Your patient feedback made this book what it is today. Thanks to the whole team who worked so hard to polish this book and find all of our mistakes.

For anyone we missed, we hope you'll accept our apologies. Any omissions were certainly not intentional.

From Eric: Dear Noelle, you're not special; you're unique, and that's so much better. Thanks for living through another book. Thanks also to the database creators and committers for providing us something to write about and make a living at.

From Luc: First, I have to thank my wonderful family and friends for making my life a charmed one from the very beginning. Second, I have to thank a handful of people who believed in me and gave me a chance in the tech industry at different stages of my career: Lucas Carlson, Marko and Saša Gargenta, Troy Howard, and my co-author Eric Redmond for inviting me on board to prepare the most recent edition of this book. My journey in this industry has changed my life and I thank all of you for crucial breakthroughs.

From Jim: First, I want to thank my family: Ruthy, your boundless patience and encouragement have been heartwarming. Emma and Jimmy, you're two smart cookies, and your daddy loves you always. Also, a special thanks to all the unsung heroes who monitor IRC, message boards, mailing lists, and bug systems ready to help anyone who needs you. Your dedication to open source keeps these projects kicking.

Preface

If we use oil extraction as a metaphor for understanding data in the contemporary world, then databases flat-out constitute—or are deeply intertwined with—all aspects of the extraction chain, from the fields to the refineries, drills, and pumps. If you want to harness the potential of data—which has perhaps become as vital to our way of life as oil—then you need to understand databases because they are quite simply the most important piece of modern data equipment.

Databases are tools, a means to an end. But like any complex tool, databases also harbor their own stories and embody their own ways of looking at the world. The better you understand databases, the more capable you'll be of tapping into the ever-growing corpus of data at our disposal. That enhanced understanding could lead to anything from undertaking fun side projects to embarking on a career change or starting your own data-driven company.

Why a NoSQL Book

What exactly does the term *NoSQL* even mean? Which types of systems does the term include? How will NoSQL impact the practice of making great software? These were questions we wanted to answer—as much for ourselves as for others.

Looking back more than a half-decade later, the rise of NoSQL isn't so much buzzworthy as it is an accepted fact. You can still read plenty of articles about NoSQL technologies on HackerNews, TechCrunch, or even WIRED, but the tenor of those articles has changed from starry-eyed prophecy ("NoSQL will change everything!") to more standard reporting ("check out this new Redis feature!"). NoSQL is now a mainstay and a steadily maturing one at that.

But don't write a eulogy for relational databases—the "SQL" in "NoSQL"—just yet. Although NoSQL databases *have* gained significant traction in the technological landscape, it's still far too early to declare "traditional" relational database models as dead or even dying. From the release of Google's BigQuery and Spanner to continued rapid development of MySQL, PostgreSQL, and others, relational databases are showing no signs of slowing down. NoSQL hasn't killed SQL; instead, the galaxy of uses for data has expanded, and both paradigms continue to grow and evolve to keep up with the demand.

So read this book as a guide to powerful, compelling databases with similar worldviews—*not* as a guide to the "new" way of doing things or as a nail in the coffin of SQL. We're writing a second edition so that a new generation of data engineers, application developers, and others can get a high-level understanding and deep dive into specific databases in one place.

Why Seven Databases

This book's format originally came to us when we read Bruce Tate's exemplary *Seven Languages in Seven Weeks [Tat10]* many years ago. That book's style of progressively introducing languages struck a chord with us. We felt teaching databases in the same manner would provide a smooth medium for tackling some of these tough NoSQL questions while also creating conceptual bridges across chapters.

What's in This Book

This book is aimed at experienced application developers, data engineers, tech enthusiasts, and others who are seeking a well-rounded understanding of the modern database landscape. Prior database experience is not strictly required, but it helps.

After a brief introduction, this book tackles a series of seven databases chapter by chapter. The databases were chosen to span five different database genres or styles, which are discussed in Chapter 1, *Introduction*, on page 1. In order, the databases covered are PostgreSQL, Apache HBase, MongoDB, Apache CouchDB, Neo4J, DynamoDB, and Redis.

Each chapter is designed to be taken as a long weekend's worth of work, split up into three days. Each day ends with exercises that expand on the topics and concepts just introduced, and each chapter culminates in a wrap-up discussion that summarizes the good and bad points about the database. You may choose to move a little faster or slower, but it's important to grasp each day's concepts before continuing. We've tried to craft examples that explore each database's distinguishing features. To really understand what these databases have to offer, you have to spend some time using them, and that means rolling up your sleeves and doing some work.

Although you may be tempted to skip chapters, we designed this book to be read linearly. Some concepts, such as mapreduce, are introduced in depth in earlier chapters and then skimmed over in later ones. The goal of this book is to attain a solid understanding of the modern database field, so we recommend you read them all.

What This Book Is Not

Before reading this book, you should know what it *won't* cover.

This Is Not an Installation Guide

Installing the databases in this book is sometimes easy, sometimes a bit of a challenge, and sometimes downright frustrating. For some databases, you'll be able to use stock packages or tools such as apt-get (on many Linux systems) or Homebrew (if you're a Mac OS user) and for others you may need to compile from source. We'll point out some useful tips here and there, but by and large you're on your own. Cutting out installation steps allows us to pack in more useful examples and a discussion of concepts, which is what you really came for anyway, right?

Administration Manual? We Think Not

In addition to installation, this book will also not cover everything you'd find in an administration manual. Each of these databases offers myriad options, settings, switches, and configuration details, most of which are well covered online in each database's official documentation and on forums such as StackOverflow. We're much more interested in teaching you useful concepts and providing full immersion than we are in focusing on the day-to-day operations. Though the characteristics of the databases can change based on operational settings—and we discuss these characteristics in some chapters—we won't be able to go into all the nitty-gritty details of all possible configurations. There simply isn't space!

A Note to Windows Users

This book is inherently about choices, predominantly open source software on *nix platforms. Microsoft environments tend to strive for an integrated environment, which limits many choices to a smaller predefined set. As such, the databases we cover are open source and are developed by (and largely *for*) users of *nix systems. This is not our own bias so much as a reflection of the current state of affairs.

Consequently, our tutorial-esque examples are presumed to be run in a *nix shell. If you run Windows and want to give it a try anyway, we recommend setting up Bash on Windows[1] or Cygwin[2] to give you the best shot at success. You may also want to consider running a Linux virtual machine.

Code Examples and Conventions

This book contains code in a variety of languages. In part, this is a consequence of the databases that we cover. We've attempted to limit our choice of languages to Ruby/JRuby and JavaScript. We prefer command-line tools to scripts, but we will introduce other languages to get the job done—such as PL/pgSQL (Postgres) and Cypher (Neo4J). We'll also explore writing some server-side JavaScript applications with Node.js.

Except where noted, code listings are provided in full, usually ready to be executed at your leisure. Samples and snippets are syntax highlighted according to the rules of the language involved. Shell commands are prefixed by $ for *nix shells or by a different token for database-specific shells (such as > in MongoDB).

Credits

Apache, Apache HBase, Apache CouchDB, HBase, CouchDB, and the HBase and CouchDB logos are trademarks of The Apache Software Foundation. Used with permission. No endorsement by The Apache Software Foundation is implied by the use of these marks.

Online Resources

The Pragmatic Bookshelf's page for this book[3] is a great resource. There you'll find downloads for all the source code presented in this book. You'll also find feedback tools such as a community forum and an errata submission form where you can recommend changes to future releases of the book.

Thanks for coming along with us on this journey through the modern database landscape.

Luc Perkins, Eric Redmond, and Jim R. Wilson
April 2018

---

1. https://msdn.microsoft.com/en-us/commandline/wsl/about
2. http://www.cygwin.com/
3. http://pragprog.com/book/pwrdata/seven-databases-in-seven-weeks

## CHAPTER 1

Introduction

The non-relational database paradigm—we'll call it *NoSQL* throughout this book, following now-standard usage—is no longer the fledgling upstart that it once was. When the NoSQL alternative to relational databases came on the scene, the "old" model was the *de facto* option for problems big and small. Today, that relational model is still going strong and for many reasons:

- Databases such as PostgreSQL, MySQL, Microsoft SQL Server, and Oracle, amongst many others, are still widely used, discussed, and actively developed.

- Knowing how to run SQL queries remains a highly sought-after skill for software engineers, data analysts, and others.

- There remains a vast universe of use cases for which a relational database is still beyond any reasonable doubt the way to go.

But at the same time, NoSQL has risen far beyond its initial upstart status and is now a fixture in the technology world. The concepts surrounding it, such as the CAP theorem, are widely discussed at programming conferences, on Hacker News, on StackOverflow, and beyond. Schemaless design, massive horizontal scaling capabilities, simple replication, new query methods that don't feel like SQL at all—these hallmarks of NoSQL have all gone mainstream. Not long ago, a Fortune 500 CTO may have looked at NoSQL solutions with bemusement if not horror; now, a CTO would be crazy not to at least consider them for some of their workloads.

In this book, we explore seven databases across a wide spectrum of database styles. We start with a relational database, PostgreSQL, largely for the sake of comparison (though Postgres is quite interesting in its own right). From there, things get a lot stranger as we wade into a world of databases united above all by what they aren't. In the process of reading this book, you will learn the various capabilities that each database presents along with some inevitable trade-offs—rich vs. fast queryability, absolute vs. eventual consistency, and so on—and how to make deeply informed decisions for your use cases.

It Starts with a Question

The central question of *Seven Databases in Seven Weeks* is this: what database or combination of databases best resolves your problem? If you walk away understanding how to make that choice, given your particular needs and resources at hand, we're happy.

But to answer that question, you'll need to understand your options. To that end, we'll take you on a deep dive—one that is both conceptual and practical —into each of seven databases. We'll uncover the good parts and point out the not so good. You'll get your hands dirty with everything from basic CRUD operations to fine-grained schema design to running distributed systems in far-away datacenters, all in the name of finding answers to these questions:

- *What type of database is this?* Databases come in a variety of genres, such as relational, key-value, columnar, document-oriented, and graph. Popular databases—including those covered in this book—can generally be grouped into one of these broad categories. You'll learn about each type and the kinds of problems for which they're best suited. We've specifically chosen databases to span these categories, including one relational database (Postgres), a key-value store (Redis), a column-oriented database (HBase), two document-oriented databases (MongoDB, CouchDB), a graph database (Neo4J), and a cloud-based database that's a difficult-to-classify hybrid (DynamoDB).

- *What was the driving force?* Databases are not created in a vacuum. They are designed to solve problems presented by real use cases. RDBMS databases arose in a world where query flexibility was more important than flexible schemas. On the other hand, column-oriented databases were built to be well suited for storing large amounts of data across several machines, while data relationships took a backseat. We'll cover use cases for each database, along with related examples.

- *How do you talk to it?* Databases often support a variety of connection options. Whenever a database has an interactive command-line interface, we'll start with that before moving on to other means. Where programming is needed, we've stuck mostly to Ruby and JavaScript, though a few other languages sneak in from time to time—such as PL/pgSQL (Postgres) and Cypher (Neo4J). At a lower level, we'll discuss protocols such as REST

(CouchDB) and Thrift (HBase). In the final chapter, we present a more complex database setup tied together by a Node.js JavaScript implementation.

- *What makes it unique?* Any database will support writing data and reading it back out again. What else it does varies greatly from one database to the next. Some allow querying on arbitrary fields. Some provide indexing for rapid lookup. Some support ad hoc queries, while queries must be planned for others. Is the data schema a rigid framework enforced by the database or merely a set of guidelines to be renegotiated at will? Understanding capabilities and constraints will help you pick the right database for the job.

- *How does it perform?* How does this database function and at what cost? Does it support sharding? How about replication? Does it distribute data evenly using consistent hashing, or does it keep like data together? Is this database tuned for reading, writing, or some other operation? How much control do you have over its tuning, if any?

- *How does it scale?* Scalability is related to performance. Talking about scalability without the context of what you want to *scale to* is generally fruitless. This book will give you the background you need to ask the right questions to establish that context. While the discussion on *how* to scale each database will be intentionally light, in these pages you'll find out whether each database is geared more for horizontal scaling (MongoDB, HBase, DynamoDB), traditional vertical scaling (Postgres, Neo4J, Redis), or something in between.

Our goal is not to guide a novice to mastery of any of these databases. A full treatment of any one of them could (and does) fill entire books. But by the end of this book, you should have a firm grasp of the strengths of each, as well as how they differ.

The Genres

Like music, databases can be broadly classified into one or more styles. An individual song may share all of the same notes with other songs, but some are more appropriate for certain uses. Not many people blast Bach's *Mass in B Minor* from an open convertible speeding down the 405. Similarly, some databases are better than others for certain situations. The question you must always ask yourself is not "Can I use this database to store and refine this data?" but rather, "Should I?"

In this section, we're going to explore five main database genres. We'll also take a look at the databases we're going to focus on for each genre.

It's important to remember most of the data problems you'll face could be solved by most or all of the databases in this book, not to mention other databases. The question is less about whether a given database style could be shoehorned to model your data and more about whether it's the best fit for your problem space, your usage patterns, and your available resources. You'll learn the art of divining whether a database is intrinsically useful to you.

Relational

The relational model is generally what comes to mind for most people with database experience. Relational database management systems (RDBMSs) are set-theory-based systems implemented as two-dimensional tables with rows and columns. The canonical means of interacting with an RDBMS is to write queries in Structured Query Language (SQL). Data values are typed and may be numeric, strings, dates, uninterpreted blobs, or other types. The types are enforced by the system. Importantly, tables can join and morph into new, more complex tables because of their mathematical basis in relational (set) theory.

There are lots of open source relational databases to choose from, including MySQL, H2, HSQLDB, SQLite, and many others. The one we cover is in Chapter 2, *PostgreSQL*, on page 9.

PostgreSQL

Battle-hardened PostgreSQL is by far the oldest and most robust database we cover. With its adherence to the SQL standard, it will feel familiar to anyone who has worked with relational databases before, and it provides a solid point of comparison to the other databases we'll work with. We'll also explore some of SQL's unsung features and Postgres's specific advantages. There's something for everyone here, from SQL novice to expert.

Key-Value

The key-value (KV) store is the simplest model we cover. As the name implies, a KV store pairs keys to values in much the same way that a map (or hashtable) would in any popular programming language. Some KV implementations permit complex value types such as hashes or lists, but this is not required. Some KV implementations provide a means of iterating through the keys, but this again is an added bonus. A file system could be considered a key-value store if you think of the file path as the key and the file contents as the value. Because the KV moniker demands so little, databases of this type can be incredibly performant in a number of scenarios but generally won't be helpful when you have complex query and aggregation needs.

As with relational databases, many open source options are available. Some of the more popular offerings include memcached, Voldemort, Riak, and two that we cover in this book: Redis and DynamoDB.

Redis

Redis provides for complex datatypes such as sorted sets and hashes, as well as basic message patterns such as publish-subscribe and blocking queues. It also has one of the most robust query mechanisms for a KV store. And by caching writes in memory before committing to disk, Redis gains amazing performance in exchange for increased risk of data loss in the case of a hardware failure. This characteristic makes it a good fit for caching noncritical data and for acting as a message broker. We leave it until the end so we can build a multidatabase application with Redis and others working together in harmony.

DynamoDB

DynamoDB is the only database in this book that is both not open source and available only as a managed cloud service.

> ## No More Riak?
>
> The first edition of *Seven Databases in Seven Weeks* had a chapter on Riak. For the second edition, we made the difficult decision to retire that chapter and replace it with the chapter on DynamoDB that you see here. There are a number of reasons for this choice:
>
> - Cloud-hosted databases are being used more and more frequently. We would be doing the current NoSQL landscape a disservice by not including a public cloud database service. We chose DynamoDB for reasons that we'll go over in that chapter.
>
> - Because we wanted to include DynamoDB (a key-value store) and stick with the "seven" theme, something had to give. With Redis, we already had a key-value store covered.
>
> - Somewhat more somberly, for commercial reasons that we won't discuss here, the future of Riak as an actively developed database and open source project is now fundamentally in doubt in ways that are true of no other database in this book.
>
> Riak is an extremely unique, intriguing, and technologically impressive database, and we strongly urge you to explore it in other venues. The official docs are a good place to start.[a]
>
> ---
>
> a.   http://docs.basho.com

Columnar

Columnar, or column-oriented, databases are so named because the important aspect of their design is that data from a given column (in the two-dimensional table sense) is stored together. By contrast, a row-oriented database (like an RDBMS) keeps information about a row together. The difference may seem inconsequential, but the impact of this design decision runs deep. In column-oriented databases, adding columns is quite inexpensive and is done on a row-by-row basis. Each row can have a different set of columns, or none at all, allowing tables to remain *sparse* without incurring a storage cost for null values. With respect to structure, columnar is about midway between relational and key-value.

In the columnar database market, there's somewhat less competition than in relational databases or key-value stores. The two most popular are HBase (which we cover in Chapter 3, *HBase*, on page 53) and Cassandra.

HBase

This column-oriented database shares the most similarities with the relational model of all the nonrelational databases we cover (though DynamoDB comes close). Using Google's BigTable paper as a blueprint, HBase is built on Hadoop and the Hadoop Distributed File System (HDFS) and designed for scaling horizontally on clusters of commodity hardware. HBase makes strong consistency guarantees and features tables with rows and columns—which should make SQL fans feel right at home. Out-of-the-box support for versioning and compression sets this database apart in the "Big Data" space.

Document

Document-oriented databases store, well, documents. In short, a document is like a hash, with a unique ID field and values that may be any of a variety of types, including more hashes. Documents can contain nested structures, and so they exhibit a high degree of flexibility, allowing for variable domains. The system imposes few restrictions on incoming data, as long as it meets the basic requirement of being expressible as a document. Different document databases take different approaches with respect to indexing, ad hoc querying, replication, consistency, and other design decisions. Choosing wisely between them requires that you understand these differences and how they impact your particular use cases.

The two major open source players in the document database market are MongoDB, which we cover in Chapter 4, *MongoDB*, on page 93, and CouchDB, covered in Chapter 5, *CouchDB*, on page 135.

MongoDB

MongoDB is designed to be *huge* (the name *mongo* is extracted from the word hu*mongo*us). Mongo server configurations attempt to remain consistent—if you write something, subsequent reads will receive the same value (until the next update). This feature makes it attractive to those coming from an RDBMS background. It also offers atomic read-write operations such as incrementing a value and deep querying of nested document structures. Using JavaScript for its query language, MongoDB supports both simple queries and complex mapreduce jobs.

CouchDB

CouchDB targets a wide variety of deployment scenarios, from the datacenter to the desktop, on down to the smartphone. Written in Erlang, CouchDB has a distinct ruggedness largely lacking in other databases. With nearly incorruptible data files, CouchDB remains highly available even in the face of intermittent connectivity loss or hardware failure. Like Mongo, CouchDB's native query language is JavaScript. Views consist of mapreduce functions, which are stored as documents and replicated between nodes like any other data.

Graph

One of the less commonly used database styles, graph databases excel at dealing with highly interconnected data. A graph database consists of nodes and relationships between nodes. Both nodes and relationships can have properties—key-value pairs—that store data. The real strength of graph databases is traversing through the nodes by following relationships.

In Chapter 6, *Neo4J*, on page 177, we discuss the most popular graph database today.

Neo4J

One operation where other databases often fall flat is crawling through self-referential or otherwise intricately linked data. This is exactly where Neo4J shines. The benefit of using a graph database is the ability to quickly traverse nodes and relationships to find relevant data. Often found in social networking applications, graph databases are gaining traction for their flexibility, with Neo4j as a pinnacle implementation.

Polyglot

In the wild, databases are often used alongside other databases. It's still common to find a lone relational database, but over time it is becoming popular to use several databases together, leveraging their strengths to create an ecosystem that is more powerful, capable, and robust than the sum of its parts. This practice, known as *polyglot persistence*, is covered in Chapter 9, *Wrapping Up*, on page 305.

Onward and Upward

Five years after the initial edition of this book, we're *still* in the midst of a Cambrian explosion of data storage options. It's hard to predict exactly what will evolve out of this explosion in the coming years but we can be fairly certain that the pure domination of any particular strategy (relational or otherwise) is unlikely. Instead, we'll see increasingly specialized databases, each suited to a particular (but certainly overlapping) set of ideal problem spaces. And just as there are jobs today that call for expertise specifically in administrating relational databases (DBAs), we are going to see the rise of their nonrelational counterparts.

Databases, like programming languages and libraries, are another set of tools that every developer should know. Every good carpenter must understand what's in their tool belt. And like any good builder, you can never hope to be a master without a familiarity of the many options at your disposal.

Consider this a crash course in the workshop. In this book, you'll swing some hammers, spin some power drills, play with some nail guns, and in the end be able to build so much more than a birdhouse. So, without further ado, let's wield our first database: PostgreSQL.

## CHAPTER 2

PostgreSQL

PostgreSQL is the hammer of the database world. It's commonly understood, often readily available, and sturdy, and it solves a surprising number of problems if you swing hard enough. No one can hope to be an expert builder without understanding this most common of tools.

PostgreSQL (or just "Postgres") is a relational database management system (or RDBMS for short). Relational databases are set-theory-based systems in which data is stored in two-dimensional tables consisting of data rows and strictly enforced column types. Despite the growing interest in newer database trends, the relational style remains the most popular and probably will for quite some time. Even in a book that focuses on non-relational "NoSQL" systems, a solid grounding in RDBMS remains essential. PostgreSQL is quite possibly the finest open source RDBMS available, and in this chapter you'll see that it provides a great introduction to this paradigm.

While the prevalence of relational databases can be partially attributed to their vast toolkits (triggers, stored procedures, views, advanced indexes), their data safety (via ACID compliance), or their mind share (many programmers speak and think relationally), query pliancy plays a central role as well. Unlike some other databases, you don't need to know in advance *how* you plan to use the data. If a relational schema is normalized, queries are flexible. You can start storing data and worrying about how exactly you'll use it later on, even changing your entire querying model over time as your needs change.

That's Post-greS-Q-L

PostgreSQL is by far the oldest and most battle-tested database in this book. It has domain-specific plug-ins for things like natural language parsing, multidimensional indexing, geographic queries, custom datatypes, and much more. It has sophisticated transaction handling and built-in stored procedures

So, What's with the Name?

PostgreSQL has existed in the current project incarnation since 1995, but its roots go back much further. The project was originally created at UC Berkeley in the early 1970s and called the Interactive Graphics and Retrieval System, or "Ingres" for short. In the 1980s, an improved version was launched post-Ingres—shortened to "Postgres." The project ended at Berkeley proper in 1993 but was picked up again by the open source community as Postgres95. It was later renamed to PostgreSQL in 1996 to denote its rather new SQL support and has retained the name ever since.

for a dozen languages, and it runs on a variety of platforms. PostgreSQL has built-in Unicode support, sequences, table inheritance, and subselects, and it is one of the most ANSI SQL-compliant relational databases on the market. It's fast and reliable, can handle terabytes of data, and has been proven to run in high-profile production projects such as Skype, Yahoo!, France's Caisse Nationale d'Allocations Familiales (CNAF), Brazil's Caixa Bank, and the United States' Federal Aviation Administration (FAA).

You can install PostgreSQL in many ways, depending on your operating system.[1] Once you have Postgres installed, create a schema called 7dbs using the following command:

```
$ createdb 7dbs
```

We'll be using the 7dbs schema for the remainder of this chapter.

Day 1: Relations, CRUD, and Joins

While we won't assume that you're a relational database expert, we do assume that you've confronted a database or two in the past. If so, odds are good that the database was relational. We'll start with creating our own schemas and populating them. Then we'll take a look at querying for values and finally explore what makes relational databases so special: the table join.

Like most databases you'll read about, Postgres provides a back-end server that does all of the work and a command-line shell to connect to the running server. The server communicates through port 5432 by default, which you can connect to the shell using the psql command. Let's connect to our 7dbs schema now:

```
$ psql 7dbs
```

---

1. http://www.postgresql.org/download/

PostgreSQL prompts with the name of the database followed by a hash mark (#) if you run as an administrator and by a dollar sign ($) as a regular user. The shell also comes equipped with perhaps the best built-in documentation that you will find in any console. Typing \h lists information about SQL commands and \? helps with psql-specific commands, namely those that begin with a backslash. You can find usage details about each SQL command in the following way (the output that follows is truncated):

```
7dbs=# \h CREATE INDEX
Command:     CREATE INDEX
Description: define a new index
Syntax:
CREATE [ UNIQUE ] INDEX [ CONCURRENTLY ] [ name ] ON table [ USING method ]
    ( { column | ( expression ) } [ opclass ] [ ASC | DESC ] [ NULLS ...
    [ WITH ( storage_parameter = value [, ... ] ) ]
    [ TABLESPACE tablespace ]
    [ WHERE predicate ]
```

Before we dig too deeply into Postgres, it would be good to familiarize yourself with this useful tool. It's worth looking over (or brushing up on) a few common commands, such as SELECT and CREATE TABLE.

Starting with SQL

PostgreSQL follows the SQL convention of calling relations TABLEs, attributes COLUMNs, and tuples ROWs. For consistency, we will use this terminology, though you may occasionally encounter the mathematical terms *relations*, *attributes*, and *tuples*. For more on these concepts, see "Mathematical Relations" in the text on page 12.

Working with Tables

PostgreSQL, being of the relational style, is a design-first database. First you design the schema; then you enter data that conforms to the definition of that schema.

On CRUD

CRUD is a useful mnemonic for remembering the basic data management operations: *Create*, *Read*, *Update*, and *Delete*. These generally correspond to inserting new records (*creating*), modifying existing records (*updating*), and removing records you no longer need (*deleting*). All of the other operations you use a database for (any crazy query you can dream up) are *read operations*. If you can CRUD, you can do just about anything. We'll use this term throughout the book.

Mathematical Relations

Relational databases are so named because they contain *relations* (tables). Tables are sets of *tuples* (rows) that map *attributes* to atomic values—for example, {name: 'Genghis Khan', died_at_age: 65}. The available attributes are defined by a *header*, which is a tuple of attributes mapped to some *domain* or constraining type (columns, for example {name: string, age: int}). That's the gist of the relational structure.

Implementations are much more practically minded than the names imply, despite sounding so mathematical. So why bring them up? We're trying to make the point that relational databases are *relational* based on mathematics. They aren't relational because tables "relate" to each other via foreign keys. Whether any such constraints exist is beside the point.

The power of the model is certainly in the math, even though the math is largely hidden from you. This magic allows users to express powerful queries while the system optimizes based on predefined patterns. RDBMSs are built atop a set theory branch called *relational algebra*—a combination of selections (WHERE ...), projections (SELECT ...), Cartesian products (JOIN ...), and more, as shown in the figure that follows.

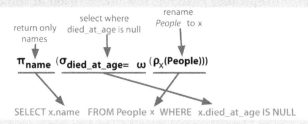

You can imagine relations as arrays of arrays, where a table is an array of rows, each of which contains an array of attribute/value pairs. One way of working with tables at the code level would be to iterate across all rows in a table and then iterate across each attribute/value pair within the row. But let's be real: that sounds like a real chore. Fortunately, relational queries are much more declarative—and fun to work with—than that. They're derived from a branch of mathematics known as *tuple relational calculus*, which can be converted to relational algebra. PostgreSQL and other RDBMSs optimize queries by performing this conversion and simplifying the algebra. You can see that the SQL in the diagram that follows is the same as in the previous diagram.

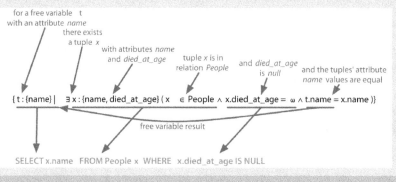

Creating a table involves giving the table a name and a list of columns with types and (optional) constraint information. Each table should also nominate a unique identifier column to pinpoint specific rows. That identifier is called a PRIMARY KEY. The SQL to create a countries table looks like this:

```
CREATE TABLE countries (
  country_code char(2) PRIMARY KEY,
  country_name text UNIQUE
);
```

This new table will store a set of rows, where each is identified by a two-character code and the name is unique. These columns both have *constraints*. The PRIMARY KEY constrains the country_code column to disallow duplicate country codes. Only one us and one gb may exist. We explicitly gave country_name a similar unique constraint, although it is not a primary key. We can populate the countries table by inserting a few rows.

```
INSERT INTO countries (country_code, country_name)
VALUES ('us','United States'), ('mx','Mexico'), ('au','Australia'),
       ('gb','United Kingdom'), ('de','Germany'), ('ll','Loompaland');
```

Let's test our unique constraint. Attempting to add a duplicate country_name will cause our unique constraint to fail, thus disallowing insertion. Constraints are how relational databases such as PostgreSQL ensure kosher data.

```
INSERT INTO countries
VALUES ('uk','United Kingdom');
```

This will return an error indicating that the Key (country_name)=(United Kingdom) already exists.

We can validate that the proper rows were inserted by reading them using the SELECT...FROM table command.

```
SELECT *
FROM countries;
 country_code | country_name
--------------+---------------
 us           | United States
 mx           | Mexico
 au           | Australia
 gb           | United Kingdom
 de           | Germany
 ll           | Loompaland
(6 rows)
```

According to any respectable map, Loompaland isn't a real place, so let's remove it from the table. You specify which row to remove using the WHERE clause. The row whose country_code equals ll will be removed.

```
DELETE FROM countries
WHERE country_code = 'll';
```

With only real countries left in the countries table, let's add a cities table. To ensure any inserted country_code also exists in our countries table, we add the REFERENCES keyword. Because the country_code column references another table's key, it's known as the *foreign key* constraint.

```
CREATE TABLE cities (
  name text NOT NULL,
  postal_code varchar(9) CHECK (postal_code <> ''),
  country_code char(2) REFERENCES countries,
  PRIMARY KEY (country_code, postal_code)
);
```

This time, we constrained the name in cities by disallowing NULL values. We constrained postal_code by checking that no values are empty strings (<> means *not equal*). Furthermore, because a PRIMARY KEY uniquely identifies a row, we created a compound key: country_code + postal_code. Together, they uniquely define a row.

Postgres also has a rich set of datatypes, by far the richest amongst the databases in this book. You've just seen three different string representations: text (a string of any length), varchar(9) (a string of variable length up to nine characters), and char(2) (a string of exactly two characters). With our schema in place, let's insert *Toronto, CA*.

```
INSERT INTO cities
VALUES ('Toronto','M4C1B5','ca');

ERROR:  insert or update on table "cities" violates foreign key constraint
  "cities_country_code_fkey"
DETAIL:  Key (country_code)=(ca) is not present in table "countries".
```

This failure is good! Because country_code REFERENCES countries, the country_code must exist in the countries table. As shown in the figure on page 15, the REFERENCES keyword constrains fields to another table's primary key. This is called *maintaining referential integrity*, and it ensures our data is always correct.

It's worth noting that NULL is valid for cities.country_code because NULL represents the lack of a value. If you want to disallow a NULL country_code reference, you would define the table cities column like this: country_code char(2) REFERENCES countries NOT NULL.

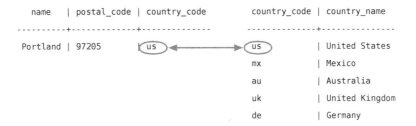

Now let's try another insert, this time with a U.S. city (quite possibly the greatest of U.S. cities).

```
INSERT INTO cities
VALUES ('Portland','87200','us');

INSERT 0 1
```

This is a successful insert, to be sure. But we mistakenly entered a postal_code that doesn't actually exist in Portland. One postal code that does exist and may just belong to one of the authors is *97206*. Rather than delete and reinsert the value, we can update it inline.

```
UPDATE cities
SET postal_code = '97206'
WHERE name = 'Portland';
```

We have now Created, Read, Updated, and Deleted table rows.

Join Reads

All of the other databases you'll read about in this book perform CRUD operations as well. What sets relational databases like PostgreSQL apart is their ability to join tables together when reading them. Joining, in essence, is an operation taking two separate tables and combining them in some way to return a single table. It's somewhat like putting together puzzle pieces to create a bigger, more complete picture.

The basic form of a join is the *inner join*. In the simplest form, you specify two columns (one from each table) to match by, using the ON keyword.

```
SELECT cities.*, country_name
FROM cities INNER JOIN countries /* or just FROM cities JOIN countries */
  ON cities.country_code = countries.country_code;
```

country_code	name	postal_code	country_name
us	Portland	97206	United States

The join returns a single table, sharing all columns' values of the cities table plus the matching country_name value from the countries table.

You can also join a table like cities that has a compound primary key. To test a compound join, let's create a new table that stores a list of venues.

A venue exists in both a *postal code* and a specific *country*. The *foreign key* must be two columns that reference both cities *primary key* columns. (MATCH FULL is a constraint that ensures either both values exist or both are NULL.)

```
CREATE TABLE venues (
  venue_id SERIAL PRIMARY KEY,
  name varchar(255),
  street_address text,
  type char(7) CHECK ( type in ('public','private') ) DEFAULT 'public',
  postal_code varchar(9),
  country_code char(2),
  FOREIGN KEY (country_code, postal_code)
    REFERENCES cities (country_code, postal_code) MATCH FULL
);
```

This venue_id column is a common primary key setup: automatically incremented integers (1, 2, 3, 4, and so on). You make this identifier using the SERIAL keyword. (MySQL has a similar construct called AUTO_INCREMENT.)

```
INSERT INTO venues (name, postal_code, country_code)
VALUES ('Crystal Ballroom', '97206', 'us');
```

Although we did not set a venue_id value, creating the row populated it.

Back to our compound join. Joining the venues table with the cities table requires *both* foreign key columns. To save on typing, you can alias the table names by following the real table name directly with an alias, with an optional AS between (for example, venues v or venues AS v).

```
SELECT v.venue_id, v.name, c.name
FROM venues v INNER JOIN cities c
  ON v.postal_code=c.postal_code AND v.country_code=c.country_code;
```

```
 venue_id |       name        |   name
----------+-------------------+----------
        1 | Crystal Ballroom  | Portland
```

You can optionally request that PostgreSQL return columns after insertion by ending the query with a RETURNING statement.

```
INSERT INTO venues (name, postal_code, country_code)
VALUES ('Voodoo Doughnut', '97206', 'us') RETURNING venue_id;
```

```
 id
----
  2
```

This provides the new venue_id without issuing another query.

The Outer Limits

In addition to inner joins, PostgreSQL can also perform *outer joins*. Outer joins are a way of merging two tables when the results of one table must always be returned, whether or not any matching column values exist on the other table.

It's easiest to give an example, but to do that, we'll create a new table named events. This one is up to you. Your events table should have these columns: a SERIAL integer event_id, a title, starts and ends (of type *timestamp*), and a venue_id (foreign key that references venues). A schema definition diagram covering all the tables we've made so far is shown in the following figure.

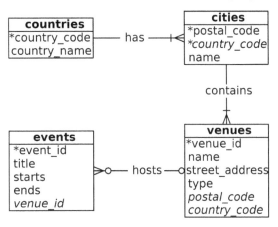

After creating the events table, INSERT the following values (timestamps are inserted as a string like *2018-02-15 17:30*) for two holidays and a club we *do not talk about*:

title	starts	ends	venue_id	event_id
Fight Club	2018-02-15 17:30:00	2018-02-15 19:30:00	2	1
April Fools Day	2018-04-01 00:00:00	2018-04-01 23:59:00		2
Christmas Day	2018-02-15 19:30:00	2018-12-25 23:59:00		3

Let's first craft a query that returns an event title and venue name as an inner join (the word INNER from INNER JOIN is not required, so leave it off here).

```
SELECT e.title, v.name
FROM events e JOIN venues v
  ON e.venue_id = v.venue_id;

     title    |       name
--------------+------------------
 Fight Club   | Voodoo Doughnut
```

INNER JOIN will return a row only *if the column values match*. Because we can't have NULL venues.venue_id, the two NULL events.venue_ids refer to nothing. Retrieving all of the events, whether or not they have a venue, requires a LEFT OUTER JOIN (shortened to LEFT JOIN).

```
SELECT e.title, v.name
FROM events e LEFT JOIN venues v
ON e.venue_id = v.venue_id;
      title        |       name
-------------------+-----------------
 Fight Club        | Voodoo Doughnut
 April Fools Day   |
 Christmas Day     |
```

If you require the inverse, all venues and only matching events, use a RIGHT JOIN. Finally, there's the FULL JOIN, which is the union of LEFT and RIGHT; you're guaranteed all values from each table, joined wherever columns match.

Fast Lookups with Indexing

The speed of PostgreSQL (and any other RDBMS) lies in its efficient management of blocks of data, reduced disk reads, query optimization, and other techniques. But those only go so far in fetching results quickly. If we select the title of *Christmas Day* from the events table, the algorithm must *scan* every row for a match to return. Without an *index*, each row must be read from disk to know whether a query should return it. See the following.

```
matches "Christmas Day"? No.──────▶LARP Club        |       2 |          1

matches "Christmas Day"? No.──────▶April Fools Day  |         |          2

matches "Christmas Day"? Yes!─────▶Christmas Day    |         |          3
```

An index is a special data structure built to avoid a full table scan when performing a query. When running CREATE TABLE commands, you may have noticed a message like this:

```
CREATE TABLE / PRIMARY KEY will create implicit index "events_pkey" \
for table "events"
```

PostgreSQL automatically creates an index on the primary key—in particular a B-tree index—where the key is the primary key value and where the value points to a row on disk, as shown in the top figure on page 19. Using the UNIQUE keyword is another way to force an index on a table column.

You can explicitly add a hash index using the CREATE INDEX command, where each value must be unique (like a hashtable or a map).

```
CREATE INDEX events_title
  ON events USING hash (title);
```

```
                    SELECT * FROM events WHERE event_id =  2;


    "events.id" hash Index          "events" Table
              1  ────────▶   LARP Club          |    2 |        1
              2  ────────▶   April Fools Day |          |        2
              3  ────────▶   Christmas Day   |          |        3
```

For less-than/greater-than/equals-to matches, we want an index more flexible than a simple hash, like a B-tree, which can match on ranged queries (see the following figure).

SELECT * FROM some_table WHERE some_number >= 2108900;

Consider a query to find all events that are on or after April 1.

```
SELECT *
FROM events
WHERE starts >= '2018-04-01';
 event_id |       title       |        starts        | ...
----------+-------------------+----------------------+-----
        2 | April Fools Day   | 2018-04-01 00:00:00  | ...
        3 | Christmas Day     | 2018-12-25 00:00:00  | ...
```

For this, a tree is the perfect data structure. To index the starts column with a B-tree, use this:

```
CREATE INDEX events_starts
  ON events USING btree (starts);
```

Now our query over a range of dates will avoid a full table scan. It makes a huge difference when scanning millions or billions of rows.

We can inspect our work with this command to list all indexes in the schema:

```
7dbs=# \di
```

It's worth noting that when you set a FOREIGN KEY constraint, PostgreSQL will *not* automatically create an index on the targeted column(s). You'll need to create an index on the targeted column(s) yourself. Even if you don't like using database constraints (that's right, we're looking at you, Ruby on Rails developers), you will often find yourself creating indexes on columns you plan to join against in order to help speed up foreign key joins.

Day 1 Wrap-Up

We sped through a lot today and covered many terms. Here's a recap:

Term	Definition
Column	A domain of values of a certain type, sometimes called an *attribute*
Row	An object comprised of a set of column values, sometimes called a *tuple*
Table	A set of rows with the same columns, sometimes called a *relation*
Primary key	The unique value that pinpoints a specific row
Foreign key	A data constraint that ensures that each entry in a column in one table uniquely corresponds to a row in another table (or even the same table)
CRUD	Create, Read, Update, Delete
SQL	Structured Query Language, the *lingua franca* of a relational database
Join	Combining two tables into one by some matching columns
Left join	Combining two tables into one by some matching columns or NULL if nothing matches the left table
Index	A data structure to optimize selection of a specific set of columns

Term	Definition
B-tree index	A good standard index; values are stored as a balanced tree data structure; very flexible; B-tree indexes are the default in Postgres
Hash index	Another good standard index in which each index value is unique; hash indexes tend to offer better performance for comparison operations than B-tree indexes but are less flexible and don't allow for things like range queries

Relational databases have been the *de facto* data management strategy for forty years—many of us began our careers in the midst of their evolution. Others may disagree, but we think that understanding "NoSQL" databases is a non-starter without rooting ourselves in this paradigm, even if for just a brief sojourn. So we looked at some of the core concepts of the relational model via basic SQL queries and undertook a light foray into some mathematical foundations. We will expound on these root concepts tomorrow.

Day 1 Homework

Find

1. Find the PostgreSQL documentation online and bookmark it.

2. Acquaint yourself with the command-line \? and \h output.

3. We briefly mentioned the MATCH FULL constraint. Find some information on the other available types of MATCH constraints.

Do

1. Select all the tables we created (and only those) from pg_class and examine the table to get a sense of what kinds of metadata Postgres stores about tables.

2. Write a query that finds the country name of the Fight Club event.

3. Alter the venues table such that it contains a Boolean column called active with a default value of TRUE.

Day 2: Advanced Queries, Code, and Rules

Yesterday we saw how to define tables, populate them with data, update and delete rows, and perform basic reads. Today we'll dig even deeper into the myriad ways that PostgreSQL can query data. We'll see how to group similar values, execute code on the server, and create custom interfaces using *views* and *rules*. We'll finish the day by using one of PostgreSQL's contributed packages to flip tables on their heads.

Aggregate Functions

An aggregate query groups results from several rows by some common criteria. It can be as simple as counting the number of rows in a table or calculating the average of some numerical column. They're powerful SQL tools and also a lot of fun.

Let's try some aggregate functions, but first we'll need some more data in our database. Enter your own country into the countries table, your own city into the cities table, and your own address as a venue (which we just named *My Place*). Then add a few records to the events table.

Here's a quick SQL tip: Rather than setting the venue_id explicitly, you can sub-SELECT it using a more human-readable title. If *Moby* is playing at the *Crystal Ballroom*, set the venue_id like this:

```
INSERT INTO events (title, starts, ends, venue_id)
  VALUES ('Moby', '2018-02-06 21:00', '2018-02-06 23:00', (
    SELECT venue_id
    FROM venues
    WHERE name = 'Crystal Ballroom'
  )
);
```

Populate your events table with the following data (to enter *Valentine's Day* in PostgreSQL, you can escape the apostrophe with two, such as Heaven''s Gate):

title	starts	ends	venue
Wedding	2018-02-26 21:00:00	2018-02-26 23:00:00	Voodoo Doughnut
Dinner with Mom	2018-02-26 18:00:00	2018-02-26 20:30:00	My Place
Valentine's Day	2018-02-14 00:00:00	2018-02-14 23:59:00	

With our data set up, let's try some aggregate queries. The simplest aggregate function is count(), which is fairly self-explanatory. Counting all titles that contain the word *Day* (note: % is a wildcard on LIKE searches), you should receive a value of 3.

```
SELECT count(title)
FROM events
WHERE title LIKE '%Day%';
```

To get the first start time and last end time of all events at the Crystal Ballroom, use min() (return the smallest value) and max() (return the largest value).

```
SELECT min(starts), max(ends)
FROM events INNER JOIN venues
  ON events.venue_id = venues.venue_id
WHERE venues.name = 'Crystal Ballroom';
```

```
        min          |         max
---------------------+---------------------
 2018-02-06 21:00:00 | 2018-02-06 23:00:00
```

Aggregate functions are useful but limited on their own. If we wanted to count all events at each venue, we could write the following for each venue ID:

```
SELECT count(*) FROM events WHERE venue_id = 1;
SELECT count(*) FROM events WHERE venue_id = 2;
SELECT count(*) FROM events WHERE venue_id = 3;
SELECT count(*) FROM events WHERE venue_id IS NULL;
```

This would be tedious (intractable even) as the number of venues grows. This is where the GROUP BY command comes in handy.

Grouping

GROUP BY is a shortcut for running the previous queries all at once. With GROUP BY, you tell Postgres to place the rows into groups and then perform some aggregate function (such as count()) on those groups.

```
SELECT venue_id, count(*)
FROM events
GROUP BY venue_id;
```

```
 venue_id | count
----------+-------
        1 |     1
        2 |     2
        3 |     1
        4 |     3
```

It's a nice list, but can we filter by the count() function? Absolutely. The GROUP BY condition has its own filter keyword: HAVING. HAVING is like the WHERE clause, except it can filter by aggregate functions (whereas WHERE cannot).

The following query SELECTs the most popular venues, those with two or more events:

```
SELECT venue_id
FROM events
GROUP BY venue_id
HAVING count(*) >= 2 AND venue_id IS NOT NULL;
```

```
 venue_id | count
----------+-------
        2 |     2
```

You can use GROUP BY without any aggregate functions. If you call SELECT...
FROM...GROUP BY on one column, you get only unique values.

```
SELECT venue_id FROM events GROUP BY venue_id;
```

This kind of grouping is so common that SQL has a shortcut for it in the
DISTINCT keyword.

```
SELECT DISTINCT venue_id FROM events;
```

The results of both queries will be identical.

GROUP BY in MySQL

If you tried to run a SELECT statement with columns not defined under a GROUP BY in
MySQL, you would be shocked to see that it works. This originally made us question
the necessity of window functions. But when we inspected the data MySQL returns
more closely, we found it will return only a random row of data along with the count,
not all relevant results. Generally, that's not useful (and quite potentially dangerous).

Window Functions

If you've done any sort of production work with a relational database in the
past, you are likely familiar with aggregate queries. They are a common SQL
staple. *Window functions*, on the other hand, are not quite so common (PostgreSQL is one of the few open source databases to implement them).

Window functions are similar to GROUP BY queries in that they allow you to
run aggregate functions across multiple rows. The difference is that they allow
you to use built-in aggregate functions without requiring every single field to
be grouped to a single row.

If we attempt to select the title column without grouping by it, we can expect
an error.

```
SELECT title, venue_id, count(*)
FROM events
GROUP BY venue_id;
```

```
ERROR:  column "events.title" must appear in the GROUP BY clause or \
        be used in an aggregate function
```

We are counting up the rows by venue_id, and in the case of *Fight Club* and
Wedding, we have two titles for a single venue_id. Postgres doesn't know *which*
title to display.

Whereas a GROUP BY clause will return one record per matching group value, a window function, which does not collapse the results per group, can return a separate record for each row. For a visual representation, see the following figure.

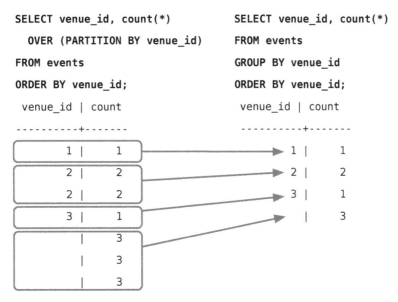

Let's see an example of the sweet spot that window functions attempt to hit.

Window functions return all matches and replicate the results of any aggregate function.

```
SELECT title, count(*) OVER (PARTITION BY venue_id) FROM events;
     title    | count
-------------+-------
 Moby        |   1
 Fight Club  |   1
 House Party |   3
 House Party |   3
 House Party |   3
(5 rows)
```

We like to think of PARTITION BY as akin to GROUP BY, but rather than grouping the results outside of the SELECT attribute list (and thus combining the results into fewer rows), it returns grouped values as any other field (calculating on the grouped variable but otherwise just another attribute). Or in SQL parlance, it returns the results of an aggregate function OVER a PARTITION of the result set.

Transactions

Transactions are the bulwark of relational database consistency. *All or nothing*, that's the transaction motto. Transactions ensure that every command of a set is executed. If anything fails along the way, all of the commands are rolled back as if they never happened.

PostgreSQL transactions follow ACID compliance, which stands for:

- Atomic (either all operations succeed or none do)
- Consistent (the data will always be in a good state and never in an inconsistent state)
- Isolated (transactions don't interfere with one another)
- Durable (a committed transaction is safe, even after a server crash)

We should note here that *consistency* in ACID is different from *consistency* in CAP (covered in Appendix 2, *The CAP Theorem*, on page 315).

Unavoidable Transactions

Up until now, every command we've executed in psql has been implicitly wrapped in a transaction. If you executed a command, such as DELETE FROM account WHERE total < 20; and the database crashed halfway through the delete, you wouldn't be stuck with half a table. When you restart the database server, that command will be rolled back.

We can wrap any transaction within a BEGIN TRANSACTION block. To verify atomicity, we'll kill the transaction with the ROLLBACK command.

```
BEGIN TRANSACTION;
  DELETE FROM events;
ROLLBACK;
SELECT * FROM events;
```

The events all remain. Transactions are useful when you're modifying two tables that you don't want out of sync. The classic example is a debit/credit system for a bank, where money is moved from one account to another:

```
BEGIN TRANSACTION;
  UPDATE account SET total=total+5000.0 WHERE account_id=1337;
  UPDATE account SET total=total-5000.0 WHERE account_id=45887;
END;
```

If something happened between the two updates, this bank just lost five grand. But when wrapped in a transaction block, the initial update is rolled back, even if the server explodes.

Stored Procedures

Every command we've seen until now has been declarative in the sense that we've been able to get our desired result set using just SQL (which is quite powerful in itself). But sometimes the database doesn't give us everything we need natively and we need to run some code to fill in the gaps. At that point, though, you need to decide *where* the code is going to run. Should it run *in* Postgres or should it run on the application side?

If you decide you want the database to do the heavy lifting, Postgres offers *stored procedures*. Stored procedures are extremely powerful and can be used to do an enormous range of tasks, from performing complex mathematical operations that aren't supported in SQL to triggering cascading series of events to pre-validating data before it's written to tables and far beyond. On the one hand, stored procedures can offer huge performance advantages. But the architectural costs can be high (and sometimes not worth it). You may avoid streaming thousands of rows to a client application, but you have also bound your application code to this database. And so the decision to use stored procedures should not be made lightly.

Caveats aside, let's create a procedure (or FUNCTION) that simplifies INSERTing a new event at a venue without needing the venue_id. Here's what the procedure will accomplish: if the venue doesn't exist, it will be created first and then referenced in the new event. The procedure will also return a Boolean indicating whether a new venue was added as a helpful bonus.

What About Vendor Lock-in?

When relational databases hit their heyday, they were the Swiss Army knife of technologies. You could store nearly anything—even programming entire projects in them (for example, Microsoft Access). The few companies that provided this software promoted use of proprietary differences and then took advantage of this corporate reliance by charging enormous license and consulting fees. This was the dreaded *vendor lock-in* that newer programming methodologies tried to mitigate in the 1990s and early 2000s.

The zeal to neuter the vendors, however, birthed maxims such as *no logic in the database*. This is a shame because relational databases are capable of so many varied data management options. Vendor lock-in has not disappeared. Many actions we investigate in this book are highly implementation-specific. However, it's worth knowing how to use databases to their fullest extent before deciding to skip tools such as stored procedures solely because they're implementation-specific.

```
postgres/add_event.sql
CREATE OR REPLACE FUNCTION add_event(
  title text,
  starts timestamp,
  ends timestamp,
  venue text,
  postal varchar(9),
  country char(2))
RETURNS boolean AS $$
DECLARE
  did_insert boolean := false;
  found_count integer;
  the_venue_id integer;
BEGIN
  SELECT venue_id INTO the_venue_id
  FROM venues v
  WHERE v.postal_code=postal AND v.country_code=country AND v.name ILIKE venue
  LIMIT 1;

  IF the_venue_id IS NULL THEN
    INSERT INTO venues (name, postal_code, country_code)
    VALUES (venue, postal, country)
    RETURNING venue_id INTO the_venue_id;

    did_insert := true;
  END IF;

  -- Note: this is a notice, not an error as in some programming languages
  RAISE NOTICE 'Venue found %', the_venue_id;

  INSERT INTO events (title, starts, ends, venue_id)
  VALUES (title, starts, ends, the_venue_id);

  RETURN did_insert;
END;
$$ LANGUAGE plpgsql;
```

You can import this external file into the current schema using the following command-line argument (if you don't feel like typing all that code).

```
7dbs=# \i add_event.sql
```

This stored procedure is run as a SELECT statement.

```
SELECT add_event('House Party', '2018-05-03 23:00',
  '2018-05-04 02:00', 'Run''s House', '97206', 'us');
```

Running it should return t (true) because this is the first use of the venue *Run's House*. This saves a client two round-trip SQL commands to the database (a SELECT and then an INSERT) and instead performs only one.

The language we used in the procedure we wrote is PL/pgSQL (which stands for Procedural Language/PostgreSQL). Covering the details of an entire

> ## Choosing to Execute Database Code
>
> This is the first of a number of places where you'll see this theme in this book: Does the code belong in your application or in the database? It's often a difficult decision, one that you'll have to answer uniquely for every application.
>
> In many cases, you'll improve performance by as much as an order of magnitude. For example, you might have a complex application-specific calculation that requires custom code. If the calculation involves many rows, a stored procedure will save you from moving thousands of rows instead of a single result. The cost is splitting your application, your code, and your tests across two different programming paradigms.

programming language is beyond the scope of this book, but you can read much more about it in the online PostgreSQL documentation.[2]

In addition to PL/pgSQL, Postgres supports three more core languages for writing procedures: Tcl (PL/Tcl), Perl (PL/Perl), and Python (PL/Python). People have written extensions for a dozen more, including Ruby, Java, PHP, Scheme, and others listed in the public documentation. Try this shell command:

```
$ createlang 7dbs --list
```

It will list the languages installed in your database. The createlang command is also used to add new languages, which you can find online.[3]

Pull the Triggers

Triggers automatically fire stored procedures when some event happens, such as an insert or update. They allow the database to enforce some required behavior in response to changing data.

Let's create a new PL/pgSQL function that logs whenever an event is updated (we want to be sure no one changes an event and tries to deny it later). First, create a logs table to store event changes. A primary key isn't necessary here because it's just a log.

```
CREATE TABLE logs (
  event_id integer,
  old_title varchar(255),
  old_starts timestamp,
  old_ends timestamp,
  logged_at timestamp DEFAULT current_timestamp
);
```

---

2. http://www.postgresql.org/docs/9.0/static/plpgsql.html
3. http://www.postgresql.org/docs/9.0/static/app-createlang.html

Next, we build a function to insert old data into the log. The OLD variable represents the row about to be changed (NEW represents an incoming row, which we'll see in action soon enough). Output a notice to the console with the event_id before returning.

postgres/log_event.sql
```
CREATE OR REPLACE FUNCTION log_event() RETURNS trigger AS $$
DECLARE
BEGIN
  INSERT INTO logs (event_id, old_title, old_starts, old_ends)
  VALUES (OLD.event_id, OLD.title, OLD.starts, OLD.ends);
  RAISE NOTICE 'Someone just changed event #%', OLD.event_id;
  RETURN NEW;
END;
$$ LANGUAGE plpgsql;
```

Finally, we create our trigger to log changes after any row is updated.

```
CREATE TRIGGER log_events
  AFTER UPDATE ON events
  FOR EACH ROW EXECUTE PROCEDURE log_event();
```

So, it turns out our party at Run's House has to end earlier than we hoped. Let's change the event.

```
UPDATE events
SET ends='2018-05-04 01:00:00'
WHERE title='House Party';

NOTICE:  Someone just changed event #9
```

And the old end time was logged.

```
SELECT event_id, old_title, old_ends, logged_at
FROM logs;

event_id |  old_title  |      old_ends       |       logged_at
---------+-------------+---------------------+------------------------
       9 | House Party | 2018-05-04 02:00:00 | 2017-02-26 15:50:31.939
```

Triggers can also be created before updates and before or after inserts.[4]

Viewing the World

Wouldn't it be great if you could use the results of a complex query just like any other table? Well, that's exactly what VIEWs are for. Unlike stored procedures, these aren't functions being executed but rather aliased queries. Let's say that we wanted to see only holidays that contain the word *Day* and have no venue. We could create a VIEW for that like this:

---

4. http://www.postgresql.org/docs/9.0/static/triggers.html

```
postgres/holiday_view_1.sql
CREATE VIEW holidays AS
  SELECT event_id AS holiday_id, title AS name, starts AS date
  FROM events
  WHERE title LIKE '%Day%' AND venue_id IS NULL;
```

Creating a view really is as simple as writing a query and prefixing it with CREATE VIEW some_view_name AS. Now you can query holidays like any other table. Under the covers it's the plain old events table. As proof, add *Valentine's Day* on *2018-02-14* to events and query the holidays view.

```
SELECT name, to_char(date, 'Month DD, YYYY') AS date
FROM holidays
WHERE date <= '2018-04-01';
```

```
      name         |         date
-------------------+--------------------
 April Fools Day   | April     01, 2018
 Valentine's Day   | February  14, 2018
```

Views are powerful tools for opening up complex queried data in a simple way. The query may be a roiling sea of complexity underneath, but all you see is a table.

If you want to add a new column to the holidays view, it will have to come from the underlying table. Let's alter the events table to have an array of associated colors.

```
ALTER TABLE events
ADD colors text ARRAY;
```

Because holidays are to have colors associated with them, let's update the VIEW query to contain the colors array.

```
CREATE OR REPLACE VIEW holidays AS
  SELECT event_id AS holiday_id, title AS name, starts AS date, colors
  FROM events
  WHERE title LIKE '%Day%' AND venue_id IS NULL;
```

Now it's a matter of setting an array or color strings to the holiday of choice. Unfortunately, we cannot update a VIEW directly.

```
UPDATE holidays SET colors = '{"red","green"}' where name = 'Christmas Day';
```

```
ERROR:  cannot update a view
HINT:  You need an unconditional ON UPDATE DO INSTEAD rule.
```

Looks like we need a RULE instead of a view.

Storing Views on Disk with Materialized Views

Though VIEWs like the holidays view mentioned previously are a convenient abstraction, they don't yield any performance gains over the SELECT queries that they alias. If you want VIEWs that *do* offer such gains, you should consider creating *materialized views*, which are different because they're stored on disk in a "real" table and thus yield performance gains because they restrict the number of tables that must be accessed to exactly one.

You can create materialized views just like ordinary views, except with a CREATE MATE-RIALIZED VIEW rather than CREATE VIEW statement. Materialized view tables are populated whenever you run the REFRESH command for them, which you can automate to run at defined intervals or in response to triggers. You can also create indexes on materialized views the same way that you can on regular tables.

The downside of materialized views is that they do increase disk space usage. But in many cases, the performance gains are worth it. In general, the more complex the query and the more tables it spans, the more performance gains you're likely to get vis-à-vis plain old SELECT queries or VIEWs.

What RULEs the School?

A RULE is a description of how to alter the parsed *query tree*. Every time Postgres runs an SQL statement, it parses the statement into a query tree (generally called an *abstract syntax tree*).

Operators and values become branches and leaves in the tree, and the tree is walked, pruned, and in other ways edited before execution. This tree is optionally rewritten by Postgres rules, before being sent on to the query planner (which also rewrites the tree to run optimally), and sends this final command to be executed. See how SQL gets executed in PostgreSQL in the figure on page 33.

In fact, a VIEW such as holidays *is* a RULE. We can prove this by taking a look at the execution plan of the holidays view using the EXPLAIN command (notice *Filter* is the WHERE clause, and *Output* is the column list).

```
EXPLAIN VERBOSE
  SELECT *
  FROM holidays;
                          QUERY PLAN
-------------------------------------------------------------------------
 Seq Scan on public.events  (cost=0.00..1.01 rows=1 width=44)
   Output: events.event_id, events.title, events.starts, events.colors
   Filter: ((events.venue_id IS NULL) AND
     ((events.title)::text ~~ '%Day%'::text))
```

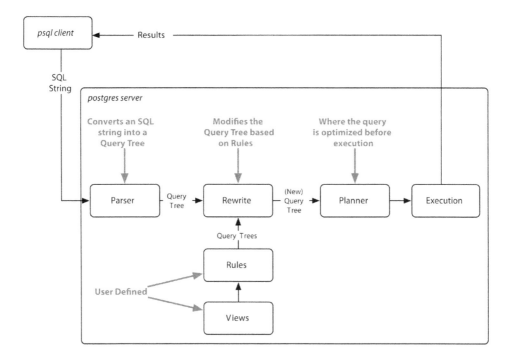

Compare that to running EXPLAIN VERBOSE on the query from which we built
the holidays VIEW. They're functionally identical.

```
EXPLAIN VERBOSE
  SELECT event_id AS holiday_id,
    title AS name, starts AS date, colors
  FROM events
  WHERE title LIKE '%Day%' AND venue_id IS NULL;

                              QUERY PLAN
--------------------------------------------------------------------------------
 Seq Scan on public.events  (cost=0.00..1.04 rows=1 width=57)
   Output: event_id, title, starts, colors
   Filter: ((events.venue_id IS NULL) AND
     ((events.title)::text ~~ '%Day%'::text))
```

So, to allow updates against our holidays view, we need to craft a RULE that tells
Postgres what to do with an UPDATE. Our rule will capture updates to the holidays
view and instead run the update on events, pulling values from the pseudore-
lations NEW and OLD. NEW functionally acts as the relation containing the values
we're setting, while OLD contains the values we query by.

postgres/create_rule.sql

```
CREATE RULE update_holidays AS ON UPDATE TO holidays DO INSTEAD
  UPDATE events
  SET title = NEW.name,
      starts = NEW.date,
      colors = NEW.colors
  WHERE title = OLD.name;
```

With this rule in place, now we can update holidays directly.

```
UPDATE holidays SET colors = '{"red","green"}' where name = 'Christmas Day';
```

Next, let's insert *New Years Day* on *2013-01-01* into holidays. As expected, we need a rule for that too. No problem.

```
CREATE RULE insert_holidays AS ON INSERT TO holidays DO INSTEAD
  INSERT INTO ...
```

We're going to move on from here, but if you'd like to play more with RULEs, try to add a DELETE RULE.

I'll Meet You at the Crosstab

For our last exercise of the day, we're going to build a monthly calendar of events, where each month in the calendar year counts the number of events in that month. This kind of operation is commonly done by a *pivot table*. These constructs "pivot" grouped data around some other output, in our case a list of months. We'll build our pivot table using the crosstab() function.

Start by crafting a query to count the number of events per month each year. PostgreSQL provides an extract() function that returns some subfield from a date or timestamp, which aids in our grouping.

```
SELECT extract(year from starts) as year,
  extract(month from starts) as month, count(*)
FROM events
GROUP BY year, month
ORDER BY year, month;
```

To use crosstab(), the query must return three columns: rowid, category, and value. We'll be using the year as an ID, which means the other fields are category (the month) and value (the count).

The crosstab() function needs another set of values to represent months. This is how the function knows how many columns we need. These are the values that become the columns (the table to *pivot* against). So let's create a table to store a list of numbers. Because we'll only need the table for a few operations, we'll create an ephemeral table, which lasts only as long as the current Postgres session, using the CREATE TEMPORARY TABLE command.

```
CREATE TEMPORARY TABLE month_count(month INT);
INSERT INTO month_count VALUES (1),(2),(3),(4),(5),
  (6),(7),(8),(9),(10),(11),(12);
```

Now we're ready to call crosstab() with our two queries.

```
SELECT * FROM crosstab(
  'SELECT extract(year from starts) as year,
     extract(month from starts) as month, count(*)
   FROM events
   GROUP BY year, month
   ORDER BY year, month',
  'SELECT * FROM month_count'
);
```

```
ERROR:  a column definition list is required for functions returning "record"
```

Oops. An error occurred. This cryptic error is basically saying that the function is returning a set of records (rows) but it doesn't know how to label them. In fact, it doesn't even know what datatypes they are.

Remember, the pivot table is using our months as categories, but those months are just integers. So, we define them like this:

```
SELECT * FROM crosstab(
  'SELECT extract(year from starts) as year,
     extract(month from starts) as month, count(*)
   FROM events
   GROUP BY year, month
   ORDER BY year, month',
  'SELECT * FROM month_count'
) AS (
  year int,
  jan int, feb int, mar int, apr int, may int, jun int,
  jul int, aug int, sep int, oct int, nov int, dec int
) ORDER BY YEAR;
```

We have one column year (which is the row ID) and twelve more columns representing the months.

year	jan	feb	mar	apr	may	jun	jul	aug	sep	oct	nov	dec
2018		5		1	1							1

Go ahead and add a couple more events on another year just to see next year's event counts. Run the crosstab() function again, and enjoy the calendar.

Day 2 Wrap-Up

Today finalized the basics of PostgreSQL. What we're starting to see is that Postgres is more than just a server for storing vanilla datatypes and querying them. Instead, it's a powerful data management engine that can reformat output data, store weird datatypes such as arrays, execute logic, and provide enough power to rewrite incoming queries.

Day 2 Homework

Find

1. Find the list of aggregate functions in the PostgreSQL docs.

2. Find a GUI program to interact with PostgreSQL, such as pgAdmin, Datagrip, or Navicat.

Do

1. Create a rule that captures DELETEs on venues and instead sets the active flag (created in the Day 1 homework) to FALSE.

2. A temporary table was not the best way to implement our event calendar pivot table. The generate_series(a, b) function returns a set of records, from a to b. Replace the month_count table SELECT with this.

3. Build a pivot table that displays every day in a single month, where each week of the month is a row and each day name forms a column across the top (seven days, starting with Sunday and ending with Saturday) like a standard month calendar. Each day should contain a count of the number of events for that date or should remain blank if no event occurs.

Day 3: Full Text and Multidimensions

We'll spend Day 3 investigating the many tools at our disposal to build a movie query system. We'll begin with the many ways PostgreSQL can search actor/movie names using fuzzy string matching. Then we'll discover the cube package by creating a movie suggestion system based on similar genres of movies we already like. Because these are all contributed packages, the implementations are special to PostgreSQL and not part of the SQL standard.

Often, when designing a relational database schema, you'll start with an entity diagram. We'll be writing a personal movie suggestion system that keeps track of movies, their genres, and their actors, as modeled in the figure on page 37.

Before we begin the Day 3 exercises, we'll need to extend Postgres by installing the following contributed packages: tablefunc, dict_xsyn, fuzzystrmatch, pg_trgm, and cube. You can refer to the website for installation instructions.[5]

---

5. http://www.postgresql.org/docs/current/static/contrib.html

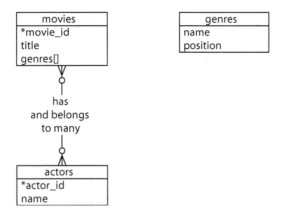

Run the following command and check that it matches the output below to ensure your contrib packages have been installed correctly:

```
$ psql 7dbs -c "SELECT '1'::cube;"
cube
------
(1)
(1 row)
```

Seek out the online docs for more information if you receive an error message.

Let's first build the database. It's often good practice to create indexes on foreign keys to speed up reverse lookups (such as what movies this actor is involved in). You should also set a UNIQUE constraint on join tables like movies_actors to avoid duplicate join values.

postgres/create_movies.sql
```
CREATE TABLE genres (
        name text UNIQUE,
        position integer
);

CREATE TABLE movies (
        movie_id SERIAL PRIMARY KEY,
        title text,
        genre cube
);

CREATE TABLE actors (
        actor_id SERIAL PRIMARY KEY,
        name text
);

CREATE TABLE movies_actors (
        movie_id integer REFERENCES movies NOT NULL,
        actor_id integer REFERENCES actors NOT NULL,
        UNIQUE (movie_id, actor_id)
);
```

```
CREATE INDEX movies_actors_movie_id ON movies_actors (movie_id);
CREATE INDEX movies_actors_actor_id ON movies_actors (actor_id);
CREATE INDEX movies_genres_cube ON movies USING gist (genre);
```

You can download the movies_data.sql file as a file alongside the book and populate the tables by piping the file into the database. Any questions you may have about the genre cube will be covered later today.

Fuzzy Searching

Opening up a system to text searches means opening your system to inaccurate inputs. You have to expect typos like "Brid of Frankstein." Sometimes, users can't remember the full name of "J. Roberts." In other cases, we just plain don't know how to spell "Benn Aflek." We'll look into a few PostgreSQL packages that make text searching easy.

It's worth noting that as we progress, this kind of string matching blurs the lines between relational queries and searching frameworks such as Lucene[6] and Elasticsearch.[7] Although some may feel that features like full-text search belong with the application code, there can be performance and administrative benefits of pushing these packages to the database, where the data lives.

SQL Standard String Matches

PostgreSQL has many ways of performing text matches but the two major default methods are LIKE and regular expressions.

I Like LIKE and ILIKE

LIKE and ILIKE are the simplest forms of text search (ILIKE is a case-insensitive version of LIKE). They are fairly universal in relational databases. LIKE compares column values against a given pattern string. The % and _ characters are wildcards: % matches any number of any characters while _ matches exactly one character.

```
SELECT title FROM movies WHERE title ILIKE 'stardust%';

      title
-------------------
 Stardust
 Stardust Memories
```

If we want to be sure the substring *stardust* is not at the end of the string, we can use the underscore (_) character as a little trick.

---

6.   http://lucene.apache.org/

7.   https://www.elastic.co/products/elasticsearch

```
SELECT title FROM movies WHERE title ILIKE 'stardust_%';
      title
-------------------
 Stardust Memories
```

This is useful in basic cases, but LIKE is limited to simple wildcards.

Regex

A more powerful string-matching syntax is a *regular expression* (regex). Regexes appear often throughout this book because many databases support them. There are entire books dedicated to writing powerful expressions—the topic is far too wide and complex to cover in depth here. Postgres conforms (mostly) to the POSIX style.

In Postgres, a regular expression match is led by the ~ operator, with the optional ! (meaning *not* matching) and * (meaning *case insensitive*). To count all movies that do *not* begin with *the*, the following case-insensitive query will work. The characters inside the string are the regular expression.

```
SELECT COUNT(*) FROM movies WHERE title !~* '^the.*';
```

You can index strings for pattern matching the previous queries by creating a text_pattern_ops operator class index, as long as the values are indexed in lowercase.

```
CREATE INDEX movies_title_pattern ON movies (lower(title) text_pattern_ops);
```

We used the text_pattern_ops because the title is of type text. If you need to index varchars, chars, or names, use the related ops: varchar_pattern_ops, bpchar_pattern_ops, and name_pattern_ops.

Bride of Levenshtein

Levenshtein is a string comparison algorithm that compares how similar two strings are by how many *steps* are required to change one string into another. Each replaced, missing, or added character counts as a step. The distance is the total number of steps away. In PostgreSQL, the levenshtein() function is provided by the fuzzystrmatch contrib package. Say we have the string *bat* and the string *fads*.

```
SELECT levenshtein('bat', 'fads');
```

The Levenshtein distance is 3 because in order to go from *bat* to *fads*, we replaced two letters (b=>f, t=>d) and added a letter (+s). Each change increments the distance. We can watch the distance close as we step closer (so to speak). The total goes down until we get zero (the two strings are equal).

```
SELECT levenshtein('bat', 'fad') fad,
  levenshtein('bat', 'fat') fat,
  levenshtein('bat', 'bat') bat;

 fad | fat | bat
-----+-----+-----
   2 |   1 |   0
```

Changes in case cost a point, too, so you may find it best to convert all strings to the same case when querying.

```
SELECT movie_id, title FROM movies
WHERE levenshtein(lower(title), lower('a hard day nght')) <= 3;

 movie_id |        title
----------+--------------------
      245 | A Hard Day's Night
```

This ensures minor differences won't over-inflate the distance.

Try a Trigram

A trigram is a group of three consecutive characters taken from a string. The pg_trgm contrib module breaks a string into as many trigrams as it can.

```
SELECT show_trgm('Avatar');

              show_trgm
--------------------------------------
 {"  a"," av","ar ",ata,ava,tar,vat}
```

Finding a matching string is as simple as counting the number of matching trigrams. The strings with the most matches are the most similar. It's useful for doing a search where you're okay with either slight misspellings or even minor words missing. The longer the string, the more trigrams and the more likely a match—they're great for something like movie titles because they have relatively similar lengths. We'll create a trigram index against movie names to start, using Generalized Index Search Tree (GIST), a generic index API made available by the PostgreSQL engine.

```
CREATE INDEX movies_title_trigram ON movies
USING gist (title gist_trgm_ops);
```

Now you can query with a few misspellings and still get decent results.

```
SELECT title
FROM movies
WHERE title % 'Avatre';

 title
---------
 Avatar
```

Trigrams are an excellent choice for accepting user input without weighing queries down with wildcard complexity.

Full-Text Fun

Next, we want to allow users to perform full-text searches based on matching words, even if they're pluralized. If a user wants to search for certain words in a movie title but can remember only some of them, Postgres supports simple natural language processing.

TSVector and TSQuery

Let's look for a movie that contains the words *night* and *day*. This is a perfect job for text search using the @@ full-text query operator.

```
SELECT title
FROM movies
WHERE title @@ 'night & day';

              title
-------------------------------
 A Hard Day's Night
 Six Days Seven Nights
 Long Day's Journey Into Night
```

The query returns titles like *A Hard Day's Night*, despite the word *Day* being in possessive form and the fact that the two words are out of order in the query. The @@ operator converts the name field into a tsvector and converts the query into a tsquery.

A tsvector is a datatype that splits a string into an array (or a *vector*) of tokens, which are searched against the given query, while the tsquery represents a query in some language, like English or French. The language corresponds to a dictionary (which we'll see more of in a few paragraphs). The previous query is equivalent to the following (if your system language is set to English):

```
SELECT title
FROM movies
WHERE to_tsvector(title) @@ to_tsquery('english', 'night & day');
```

You can take a look at how the vector and the query break apart the values by running the conversion functions on the strings outright.

```
SELECT to_tsvector('A Hard Day''s Night'),
  to_tsquery('english', 'night & day');

       to_tsvector          |    to_tsquery
----------------------------+------------------
 'day':3 'hard':2 'night':5 | 'night' & 'day'
```

The tokens on a tsvector are called *lexemes* and are coupled with their positions in the given phrase.

You may have noticed the tsvector for *A Hard Day's Night* did not contain the lexeme *a*. Moreover, simple English words such as *a* are missing if you try to query by them.

```
SELECT *
FROM movies
WHERE title @@ to_tsquery('english', 'a');
```

```
NOTICE:  text-search query contains only stop words or doesn't \
      contain lexemes, ignored
```

Common words such as *a* are called *stop words* and are generally not useful for performing queries. The English dictionary was used by the parser to normalize our string into useful English components. In your console, you can view the output of the stop words under the English tsearch_data directory.

```
$ cat `pg_config --sharedir`/tsearch_data/english.stop
```

We could remove *a* from the list, or we could use another dictionary like simple that just breaks up strings by nonword characters and makes them lowercase. Compare these two vectors:

```
SELECT to_tsvector('english', 'A Hard Day''s Night');
     to_tsvector
--------------------------
'day':3 'hard':2 'night':5
SELECT to_tsvector('simple', 'A Hard Day''s Night');
            to_tsvector
---------------------------------------
'a':1 'day':3 'hard':2 'night':5 's':4
```

With simple, you can retrieve any movie containing the lexeme *a*.

Other Languages

Because Postgres is doing some natural language processing here, it only makes sense that different configurations would be used for different languages. All of the installed configurations can be viewed with this command:

```
7dbs=# \dF
```

Dictionaries are part of what Postgres uses to generate tsvector lexemes (along with stop words and other tokenizing rules we haven't covered called *parsers* and *templates*). You can view your system's list here:

```
7dbs=# \dFd
```

You can test any dictionary outright by calling the ts_lexize() function. Here we find the English stem word of the string *Day's*.

```
SELECT ts_lexize('english_stem', 'Day''s');
```

```
 ts_lexize
-----------
 {day}
```

Finally, the previous full-text commands work for other languages, too. If you have German installed, try this:

```
SELECT to_tsvector('german', 'was machst du gerade?');
```

```
     to_tsvector
--------------------
 'gerad':4 'mach':2
```

Because *was* (what) and *du* (you) are common, they are marked as stop words in the German dictionary, while *machst* (doing) and *gerade* (at the moment) are stemmed.

Indexing Lexemes

Full-text search is powerful. But if we don't index our tables, it's also slow. The EXPLAIN command is a powerful tool for digging into how queries are internally planned.

```
EXPLAIN
SELECT *
FROM movies
WHERE title @@ 'night & day';
```

```
                              QUERY PLAN
-----------------------------------------------------------------------
 Seq Scan on movies  (cost=0.00..815.86 rows=3 width=171)
   Filter: (title @@ 'night & day'::text)
```

Note the line *Seq Scan on movies*. That's rarely a good sign in a query because it means a whole table scan is taking place; each row will be read. That usually means that you need to create an index.

We'll use Generalized Inverted iNdex (GIN)—like GIST, it's an index API—to create an index of lexeme values we can query against. The term *inverted index* may sound familiar to you if you've ever used a search engine like Lucene or Sphinx. It's a common data structure to index full-text searches.

```
CREATE INDEX movies_title_searchable ON movies
USING gin(to_tsvector('english', title));
```

With our index in place, let's try to search again.

```
EXPLAIN
SELECT *
FROM movies
WHERE title @@ 'night & day';
                        QUERY PLAN
--------------------------------------------------------------------------
 Seq Scan on movies  (cost=0.00..815.86 rows=3 width=171)
   Filter: (title @@ 'night & day'::text)
```

What happened? Nothing. The index is there, but Postgres isn't using it because our GIN index specifically uses the english configuration for building its tsvectors, but we aren't specifying that vector. We need to specify it in the WHERE clause of the query.

```
EXPLAIN
SELECT *
FROM movies
WHERE to_tsvector('english',title) @@ 'night & day';
```

That will return this query plan:

```
                        QUERY PLAN
-----------------------------------------------------------------
 Bitmap Heap Scan on movies  (cost=20.00..24.26 rows=1 width=171)
   Recheck Cond: (to_tsvector('english'::regconfig, title) @@
   '''night'' & ''day'''::tsquery)
   -> Bitmap Index Scan on movies_title_searchable
       (cost=0.00..20.00 rows=1 width=0)
       Index Cond: (to_tsvector('english'::regconfig, title) @@
       '''night'' & ''day'''::tsquery)
```

EXPLAIN is important to ensure indexes are used as you expect them. Otherwise, the index is just wasted overhead.

Metaphones

We've inched toward matching less specific inputs. LIKE and regular expressions require crafting patterns that can match strings precisely according to their format. Levenshtein distance allows you to find matches that contain minor misspellings but must ultimately be very close to the same string. Trigrams are a good choice for finding reasonable misspelled matches. Finally, full-text searching allows natural language flexibility in that it can ignore minor words such as *a* and *the* and can deal with pluralization. Sometimes we just don't know how to spell words correctly but we know how they sound.

We love Bruce Willis and would love to see what movies he's in. Unfortunately, we can't remember exactly how to spell his name, so we sound it out as best we can.

```
SELECT *
FROM actors
WHERE name = 'Broos Wils';
```

Even a trigram is no good here (using % rather than =).

```
SELECT *
FROM actors
WHERE name % 'Broos Wils';
```

Enter the metaphones, which are algorithms for creating a string representation of word sounds. You can define how many characters are in the output string. For example, the seven-character metaphone of the name Aaron Eckhart is *ARNKHRT*.

To find all films with actors with names sounding like Broos Wils, we can query against the metaphone output. Note that NATURAL JOIN is an INNER JOIN that automatically joins ON matching column names (for example, movies.actor_id= movies_actors.actor_id).

```
SELECT title
FROM movies NATURAL JOIN movies_actors NATURAL JOIN actors
WHERE metaphone(name, 6) = metaphone('Broos Wils', 6);
           title
----------------------------
 The Fifth Element
 Twelve Monkeys
 Armageddon
 Die Hard
 Pulp Fiction
 The Sixth Sense
:
```

If you peek at the online documentation, you'll see the *fuzzystrmatch* module contains other functions: dmetaphone() (double metaphone), dmetaphone_alt() (for alternative name pronunciations), and soundex() (a really old algorithm from the 1880s made by the U.S. Census to compare common American surnames).

You can dissect the functions' representations by selecting their output.

```
SELECT name, dmetaphone(name), dmetaphone_alt(name),
  metaphone(name, 8), soundex(name)
FROM actors;
```

name	dmetaphone	dmetaphone_alt	metaphone	soundex
50 Cent	SNT	SNT	SNT	C530
Aaron Eckhart	ARNK	ARNK	ARNKHRT	A652
Agatha Hurle	AK0R	AKTR	AK0HRL	A236

There is no single best function to choose, and the optimal choice depends on your dataset and use case.

Combining String Matches

With all of our string searching ducks in a row, we're ready to start combining them in interesting ways.

One of the most flexible aspects of metaphones is that their outputs are just strings. This allows you to mix and match with other string matchers.

For example, we could use the trigram operator against metaphone() outputs and then order the results by the lowest Levenshtein distance. This means "Get me names that sound the most like Robin Williams, in order."

```
SELECT * FROM actors
WHERE metaphone(name,8) % metaphone('Robin Williams',8)
ORDER BY levenshtein(lower('Robin Williams'), lower(name));
```

```
 actor_id | name
----------+------------------
     4093 | Robin Williams
     2442 | John Williams
     4479 | Steven Williams
     4090 | Robin Shou
```

Be warned, though, that unbridled exploitation of this flexibility can yield funny results.

```
SELECT * FROM actors WHERE dmetaphone(name) % dmetaphone('Ron');
```

This will return a result set that includes actors like Renée Zellweger, Ringo Starr, and Randy Quaid.

The combinations are vast, limited only by your experimentations.

Genres as a Multidimensional Hypercube

The last contributed package we investigate is cube. We'll use the cube datatype to map a movie's genres as a multidimensional vector. We will then use methods to efficiently query for the closest points within the boundary of a hypercube to give us a list of similar movies.

As you may have noticed in the beginning of Day 3, we created a column named genres of type cube. Each value is a point in 18-dimensional space with each dimension representing a genre. Why represent movie genres as points in n-dimensional space? Movie categorization is not an exact science, and many movies are not 100 percent comedy or 100 percent tragedy—they are something in between.

In our system, each genre is scored from (the totally arbitrary numbers) 0 to 10 based on how strong the movie is within that genre—with 0 being nonexistent and 10 being the strongest.

Star Wars, for example, has a genre vector of (0,7,0,0,0,0,0,0,0,7,0,0,0,0,10,0,0,0). The genres table describes the position of each dimension in the vector. We can decrypt its genre values by extracting the cube_ur_coord(vector,dimension) using each genres.position. For clarity, we filter out genres with scores of 0.

```
SELECT name,
  cube_ur_coord('(0,7,0,0,0,0,0,0,0,7,0,0,0,0,10,0,0,0)', position) as score
FROM genres g
WHERE cube_ur_coord('(0,7,0,0,0,0,0,0,0,7,0,0,0,0,10,0,0,0)', position) > 0;
```

```
  name      | score
-----------+-------
 Adventure |    7
 Fantasy   |    7
 SciFi     |   10
```

We will find similar movies by finding the nearest points. To understand why this works, we can envision two movies on a two-dimensional genre graph, like the graph shown below. If your favorite movie is *Animal House*, you'll probably want to see *The 40-Year-Old Virgin* more than *Oedipus*—a story famously lacking in comedy. In our two-dimensional universe, it's a simple nearest-neighbor search to find likely matches.

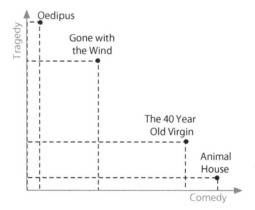

We can extrapolate this into more dimensions with more genres, be it 2, 3, or 18. The principle is the same: a nearest-neighbor match to the nearest points in genre space will yield the closest genre matches.

The nearest matches to the genre vector can be discovered by the cube_distance(point1, point2). Here we can find the distance of all movies to the *Star Wars* genre vector, nearest first.

```
SELECT *,
  cube_distance(genre, '(0,7,0,0,0,0,0,0,0,7,0,0,0,0,10,0,0,0)') dist
FROM movies
ORDER BY dist;
```

We created the movies_genres_cube cube index earlier when we created the tables. However, even with an index, this query is still relatively slow because it requires a full-table scan. It computes the distance on every row and then sorts them.

Rather than compute the distance of every point, we can instead focus on likely points by way of a *bounding cube*. Just like finding the closest five towns on a map will be faster on a state map than a world map, bounding reduces the points we need to look at.

We use cube_enlarge(cube,radius,dimensions) to build an 18-dimensional cube that is some length (radius) wider than a point.

Let's view a simpler example. If we built a two-dimensional square one unit around a point (1,1), the lower-left point of the square would be at (0,0), and the upper-right point would be (2,2).

```
SELECT cube_enlarge('(1,1)',1,2);
```

```
 cube_enlarge
---------------
 (0, 0),(2, 2)
```

The same principle applies in any number of dimensions. With our bounding hypercube, we can use a special cube operator, @>, which means *contains*. This query finds the distance of all points contained within a five-unit cube of the *Star Wars* genre point.

```
SELECT title,
  cube_distance(genre, '(0,7,0,0,0,0,0,0,0,7,0,0,0,0,10,0,0,0)') dist
FROM movies
WHERE cube_enlarge('(0,7,0,0,0,0,0,0,0,7,0,0,0,0,10,0,0,0)'::cube, 5, 18)
  @> genre
ORDER BY dist;
```

```
                      title                       |       dist
--------------------------------------------------+------------------
 Star Wars                                         |                0
 Star Wars: Episode V - The Empire Strikes Back    |                2
 Avatar                                            |                5
 Explorers                                         | 5.74456264653803
 Krull                                             | 6.48074069840786
 E.T. The Extra-Terrestrial                        | 7.61577310586391
```

Using a subselect, we can get the genre by movie name and perform our calculations against that genre using a table alias.

```
SELECT m.movie_id, m.title
FROM movies m, (SELECT genre, title FROM movies WHERE title = 'Mad Max') s
WHERE cube_enlarge(s.genre, 5, 18) @> m.genre AND s.title <> m.title
ORDER BY cube_distance(m.genre, s.genre)
LIMIT 10;

 movie_id |            title
----------+----------------------------
     1405 | Cyborg
     1391 | Escape from L.A.
     1192 | Mad Max Beyond Thunderdome
     1189 | Universal Soldier
     1222 | Soldier
     1362 | Johnny Mnemonic
      946 | Alive
      418 | Escape from New York
     1877 | The Last Starfighter
     1445 | The Rocketeer
```

This method of movie suggestion is not perfect, but it's an excellent start. We will see more dimensional queries in later chapters, such as two-dimensional geographic searches in MongoDB (see *GeoSpatial Queries*, on page 130).

Day 3 Wrap-Up

Today we jumped headlong into PostgreSQL's flexibility in performing string searches and used the cube package for multidimensional searching. Most importantly, we caught a glimpse of the nonstandard extensions that put PostgreSQL at the top of the open source RDBMS field. There are dozens (if not hundreds) more extensions at your disposal, from geographic storage to cryptographic functions, custom datatypes, and language extensions. Beyond the core power of SQL, contrib packages make PostgreSQL shine.

Day 3 Homework

Find

1. Find the online documentation listing all contributed packages bundled into Postgres. Read up on two that you could imagine yourself using in one of your projects.

2. Find the online POSIX regex documentation (it will also come in handy in future chapters).

Do

1. Create a stored procedure that enables you to input a movie title or an actor's name and then receive the top five suggestions based on either movies the actor has starred in or films with similar genres.

2. Expand the movies database to track user comments and extract keywords (minus English stopwords). Cross-reference these keywords with actors' last names and try to find the most talked-about actors.

Wrap-Up

If you haven't spent much time with relational databases, we highly recommend digging deeper into PostgreSQL, or another relational database, before deciding to scrap it for a newer variety. Relational databases have been the focus of intense academic research and industrial improvements for more than forty years, and PostgreSQL is one of the top open source relational databases to benefit from these advancements.

PostgreSQL's Strengths

PostgreSQL's strengths are as numerous as any relational model: years of research and production use across nearly every field of computing, flexible queryability, and very consistent and durable data. Most programming languages have battle-tested driver support for Postgres, and many programming models, like object-relational mapping (ORM), assume an underlying relational database.

But the real crux of the matter is the flexibility of the join. You don't need to know how you plan to actually query your model because you can always perform some joins, filters, views, and indexes—odds are good that you will always have the ability to extract the data you want. In the other chapters of this book that assumption will more or less fly out the window.

PostgreSQL is fantastic for what we call "Stepford data" (named for *The Stepford Wives*, a story about a neighborhood where nearly everyone was consistent in style and substance), which is data that is fairly homogeneous and conforms well to a structured schema.

Furthermore, PostgreSQL goes beyond the normal open source RDBMS offerings, such as powerful schema constraint mechanisms. You can write your own language extensions, customize indexes, create custom datatypes, and even overwrite the parsing of incoming queries. And where other open source databases may have complex licensing agreements, PostgreSQL is open source in its purest form. No one owns the code. Anyone can do pretty much anything they want with the project (other than hold authors liable). The development and distribution are completely community supported. If you are a fan of free(dom) software, you have to respect their general resistance to cashing in on an amazing product.

PostgreSQL's Weaknesses

Although relational databases have been undeniably the most successful style of database over the years, there are cases where it may not be a great fit.

Postgres and JSON

Although we won't delve too deeply into it here given that we cover two other databases in this book that were explicitly created to handle unstructured data, we'd be remiss in not mentioning that Postgres has offered support for JSON since version 9.3. Postgres offers two different formats for this: JSON and JSONB (the json and jsonb types, respectively). The crucial difference between them is that the json type stores JSON as text while jsonb stores JSON using a decomposed binary format; json is optimized for faster data input while jsonb is optimized for faster processing.

With Postgres, you can perform operations like this:

```
CREATE TABLE users (
  username TEXT,
  data     JSON
);
INSERT INTO users VALUES ('wadeboggs107', '{ "AVG": 0.328, "HR": 118, "H": 3010 }');
SELECT data->>'AVG' AS lifetime_batting_average FROM users;

 lifetime_batting_average
--------------------------
 0.328
```

If your use case requires a mixture of structured and unstructured (or less structured) datatypes—or even requires *only* unstructured datatypes—then Postgres may provide a solution.

Partitioning is not one of the strengths of relational databases such as PostgreSQL. If you need to scale out rather than up—multiple parallel databases rather than a single beefy machine or cluster—you may be better served looking elsewhere (although clustering capabilities have improved in recent releases). Another database might be a better fit if:

- You don't truly require the overhead of a full database (perhaps you only need a cache like Redis).

- You require very high-volume reads and writes as key values.

- You need to store only large BLOBs of data.

Parting Thoughts

A relational database is an excellent choice for query flexibility. While PostgreSQL requires you to design your data up front, it makes no assumptions about how you use that data. As long as your schema is designed in a fairly normalized way, without duplication or storage of computable values, you should generally be all set for any queries you might need to create. And if you include the correct modules, tune your engine, and index well, it will perform amazingly well for multiple terabytes of data with very small resource consumption. Finally, to those for whom data safety is paramount, PostgreSQL's ACID-compliant transactions ensure your commits are completely atomic, consistent, isolated, and durable.

## CHAPTER 3

HBase

Apache HBase is made for big jobs, like a nail gun. You would never use HBase to catalog your corporate sales list or build a to-do list app for fun, just like you'd never use a nail gun to build a doll house. If the size of your dataset isn't many, many gigabytes at the very least then you should probably use a less heavy-duty tool.

At first glance, HBase looks a lot like a relational database, so much so that if you didn't know any better, you might think that it is one. In fact, the most challenging part of learning HBase isn't the technology; it's that many of the words used in HBase are deceptively familiar. For example, HBase stores data in buckets it calls *tables*, which contain *cells* that appear at the intersection of *rows* and *columns*. Sounds like a relational database, right?

Wrong! In HBase, tables don't behave like relations, rows don't act like records, and columns are completely variable and not enforced by any predefined schema. Schema design is still important, of course, because it informs the performance characteristics of the system, but it won't keep your house in order—that task falls to you and how your applications use HBase. In general, trying to shoehorn HBase into an RDBMS-style system is fraught with nothing but peril and a certain path to frustration and failure. HBase is the evil twin, the bizarro doppelgänger, if you will, of RDBMS.

On top of that, unlike relational databases, which sometimes have trouble scaling out, HBase doesn't scale *down*. If your production HBase cluster has fewer than five nodes, then, quite frankly, you're doing it wrong. HBase is not the right database for some problems, particularly those where the amount of data is measured in megabytes, or even in the low gigabytes.

So why would you use HBase? Aside from scalability, there are a few reasons. To begin with, HBase has some built-in features that other databases lack, such as versioning, compression, garbage collection (for expired data), and in-memory tables. Having these features available right out of the box means less code that you have to write when your requirements demand them. HBase also makes strong consistency guarantees, making it easier to transition from relational databases for some use cases. Finally, HBase guarantees atomicity at the row level, which means that you can have strong consistency guarantees at a crucial level of HBase's data model.

For all of these reasons, HBase really shines as the cornerstone of a large-scale online analytics processing system. While individual operations may sometimes be slower than equivalent operations in other databases, scanning through enormous datasets is an area where HBase truly excels. For genuinely big queries, HBase often outpaces other databases, which helps to explain why HBase is often used at big companies to back heavy-duty logging and search systems.

Introducing HBase

HBase is a *column-oriented* database that prides itself on its ability to provide both consistency and scalability. It is based on Bigtable, a high-performance, proprietary database developed by Google and described in the 2006 white paper "Bigtable: A Distributed Storage System for Structured Data."[1] Initially created for natural language processing, HBase started life as a contrib package for Apache Hadoop. Since then, it has become a top-level Apache project.

 Luc says:
Hosted HBase with Google Cloud Bigtable

As you'll see later in this chapter, HBase can be tricky to administer. Fortunately, there's now a compelling option for those who want to utilize the power of HBase with very little operational burden: Google's Cloud Bigtable, which is part of its Cloud Platform suite of products. Cloud Bigtable isn't 100% compatible with HBase but as of early 2018 it's very close—close enough that you may be able to migrate many existing HBase applications over.

If you find the basic value proposition of, for example, Amazon's cloud-based DynamoDB compelling and you think HBase is a good fit for a project, then Cloud Bigtable might be worth checking out. You can at least be assured that it's run by the same company that crafted the concepts behind HBase (and the folks at Google do seem to know a thing or two about scale).

---

1. http://research.google.com/archive/bigtable.html

On the architecture front, HBase is designed to be fault tolerant. Hardware failures may be uncommon in individual machines but, in large clusters, node failure is the norm (as are network issues). HBase can gracefully recover from individual server failures because it uses both *write-ahead logging*, which writes data to an in-memory log before it's written (so that nodes can use the log for recovery rather than disk), and *distributed configuration*, which means that nodes can rely on each other for configuration rather than on a centralized source.

Additionally, HBase lives in the Hadoop ecosystem, where it benefits from its proximity to other related tools. Hadoop is a sturdy, scalable computing platform that provides a distributed file system and MapReduce capabilities. Wherever you find HBase, you'll find Hadoop and other infrastructural components that you can use in your own applications, such as Apache Hive, a data warehousing tool, and Apache Pig, a parallel processing tool (and *many* others).

Finally, HBase is actively used and developed by a number of high-profile companies for their "Big Data" problems. Notably, Facebook uses HBase for a variety of purposes, including for Messages, search indexing, and stream analysis. Twitter uses it to power its people search capability, for monitoring and performance data, and more. Airbnb uses it as part of their realtime stream processing stack. Apple uses it for...something, though they won't publicly say what. The parade of companies using HBase also includes the likes of eBay, Meetup, Ning, Yahoo!, and many others.

With all of this activity, new versions of HBase are coming out at a fairly rapid clip. At the time of this writing, the current stable version is 1.2.1, so that's what you'll be using. Go ahead and download HBase, and we'll get started.

Day 1: CRUD and Table Administration

Today's goal is to learn the nuts and bolts of working with HBase. You'll get a local instance of HBase running in standalone mode (rather than in distributed mode), and then you'll use the HBase shell to create and alter tables and to insert and modify data using basic CRUD-style commands. After that, you'll explore how to perform some of those operations programmatically by using the HBase Java API in JRuby. Along the way, you'll uncover some HBase architectural concepts, such as the relationship between rows, column families, columns, and values in a table. Just bear in mind that these concepts in HBase are subtly different from their counterparts in relational databases.

According to most HBase admins out there, a fully operational, production-quality HBase cluster should really consist of no fewer than five nodes. But this bulky of a setup would be overkill for our needs (and for our laptops). Fortunately, HBase supports three running modes:

- *Standalone* mode is a single machine acting alone.
- *Pseudo-distributed* mode is a single node pretending to be a cluster.
- *Fully distributed* mode is a cluster of nodes working together.

For most of this chapter, you'll be running HBase in standalone mode. Yet even that can be a bit of a challenge, especially compared to other databases in this book, such as Redis or MongoDB. So although we won't cover every aspect of installation and administration, we'll give some relevant troubleshooting tips where appropriate.

Configuring HBase

Before you can use HBase, you need to provide it with some configuration, as HBase doesn't really have an "out-of-the-box" mode. Configuration settings for HBase are kept in a file called hbase-site.xml, which can be found in the ${HBASE_HOME}/conf directory. Note that HBASE_HOME is an environment variable pointing to the directory where you've installed HBase. Make sure to set this variable now, preferably in your .bash_profile or similar file so that it persists across shell sessions.

Initially, this hbase-site.xml file contains just an empty <configuration> tag. You can add any number of property definitions to your configuration using this format:

```
<property>
  <name>some.property.name</name>
  <value>A property value</value>
</property>
```

The hbase-default.xml File

Another way of installing HBase is to clone the project directory locally using Git, either from the Apache repository at http://git.apache.org/hbase.git or from the mirror repository on GitHub at https://github.com/apache/hbase.

If you install HBase this way, you'll find an hbase-default.xml file in the hbase-common/src/main/resources subdirectory. This is a very handy file that lists all of the available configurable parameters for HBase—and there are many!—along with default values and descriptions for each parameter.

You can also see the contents of this file in your browser on GitHub.[a]

---

a.   https://github.com/apache/hbase/blob/master/hbase-common/src/main/resources/hbase-default.xml

By default, HBase uses a temporary directory to store its data files. This means you'll lose *all your data* whenever the operating system decides to reclaim the disk space. To keep your data around, you should specify a non-ephemeral storage location. Set the hbase.rootdir property to an appropriate path like so:

```
<property>
  <name>hbase.rootdir</name>
  <value>file:///path/to/hbase</value>
</property>
```

Here's an example configuration:

```
<property>
  <name>hbase.rootdir</name>
  <value>file://</value>
</property>
```

To start HBase, open a terminal (command prompt) and run this command:

```
$ ${HBASE_HOME}/bin/start-hbase.sh
```

To shut down HBase at any time, use the stop-hbase.sh command in the same directory.

If anything goes wrong, take a look at the most recently modified files in the ${HBASE_HOME}/logs directory. On *nix-based systems, the following command will pipe the latest log data to the console as it's written:

```
$ cd ${HBASE_HOME}
$ find ./logs -name "hbase-*.log" -exec tail -f {} \;
```

The HBase Shell

The HBase shell is a JRuby-based command-line program you can use to interact with HBase. In the shell, you can add and remove tables, alter table schemas, add or delete data, and perform a bunch of other tasks. Later, we'll explore other means of connecting to HBase, but for now the shell will be our home.

With HBase running, open a terminal and fire up the HBase shell:

```
$ ${HBASE_HOME}/bin/hbase shell
```

To confirm that it's working properly, try asking it for version information. That should output a version number and hash, and a timestamp for when the version was released.

```
hbase> version
1.2.1, r8d8a7107dc4ccbf36a92f64675dc60392f85c015, Wed Mar 30 11:19:21 CDT 2016
```

You can enter help at any time to see a list of available commands or to get usage information about a particular command.

Next, execute the status command to see how your HBase server is holding up.

```
hbase> status
1 active master, 0 backup masters, 1 servers, 0 dead, 2.0000 average load
```

If an error occurs for any of these commands or if the shell hangs, a connection problem could be to blame. HBase does its best to automatically configure its services based on your network setup, but sometimes it gets it wrong. If you're seeing these symptoms, check the HBase network settings.

HBase Network Settings

By default, HBase tries to make its services available to external clients, but in our case, we only need to connect from the same machine. So it might help to add some or all of the following properties to your hbase-site.xml file (your mileage may vary). Note that the values in the following table will help only if you plan to connect locally and not remotely:

property name	value
hbase.master.dns.interface	lo
hbase.master.info.bindAddress	127.0.0.1
hbase.regionserver.info.bindAddress	127.0.0.1
hbase.regionserver.dns.interface	lo
hbase.zookeeper.dns.interface	lo

The properties tell HBase how to establish connections for the master server and region servers (both of which we'll discuss later) and for ZooKeeper (which HBase uses as a configuration service). The properties with the value "lo" refer to the so-called *loopback* interface. On *nix systems, the loopback interface is not a real network interface (like your Ethernet or wireless cards) but rather a software-only interface for the computer to use to connect to itself. The bindAddress properties tell HBase which IP address to try to listen on.

Creating a Table

Most programming languages have some concept of a key/value *map*. Java-Script has objects, Ruby has hashes, Go has maps, Python has dictionaries, Java has hashmaps, and so on. A table in HBase is basically a big map—well, more accurately, a *map of maps*.

In an HBase table, keys are arbitrary strings that each map to a *row* of data. A row is itself a map in which keys are called *columns* and values are stored as uninterpreted arrays of bytes. Columns are grouped into *column families*, so a column's full name consists of two parts: the column family name and the *column qualifier*. Often these are concatenated together using a colon (for example, family:qualifier).

Here's what a simple HBase table might look like if it were a Python dictionary:

```
hbase_table = {                  # Table
  'row1': {                      # Row key
    'cf1:col1': 'value1',        # Column family, column, and value
    'cf1:col2': 'value2',
    'cf2:col1': 'value3'
  },
  'row2': {
    # More row data
  }
}
queried_value = hbase_table['row1']['cf1:col1'] # 'value1'
```

For a more visual illustration, take a look at the following diagram.

	row keys	column family "color"	column family "shape"
row	"first"	"red": "#F00" "blue": "#00F" "yellow": "#FF0"	"square": "4"
row	"second"		"triangle": "3" "square": "4"

In this figure, we have a hypothetical table with two column families: color and shape. The table has two rows—denoted by dashed boxes—identified by their row keys: first and second. Looking at just the first row, you see that it has three columns in the color column family (with qualifiers red, blue, and yellow) and one column in the shape column family (square). The combination of row key and column name (including both family and qualifier) creates an address for locating data. In this example, the tuple first/color:red points us to the value '#F00'.

Now let's take what you've learned about table structure and use it to do something fun—you're going to make a wiki! There are lots of juicy info bits you might want to associate with a wiki, but you'll start with the bare minimum. A wiki contains pages, each of which has a unique title string and contains some article text.

Use the create command to make our wiki table in the HBase shell:

```
hbase> create 'wiki', 'text'
0 row(s) in 1.2160 seconds
```

Here, we're creating a table called wiki with a single column family called text. The table is currently empty; it has no rows and thus no columns. Unlike a relational database, in HBase a column is specific to the row that contains it. Columns don't have to be predefined in something like a CREATE TABLE declaration in SQL. For our purposes here, though, we'll stick to a schema, even though it isn't predefined. When we start adding rows, we'll add columns to store data at the same time.

Visualizing our table architecture, we arrive at something like the following figure.

By our own convention, we expect each row to have exactly one column within the text family, qualified by the empty string ("). So, the full column name containing the text of a page will be 'text:'.

For our wiki table to be useful, it's of course going to need content, so let's add some!

Inserting, Updating, and Retrieving Data

Our wiki needs a Home page, so we'll start with that. To add data to an HBase table, use the put command:

```
hbase> put 'wiki', 'Home', 'text:', 'Welcome to the wiki!'
```

This command inserts a new row into the wiki table with the key 'Home', adding 'Welcome to the wiki!' to the column called 'text:'. Note the colon at the end of the column name. This is actually a requirement in HBase if you don't specify a column family in addition to a column (in this case, you're specifying *no column family*).

We can query the data for the 'Home' row using get, which requires two parameters: the table name and the row key. You can optionally specify a list of columns to return. Here, we'll fetch the value of the text: column:

```
hbase> get 'wiki', 'Home', 'text:'
COLUMN      CELL
 text:      timestamp=1295774833226, value=Welcome to the wiki!
1 row(s) in 0.0590 seconds
```

Notice the timestamp field in the output. HBase stores an integer timestamp for all data values, representing time in milliseconds since the epoch (00:00:00 UTC on January 1, 1970). When a new value is written to the same cell, the old value hangs around, indexed by its timestamp. This is a pretty awesome feature, and one that is unique to HBase amongst the databases in this book. Most databases require you to specifically handle historical data yourself, but in HBase, versioning is baked right in!

Finally, let's perform a scan operation:

```
hbase> scan 'wiki'
```

Scan operations simply return all rows in the entire table. Scans are powerful and great for development purposes but they are also a very blunt instrument, so use them with care. We don't have much data in our wiki table so it's perfectly fine, but if you're running HBase in production, stick to more precise reads or you'll put a lot of undue strain on your tables.

Putting and Getting

The put and get commands allow you to specify a timestamp explicitly. If using milliseconds since the epoch doesn't strike your fancy, you can specify another integer value of your choice. This gives you an extra dimension to work with if you need it. If you don't specify a timestamp, HBase will use the current time when inserting, and it will return the most recent version when reading.

Luc says:

Rows Are Like Mini Databases

Rows in HBase are a bit tough to fully understand at first because rows tend to be much more "shallow" in other databases. In relational databases, for example, rows contain any number of column values but not metadata such as timestamps, and they don't contain the kind of depth that HBase rows do (like the Python dictionary in the previous example).

I recommend thinking of HBase rows as being a tiny database in their own right. Each cell in the database can have many different values associated with it (like a mini timeseries database). When you fetch a row in HBase, you're not fetching a set of values; you're fetching a small world.

Altering Tables

So far, our wiki schema has pages with titles, text, and an integrated version history but nothing else. Let's expand our requirements to include the following:

- In our wiki, a page is uniquely identified by its title.
- A page can have unlimited revisions.
- A revision is identified by its timestamp.
- A revision contains text and optionally a commit comment.
- A revision was made by an author, identified by name.

Visually, our requirements can be sketched as you see in the following figure.

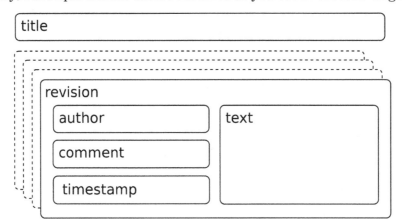

In this abstract representation of our requirements for a page, we see that each revision has an author, a commit comment, some article text, and a timestamp. The title of a page is not part of a revision because it's the identifier we use to denote revisions belonging to the same page and thus cannot change. If you *did* want to change the title of a page, you'd need to write a whole new row.

Mapping our vision to an HBase table takes a somewhat different form, as illustrated in the figure that follows.

keys (title)	family "text"	family "revision"
row (page) "first page"	"". "..."	"author": "..." "comment": "..."
row (page) "second page"	"". "..."	"author": "..." "comment": "..."

Our wiki table uses the title as the row key and will group other page data into two column families called text and revision. The text column family is the same as before; we expect each row to have exactly one column, qualified by the empty string ('), to hold the article contents. The job of the revision column family is to hold other revision-specific data, such as the author and commit comment.

Defaults

We created the wiki table with no special options, so all the HBase default values were used. One such default value is to keep only three VERSIONS of column values, so let's increase that. To make schema changes, first we have to take the table offline with the disable command.

```
hbase> disable 'wiki'
0 row(s) in 1.0930 seconds
```

Now we can modify column family characteristics using the alter command.

```
hbase> alter 'wiki', { NAME => 'text', VERSIONS =>
hbase*   org.apache.hadoop.hbase.HConstants::ALL_VERSIONS }
0 row(s) in 0.0430 seconds
```

Here, we're instructing HBase to alter the text column family's VERSIONS attribute. There are a number of other attributes we could have set, some of which we'll discuss in Day 2. The hbase* line means that it's a continuation of the previous line.

Altering a Table

Operations that alter column family characteristics can be very expensive because HBase has to create a new column family with the chosen specifications and then copy all the data over. In a production system, this may incur significant downtime. For this reason, the sooner you settle on column family options the better.

With the wiki table still disabled, let's add the revision column family, again using the alter command:

```
hbase> alter 'wiki', { NAME => 'revision', VERSIONS =>
hbase*    org.apache.hadoop.hbase.HConstants::ALL_VERSIONS }
0 row(s) in 0.0660 seconds
```

Just as before, with the text family, we're only adding a revision *column family* to the table schema, not individual *columns*. Though we expect each row to eventually contain a revision:author and revision:comment, it's up to the client to honor this expectation; it's not written into any formal schema. If someone wants to add a revision:foo for a page, HBase won't stop them.

Moving On

With these additions in place, let's reenable our wiki:

```
hbase> enable 'wiki'
0 row(s) in 0.0550 seconds
```

Now that our wiki table has been modified to support our growing requirements list, we can start adding data to columns in the revision column family.

Adding Data Programmatically

As you've seen, the HBase shell is great for tasks such as manipulating tables. Sadly, the shell's data insertion support isn't the best. The put command allows you to set only one column value at a time, and in our newly updated schema, we need to add multiple column values simultaneously so they all share the same timestamp. We're going to need to start scripting.

The following script can be executed directly in the HBase shell because the shell is also a JRuby interpreter. When run, it adds a new version of the text for the Home page, setting the author and comment fields at the same time. JRuby runs on the Java virtual machine (JVM), giving it access to the HBase Java code. These examples will *not* work with non-JVM Ruby.

```
hbase/put_multiple_columns.rb
import 'org.apache.hadoop.hbase.client.HTable'
import 'org.apache.hadoop.hbase.client.Put'

def jbytes(*args)
  args.map {|arg| arg.to_s.to_java_bytes}
end

table = HTable.new(@hbase.configuration, "wiki")

p = Put.new(*jbytes("Home"))

p.add(*jbytes("text", "", "Hello world"))
p.add(*jbytes("revision", "author", "jimbo"))
p.add(*jbytes("revision", "comment", "my first edit"))

table.put(p)
```

The import lines bring references to useful HBase classes into the shell. This saves us from having to write out the full namespace later. Next, the jbytes() function takes any number of arguments and returns an array converted to Java byte arrays, as the HBase API methods demand.

After that, we create a local variable (table) pointing to our wiki table, using the @hbase administration object for configuration information.

Next, we stage a commit operation by creating and preparing a new instance of a Put object, which takes the row to be modified. In this case, we're sticking with the Home page we've been working with thus far. Finally, we add() properties to our Put instance and then call on the table object to execute the put operation we've prepared. The add() method has several forms; in our case, we used the three-argument version: add(column_family, column_qualifier, value).

Why Column Families?

You may be tempted to build your whole structure without column families. Why not just store all of a row's data in a single column family? That solution would be simpler to implement. But there are downsides to avoiding column families. One of them is that you'd miss out on fine-grained performance tuning. Each column family's performance options are configured independently. These settings affect things such as read and write speed and disk space consumption.

The other advantage to keep in mind is that column families are stored in different directories. When reading row data in HBase, you can potentially target your reads to specific column families within the row and thus avoid unnecessary cross-directory lookups, which can provide a speed boost, especially in read-heavy workloads.

All operations in HBase are atomic at the *row level*. No matter how many columns are affected, the operation will have a consistent view of the particular row being accessed or modified. This design decision helps clients reason intelligently about the data.

Our put operation affects several columns and doesn't specify a timestamp, so all column values will have the same timestamp (the current time in milliseconds). Let's verify by invoking get.

```
hbase> get 'wiki', 'Home'
COLUMN                CELL
 revision:author      timestamp=1296462042029, value=jimbo
 revision:comment     timestamp=1296462042029, value=my first edit
 text:                timestamp=1296462042029, value=Hello world
3 row(s) in 0.0300 seconds
```

As you can see, each column value listed previously has the same timestamp.

Day 1 Wrap-Up

Today, you got a firsthand look at a running HBase server. You learned how to configure it and monitor log files for troubleshooting. And using the HBase shell you performed basic administration and data manipulation tasks.

In providing a basic data model for a wiki storage engine, you explored schema design in HBase. You learned how to create tables and manipulate column families. Designing an HBase schema means making choices about column family options and, just as important, our semantic interpretation of features such as timestamps and row keys.

You also started poking around in the HBase Java API by executing JRuby code in the shell. In Day 2, you'll take this a step further, using the shell to run custom scripts for big jobs such as data import.

At this point, we hope you've been able to uncouple your thinking from relational database terms such as *table*, *row*, and *column*. By all means, don't *forget* those terms; just suspend their meaning in your head for a while longer, as the difference between how HBase uses these terms and what they mean in other systems will become even starker as we delve deeper into HBase's features.

Day 1 Homework

HBase documentation online generally comes in two flavors: extremely technical and nonexistent. There are some decent "getting started" guides out there, but there's a chance you may need to spend some time trawling through Javadoc or source code to find answers.

Find

1. Figure out how to use the shell to do the following:

   • Delete individual column values in a row
   • Delete an entire row

2. Bookmark the HBase API documentation for the version of HBase you're using.

Do

1. Create a function called put_many() that creates a Put instance, adds any number of column-value pairs to it, and commits it to a table. The signature should look like this:

   ```
   def put_many(table_name, row, column_values)
     # your code here
   end
   ```

2. Define your put_many() function by pasting it in the HBase shell, and then call it like so:

   ```
   hbase> put_many 'wiki', 'Some title', {
   hbase*    "text:" => "Some article text",
   hbase*    "revision:author" => "jschmoe",
   hbase*    "revision:comment" => "no comment" }
   ```

Day 2: Working with Big Data

With Day 1's table creation and manipulation under our belts, it's time to start adding some serious data to our wiki table. Today, you'll script against the HBase APIs, ultimately streaming Wikipedia content right into our wiki! Along the way, you'll pick up some performance tricks for making faster import jobs. Finally, you'll poke around in HBase's internals to see how it partitions data into regions, achieving a series of both performance and disaster recovery goals.

Importing Data, Invoking Scripts

One common problem people face when trying a new database system is how to migrate data into it. Handcrafting Put operations with static strings, as you did in Day 1, is all well and good, but you can do better.

Fortunately, pasting commands into the shell is not the only way to execute them. When you start the HBase shell from the command line, you can specify the name of a JRuby script to run. HBase will execute that script as though it were entered directly into the shell. The syntax looks like this:

```
$ ${HBASE_HOME}/bin/hbase shell <your_script> [<optional_arguments> ...]
```

Because we're interested specifically in "Big Data," let's create a script for importing Wikipedia articles into our wiki table. The WikiMedia Foundation, which oversees Wikipedia, Wictionary, and other projects, periodically publishes data dumps we can use. These dumps are in the form of enormous XML files. Here's an example record from the English Wikipedia:

```
<page>
  <title>Anarchism</title>
  <id>12</id>
  <revision>
    <id>408067712</id>
    <timestamp>2011-01-15T19:28:25Z</timestamp>
    <contributor>
      <username>RepublicanJacobite</username>
      <id>5223685</id>
    </contributor>
    <comment>Undid revision 408057615 by [[Special:Contributions...</comment>
    <text xml:space="preserve">{{Redirect|Anarchist|the fictional character|
...
[[bat-smg:Anarkėzmos]]
    </text>
  </revision>
</page>
```

Because we have such incredible foresight, the individual items in these XML files contain all the information we've already accounted for in our schema: title (row key), text, timestamp, and author. We ought to be able to write a script to import revisions without too much trouble.

Streaming XML

First things first: We'll need to parse the huge XML files in a streaming fashion, so let's start with that. The basic outline for parsing an XML file in JRuby, record by record, looks like this:

```
hbase/basic_xml_parsing.rb
import 'javax.xml.stream.XMLStreamConstants'

factory = javax.xml.stream.XMLInputFactory.newInstance
reader = factory.createXMLStreamReader(java.lang.System.in)

while reader.has_next

  type = reader.next
```

```
  if type == XMLStreamConstants::START_ELEMENT
    tag = reader.local_name
    # do something with tag
  elsif type == XMLStreamConstants::CHARACTERS
    text = reader.text
    # do something with text
  elsif type == XMLStreamConstants::END_ELEMENT
    # same as START_ELEMENT
  end

end
```

Breaking this down, there are a few parts worth mentioning. First, we produce an XMLStreamReader and wire it up to java.lang.System.in, which means it will be reading from standard input.

Next, we set up a while loop, which will continuously pull out tokens from the XML stream until there are none left. Inside the while loop, we process the current token. What happens then depends on whether the token is the start of an XML tag, the end of a tag, or the text in between.

Streaming Wikipedia

Now we can combine this basic XML processing framework with our previous exploration of the HTable and Put interfaces you explored previously. Here is the resultant script. Most of it should look familiar, and we will discuss a few novel parts.

hbase/import_from_wikipedia.rb
```
require 'time'

import 'org.apache.hadoop.hbase.client.HTable'
import 'org.apache.hadoop.hbase.client.Put'
import 'javax.xml.stream.XMLStreamConstants'

def jbytes(*args)
  args.map { |arg| arg.to_s.to_java_bytes }
end

factory = javax.xml.stream.XMLInputFactory.newInstance
reader = factory.createXMLStreamReader(java.lang.System.in)

document = nil
buffer = nil
count = 0

table = HTable.new(@hbase.configuration, 'wiki')
table.setAutoFlush(false)

while reader.has_next
  type = reader.next
```

```
  if type == XMLStreamConstants::START_ELEMENT

    case reader.local_name
    when 'page' then document = {}
    when /title|timestamp|username|comment|text/ then buffer = []
    end

  elsif type == XMLStreamConstants::CHARACTERS

    buffer << reader.text unless buffer.nil?

  elsif type == XMLStreamConstants::END_ELEMENT

    case reader.local_name
    when /title|timestamp|username|comment|text/
      document[reader.local_name] = buffer.join
    when 'revision'
      key = document['title'].to_java_bytes
      ts = (Time.parse document['timestamp']).to_i

      p = Put.new(key, ts)
      p.add(*jbytes("text", "", document['text']))
      p.add(*jbytes("revision", "author", document['username']))
      p.add(*jbytes("revision", "comment", document['comment']))
      table.put(p)

      count += 1
      table.flushCommits() if count % 10 == 0
      if count % 500 == 0
        puts "#{count} records inserted (#{document['title']})"
      end
    end
  end
end
end

table.flushCommits()
exit
```

A few things to note in the preceding snippet:

- Several new variables were introduced:

  - document holds the current article and revision data.

  - buffer holds character data for the current field within the document (text, title, author, and so on).

  - count keeps track of how many articles you've imported so far.

- Pay special attention to the use of table.setAutoFlush(false). In HBase, data is *automatically flushed* to disk periodically. This is preferred in most applications. By disabling autoflush in our script, any put operations you execute will be buffered until you call table.flushCommits(). This allows you to batch writes together and execute them when it's convenient for you.

- If the start tag is a <page>, then reset document to an empty hash. Otherwise, if it's another tag you care about, reset buffer for storing its text.

- We handle character data by appending it to the buffer.

- For most closing tags, you just stash the buffered contents into the document. If the closing tag is a </revision>, however, you create a new Put instance, fill it with the document's fields, and submit it to the table. After that, you use flushCommits() if you haven't done so in a while and report progress to stdout.

Compression and Bloom Filters

We're almost ready to run the script; we just have one more bit of housecleaning to do first. The text column family is going to contain big blobs of text content. Reading those values will take much longer than values like Hello world or Welcome to the wiki! from Day 1. HBase enables us to compress that data to speed up reads:

```
hbase> alter 'wiki', {NAME=>'text', COMPRESSION=>'GZ', BLOOMFILTER=>'ROW'}
0 row(s) in 0.0510 seconds
```

HBase supports two compression algorithms: Gzip (GZ) and Lempel-Ziv-Oberhumer (LZO). The HBase community highly recommends using LZO over Gzip pretty much unilaterally, but here we're using Gzip. Why is that?

The problem with LZO for our purposes here is the implementation's license. While open source, LZO is not compatible with Apache's licensing philosophy, so LZO can't be bundled with HBase. Detailed instructions are available online for installing and configuring LZO support. If you want high-performance compression, use LZO in your own projects.

A *Bloom filter* is a really cool data structure that efficiently answers the question "Have I ever seen this thing before?" and is used to prevent expensive queries that are doomed to fail (that is, to return no results). Originally developed by Burton Howard Bloom in 1970 for use in spell-checking applications, Bloom filters have become popular in data storage applications for determining quickly whether a key exists.

HBase supports using Bloom filters to determine whether a particular column exists for a given row key (BLOOMFILTER=>'ROWCOL') or just whether a given row key exists at all (BLOOMFILTER=>'ROW'). The number of columns within a column family and the number of rows are both potentially unbounded. Bloom filters offer a fast way of determining whether data exists before incurring an expensive disk read.

How Do Bloom Filters Work?

Without going too deep into implementation details, a Bloom filter manages a statically sized array of bits initially set to 0. Each time a new blob of data is presented to the filter, some of the bits are flipped to 1. Determining which bits to flip depends on generating a hash from the data and turning that hash into a set of bit positions.

Later, to test whether the filter has been presented with a particular blob in the past, the filter figures out which bits would have to be 1 and checks them. If any are 0, then the filter can unequivocally say "no." If all of the bits are 1, then it reports "yes." Chances are it has been presented with that blob before, but false positives are increasingly likely as more blobs are entered.

This is the trade-off of using a Bloom filter as opposed to a simple hash. A hash will never produce a false positive, but the space needed to store that data is unbounded. Bloom filters use a constant amount of space but will occasionally produce false positives at a predictable rate based on saturation. False positives aren't a huge deal, though; they just mean that the filter *says* a value is likely to be there, but you will eventually find out that it isn't.

Engage!

Now that we've dissected the script a bit and added some powerful capabilities to our table, we're ready to kick off the script. Remember that these files are enormous, so downloading and unzipping them is pretty much out of the question. So, what are we going to do?

Fortunately, through the magic of *nix pipes, we can download, extract, and feed the XML into the script all at once. The command looks like this:

```
$ curl https://url-for-the-data-dump.com | bzcat | \
${HBASE_HOME}/bin/hbase shell import_from_wikipedia.rb
```

Note that you should replace the preceding dummy URL with the URL of a WikiMedia Foundation dump file of some kind.[2] You should use [project]-latest-pages-articles.xml.bz2 for either the English Wikipedia (~12.7 GB)[3] or the English Wiktionary (~566 MB).[4] These files contain all of the most recent revisions of pages in the Main namespace. That is, they omit user pages, discussion pages, and so on.

Plug in the URL and run it! You should start seeing output like this shortly:

---

2. https://dumps.wikimedia.org/enwiki/latest
3. https://dumps.wikimedia.org/enwiki/latest/enwiki-latest-pages-articles.xml.bz2
4. https://dumps.wikimedia.org/enwiktionary/latest/enwiktionary-latest-pages-articles.xml.bz2

```
500 records inserted (Ashmore and Cartier Islands)
1000 records inserted (Annealing)
1500 records inserted (Ajanta Caves)
```

The script will happily chug along as long as you let it or until it encounters an error, but you'll probably want to shut it off after a while. When you're ready to kill the script, press Ctrl+C. For now, though, let's leave it running so we can take a peek under the hood and learn about how HBase achieves its horizontal scalability.

Introduction to Regions and Monitoring Disk Usage

In HBase, rows are kept in order, sorted by the row key. A region is a chunk of rows, identified by the starting key (inclusive) and ending key (exclusive). Regions never overlap, and each is assigned to a specific region server in the cluster. In our simplistic standalone server, there is only one region server, which will always be responsible for all regions. A fully distributed cluster would consist of many region servers.

So, let's take a look at your HBase server's disk usage, which will give us insight into how the data is laid out. You can inspect HBase's disk usage by opening a command prompt to the data/default directory in the hbase.rootdir location you specified earlier and executing the du command. du is a standard *nix command-line utility that tells you how much space is used by a directory and its children, recursively. The -h option tells du to report numbers in human-readable form.

Here's what ours looked like after about 68 MB worth of pages (out of over 560 MB total or about 160,000 pages) had been inserted and the import was still running:

```
$ du -h
4.0K    ./wiki/.tabledesc
  0B    ./wiki/.tmp
  0B    ./wiki/1e157605a0e5a1493e4cc91d7e368b05/.tmp
  0B    ./wiki/1e157605a0e5a1493e4cc91d7e368b05/recovered.edits
 11M    ./wiki/1e157605a0e5a1493e4cc91d7e368b05/revision
 64M    ./wiki/1e157605a0e5a1493e4cc91d7e368b05/text
 75M    ./wiki/1e157605a0e5a1493e4cc91d7e368b05
 75M    ./wiki
 75M    .
```

This output tells us a lot about how much space HBase is using and how it's allocated. The lines starting with /wiki describe the space usage for the wiki table. The long-named subdirectory 1e157605a0e5a1493e4cc91d7e368b05 represents an individual region (the only region so far). Under that, the directories /text and /revision correspond to the text and revision column families, respectively. Finally, the last line sums up all these values, telling us that HBase is using 75 MB of disk space. We can safely ignore the .tmp and recovered.edits for now.

One more thing. In the directory that you specified using the hbase.rootdir variable, you'll find three folders named MasterProcWALs, WALs, and oldWALs. These folders hold write-ahead log (WAL) files. HBase uses write-ahead logging to provide protection against node failures. This is a fairly typical disaster recovery technique. For instance, write-ahead logging in file systems is called *journaling*. In HBase, logs are appended to the WAL before any edit operations (put and increment) are persisted to disk.

For performance reasons, edits are not necessarily written to disk immediately. The system does much better when I/O is buffered and written to disk in chunks. If the *region server* responsible for the affected region were to crash during this limbo period, HBase would use the WAL to determine which operations were successful and take corrective action. Without a WAL, a region server crash would mean that that not-yet-written data would be simply lost.

Writing to the WAL is optional and enabled by default. Edit classes such as Put and Increment have a setter method called setWriteToWAL() that can be used to exclude the operation from being written to the WAL. Generally you'll want to keep the default option, but in some instances it might make sense to change it. For example, if you're running an import job that you can rerun any time, such as our Wikipedia import script, you might prioritize the performance benefit of disabling WAL writes over disaster recovery protection.

Regional Interrogation

If you let the script run long enough, you'll see HBase split the table into multiple regions. Here's our du output again, after about 280 MB worth of data (roughly 2.1 million pages) has been written to the wiki table:

```
$ du -h
4.0K    ./wiki/.tabledesc
  0B    ./wiki/.tmp
  0B    ./wiki/48576fdcfcb9b29257fb93d33dbeda90/.tmp
  0B    ./wiki/48576fdcfcb9b29257fb93d33dbeda90/recovered.edits
132M    ./wiki/48576fdcfcb9b29257fb93d33dbeda90/revision
145M    ./wiki/48576fdcfcb9b29257fb93d33dbeda90/text
277M    ./wiki/48576fdcfcb9b29257fb93d33dbeda90
  0B    ./wiki/bd36620826a14025a35f1fe5e928c6c9/.tmp
  0B    ./wiki/bd36620826a14025a35f1fe5e928c6c9/recovered.edits
134M    ./wiki/bd36620826a14025a35f1fe5e928c6c9/revision
113M    ./wiki/bd36620826a14025a35f1fe5e928c6c9/text
```

```
247M    ./wiki/bd36620826a14025a35f1fe5e928c6c9
1.0G    ./wiki
1.0G    .
```

The biggest change is that the old region (1e157605a0e5a1493e4cc91d7e368b05) is now gone and has been replaced by two new regions (48576fd... and bd36620....). In our stand-alone server, all the regions are served by our single server, but in a distributed environment these would be parceled across multiple *region* servers.

This raises a few questions, such as "How do the region servers know which regions they're responsible for serving?" and "How can you find which region (and, by extension, which region server) is serving a given row?"

If we drop back into the HBase shell, we can query the hbase:meta to find out more about the current regions. hbase:meta is a special table whose sole purpose is to keep track of all the user tables and which region servers are responsible for serving the regions of those tables.

```
hbase> scan 'hbase:meta', { COLUMNS => ['info:server', 'info:regioninfo'] }
```

Even for a small number of regions, you should get a lot of output. Let's just focus on the rows that begin with wiki for now. Here's a fragment of ours, formatted and truncated for readability:

```
ROW
  wiki,,1487399747176.48576fdcfcb9b29257fb93d33dbeda90.

COLUMN+CELL
  column=info:server, timestamp=..., value=localhost.localdomain:35552
  column=info:regioninfo, timestamp=1487399747533, value={
    ENCODED => 48576fdcfcb9b29257fb93d33dbeda90,
    NAME => 'wiki,,1487399747176.48576fdcfcb9b29257fb93d33dbeda90.',
    STARTKEY => '', ENDKEY => 'lacrimamj'}

ROW
  wiki,lacrimamj,1487399747176.bd36620826a14025a35f1fe5e928c6c9.

COLUMN+CELL
  column=info:server, timestamp=..., value=localhost.localdomain:35552
  column=info:regioninfo, timestamp=1487399747533, value={
    ENCODED => bd36620826a14025a35f1fe5e928c6c9,
    NAME => 'wiki,lacrimamj,1487399747176.bd36620826a14025a35f1fe5e928c6c9.',
    STARTKEY => 'lacrimamj',
    ENDKEY => ''}
```

Both of the regions listed previously are served by the same server, localhost.localdomain:35552. The first region starts at the empty string row ('') and ends with 'lacrimamj'. The second region starts at 'lacrimamj' and goes to '' (that is, to the end of the available keyspace).

STARTKEY is inclusive, while ENDKEY is exclusive. So, if you were looking for the 'Demographics of Macedonia' row, you'd find it in the first region.

Because rows are kept in sorted order, we can use the information stored in hbase:meta to look up the region and server where any given row should be found. But where is the hbase:meta table stored?

It turns out that the hbase:meta table can also be split into regions and served by region servers just like any other table would be. If you run the load script as long as we have, this may or may not happen on your machine; you may have this table stored in only one region. To find out which servers have which parts of the hbase:meta table, look at the results of the preceding scan query but pay attention to the rows that begin with hbase:namespace.

```
ROW
  hbase:namespace,,1486625601612.aa5b4cfb7204bfc50824dee1886103c5.
COLUMN+CELL
  column=info:server, timestamp=..., value=localhost.localdomain:35552
  column=info:regioninfo, timestamp=1486625602069, value={
    ENCODED => aa5b4cfb7204bfc50824dee1886103c5,
    NAME => 'hbase:namespace,,1486625601612.aa5b4cfb7204bfc50824dee1886103c5.',
    STARTKEY => '',
    ENDKEY => ''}
```

In this case, the entire keyspace (beginning with '' and ending with '') is stored in the aa5b4cfb7204bfc50824dee1886103c5, which is on disk on our machine in the data/hbase/namespace/aa5b4cfb7204bfc50824dee1886103c5 subdirectory of our HBase data folder (your region name will vary).

Describe Your Tables

To see other metadata associated with an HBase table, use the describe command, like so:

```
hbase> describe 'wiki'
hbase> describe 'hbase:meta'
```

This will tell you whether the table is currently enabled and provide a lot of information about each column family in the table, including any Bloom filters that you've applied, which compression is used, and so on.

The assignment of regions to region servers, including hbase:meta regions, is handled by the *master* node, often referred to as HBaseMaster. The master server can also be a region server, performing both duties simultaneously.

When a region server fails, the master server steps in and reassigns responsibility for regions previously assigned to the failed node. The new stewards of those regions would look to the WAL to see what, if any, recovery steps are needed. If the master server fails, responsibility defers to any of the other region servers that step up to become the master.

Scanning One Table to Build Another

Once you've stopped the import script from running, we can move on to the next task: extracting information from the imported wiki contents.

Wiki syntax is filled with links, some of which link internally to other articles and some of which link to external resources. This interlinking contains a wealth of topological data. Let's capture it!

Our goal is to capture the relationships between articles as directional links, pointing one article *to* another or receiving a link *from* another. An internal article link in wikitext looks like this: *[[<target name>|<alt text>]]*, where *<target name>* is the article to link to, and *<alt text>* is the alternative text to display (optional).

For example, if the text of the article on *Star Wars* contains the string *"[[Yoda|jedi master]]"*, we want to store that relationship twice—once as an outgoing link from *Star Wars* and once as an incoming link to Yoda. Storing the relationship twice means that it's fast to look up both a page's outgoing links and its incoming links.

To store this additional link data, we'll create a new table. Head over to the shell and enter this:

```
hbase> create 'links', {
  NAME => 'to', VERSIONS => 1, BLOOMFILTER => 'ROWCOL'
},{
  NAME => 'from', VERSIONS => 1, BLOOMFILTER => 'ROWCOL'
}
```

In principle, we could have chosen to shove the link data into an existing column family or merely added one or more additional column families to the wiki table rather than create a new one. When you create a separate table, this has the advantage that the tables have separate regions, which in turn means that the cluster can more effectively split regions as necessary.

The general guidance for column families in the HBase community is to try to keep the number of families per table down. You can do this either by combining more columns into the same families or by putting families in different tables entirely. The choice is largely decided by whether and how often clients will need to get an entire row of data (as opposed to needing just a few column values).

For the wiki application we've been developing, the text and revision column families need to be on the same table so when you put new revisions in, the metadata and the text share the same timestamp. The links content, by contrast, will never have the same timestamp as the article from which the data came. Further, most client actions will be interested either in the article text or in the extracted information about article links but probably not in both at the same time. So, splitting out the to and from column families into a separate table makes sense.

Constructing the Scanner

With the links table created, we're ready to implement a script that'll scan all the rows of the wiki table. Then, for each row, it'll retrieve the wikitext and parse out the links. Finally, for each link found, it'll create incoming and outgoing link table records. The bulk of this script should be pretty familiar to you by now. Most of the pieces are recycled, and we'll discuss the few novel bits.

```ruby
hbase/generate_wiki_links.rb
import 'org.apache.hadoop.hbase.client.HTable'
import 'org.apache.hadoop.hbase.client.Put'
import 'org.apache.hadoop.hbase.client.Scan'
import 'org.apache.hadoop.hbase.util.Bytes'

def jbytes(*args)
  return args.map { |arg| arg.to_s.to_java_bytes }
end

wiki_table = HTable.new(@hbase.configuration, 'wiki')
links_table = HTable.new(@hbase.configuration, 'links')
links_table.setAutoFlush(false)

scanner = wiki_table.getScanner(Scan.new)

linkpattern = /\[\[([^\[\]\|]\|\:\#][^\[\]\|\:]*)(?:\|(([^\[\]\|]+))?\]\]/
count = 0

while (result = scanner.next())
  title = Bytes.toString(result.getRow())
  text = Bytes.toString(result.getValue(*jbytes('text', '')))
  if text
    put_to = nil
    text.scan(linkpattern) do |target, label|
      unless put_to
        put_to = Put.new(*jbytes(title))
        put_to.setWriteToWAL( false )
      end

      target.strip!
      target.capitalize!

      label = '' unless label
      label.strip!
```

```
        put_to.add(*jbytes("to", target, label))
        put_from = Put.new(*jbytes(target))
        put_from.add(*jbytes("from", title, label))
        put_from.setWriteToWAL(false)
        links_table.put(put_from)
      end
      links_table.put(put_to) if put_to
      links_table.flushCommits()
    end

    count += 1
    puts "#{count} pages processed (#{title})" if count % 500 == 0
end

links_table.flushCommits()
exit
```

A few things to note in this script:

- First, we grab a Scan object, which we'll use to scan through the wiki table.

- Extracting row and column data requires some byte wrangling but generally isn't too bad either.

- Each time the linkpattern appears in the page text, we extract the target article and text of the link and then use those values to add to our Put instances.

- Finally, we tell the table to execute our accumulated Put operations. It's possible (though unlikely) for an article to contain no links at all, which is the reason for the if put_to clause.

- Using setWriteToWAL(false) for these puts is a judgment call. Because this exercise is for educational purposes and because you could simply rerun the script if anything went wrong, we'll take the speed bonus and accept our fate should the node fail.

Running the Script

If you're ready to throw caution to the wind, run the script.

```
${HBASE_HOME}/bin/hbase shell generate_wiki_links.rb
```

It should produce output like this:

```
500 pages processed (10 petametres)
1000 pages processed (1259)
1500 pages processed (1471 BC)
2000 pages processed (1683)
...
```

As with the previous script, you can let it run as long as you like, even to completion. If you want to stop it, press Ctrl+C.

You can monitor the disk usage of the script using du as we've done before. You'll see new entries for the links table we just created, and the size counts will increase as the script runs.

Examining the Output

We just created a scanner programmatically to perform a sophisticated task. Now we'll use the shell's scan command to simply dump part of a table's contents to the console. For each link the script finds in a text: blob, it will indiscriminately create both to and from entries in the links table. To see the kinds of links being created, head over to the shell and scan the table.

```
hbase> scan 'links', STARTROW => "Admiral Ackbar", ENDROW => "It's a Trap!"
```

You should get a whole bunch of output. Of course, you can use the get command to see the links for just a single article.

```
hbase> get 'links', 'Addition'
COLUMN                                    CELL
 from:+                                    timestamp=1487402389072, value=
 from:0                                    timestamp=1487402390828, value=
 from:Addition                             timestamp=1487402391595, value=
 from:Appendix:Basic English word list    timestamp=1487402393334, value=
 ...
```

The structure of the wiki table is highly regular, with each row consisting of the same columns. As you recall, each row has text:, revision:author, and revision:comment columns. The links table has no such regularity. Each row may have one column or hundreds. And the variety of column names is as diverse as the row keys themselves (titles of Wikipedia articles). That's okay! HBase is a so-called sparse data store for exactly this reason.

To find out just how many rows are now in your table, you can use the count command.

```
hbase> count 'wiki', INTERVAL => 100000, CACHE => 10000
Current count: 100000, row: Nov-Zelandon
Current count: 200000, row: adiudicamur
Current count: 300000, row: aquatores
Current count: 500000, row: coiso
...
Current count: 1300000, row: occludesti
Current count: 1400000, row: plendonta
Current count: 1500000, row: receptarum
Current count: 1900000, row: ventilators
2179230 row(s) in 17.3440 seconds
```

Because of its distributed architecture, HBase doesn't immediately know how many rows are in each table. To find out, it has to count them (by performing a table scan). Fortunately, HBase's region-based storage architecture lends itself to fast distributed scanning. So, even if the operation at hand requires a table scan, we don't have to worry quite as much as we would with other databases.

Day 2 Wrap-Up

Whew, that was a pretty big day! You learned how to write an import script for HBase that parses data out of a stream of XML. Then you used those techniques to stream Wikipedia dumps directly into your wiki table.

You learned more of the HBase API, including some client-controllable performance levers such as setAutoFlush(), flushCommits(), and setWriteToWAL(). Along those lines, we discussed some HBase architectural features such as disaster recovery, provided via the write-ahead log.

Speaking of architecture, you discovered table regions and how HBase divvies up responsibility for them among the region servers in the cluster. We scanned the hbase:meta table to get a feel for HBase internals.

Finally, we discussed some of the performance implications of HBase's sparse design. In so doing, we touched on some community best practices regarding the use of columns, families, and tables.

Day 2 Homework

Find

1. Find a discussion or article describing the pros and cons of compression in HBase.

2. Find an article explaining how Bloom filters work in general and how they benefit HBase.

3. Aside from the algorithm, what other column family options relate to compression?

4. How does the type of data and expected usage patterns inform column family compression options?

Do

Expanding on the idea of data import, let's build a database containing nutrition facts.

Download the MyPyramid Raw Food Data set from Data.gov[5] and extract the zipped contents to Food_Display_Table.xml.

This data consists of many pairs of <Food_Display_Row> tags. Inside these, each row has a <Food_Code> (integer value), <Display_Name> (string), and other facts about the food in appropriately named tags.

1. Create a new table called foods with a single column family to store the facts. What should you use for the row key? What column family options make sense for this data?

2. Create a new JRuby script for importing the food data. Use the streaming XML parsing style we used earlier for the Wikipedia import script and tailor it to the food data. Pipe the food data into your import script on the command line to populate the table.

3. Using the HBase shell, query the foods table for information about your favorite foods.

Day 3: Taking It to the Cloud

On Days 1 and 2, you got quite a lot of hands-on experience using HBase in standalone mode. Our experimentation so far has focused on accessing a single local server. But in reality, if you choose to use HBase, you'll want to have a good-sized cluster in order to realize the performance benefits of its distributed architecture. And nowadays, there's also an increasingly high chance that you'll want to run it in the cloud.

Here on Day 3, let's turn our attention toward operating and interacting with a remote HBase cluster. First, you'll deploy an HBase cluster on Amazon Web Services' Elastic MapReduce platform (more commonly known as AWS and EMR, respectively) using AWS's command-line tool, appropriately named aws. Then, you'll connect directly to our remote HBase cluster using Secure Shell (SSH) and perform some basic operations.

Initial AWS and EMR Setup

EMR is a managed Hadoop platform for AWS. It enables you to run a wide variety of servers in the Hadoop ecosystem—Hive, Pig, HBase, and many others—on EC2 without having to engage in a lot of the nitty-gritty details usually associated with managing those systems.

---

5. https://www.cnpp.usda.gov/Innovations/DataSource/MyFoodapediaData.zip

Warning! AWS Isn't Free

Whenever you're using AWS—or any other cloud provider—always keep in mind that you're using paid services. The exercise that you're about to go through will *probably* be free for you, but it may end up costing a few units of whatever your local currency happens to be. You're free to leave the cluster running, especially if you want to do the Day 3 homework in the next section, but we recommend terminating it whenever you're done so that you don't rack up unwanted costs. To do so at any time, use the terminate-clusters command (more on setting a CLUSTER_ID environment variable later in this section):

```
$ aws emr terminate-clusters \
  --cluster-ids ${CLUSTER_ID}
```

You can also set up a usage-based alarm using AWS's CloudWatch service in case you want some extra assurance that you won't end up with any unpleasant billing surprises.[a]

---

a. http://docs.aws.amazon.com/AmazonCloudWatch/latest/monitoring/monitor_estimated_charges_with_cloudwatch.html

Before you can get started spinning up an HBase cluster, you'll need to sign up for an AWS account.[6] Once you've created an account, log into the IAM service in the AWS console[7] and create a new user by clicking Add User.

During the user creation process, select "Programmatic access" and then click "Attach existing policies directly." Select the following policies: IAMFullAccess, AmazonEC2FullAccess, and AmazonElasticMapReduceFullAccess. Then, fetch your AWS access key and secret key from a different section of the console.[8] With that information in hand, install the aws tool using pip and then run aws --version to ensure that the tool installed properly. To configure the client, just run:

```
$ aws configure
```

This will prompt you to enter your access key and secret key and two other pieces of information: a default region name (basically which AWS datacenter you'd like to use) and a default output format. Input us-east-1 and json respectively (though feel free to select a different region if you'd like; the authors happen to be partial to us-west-1 in Oregon). To make sure that your setup is now in place, run aws emr list-clusters, which lists the clusters you've created in EMR. That should return an empty list:

---

6. http://aws.amazon.com/
7. https://console.aws.amazon.com/iam
8. https://console.aws.amazon.com/iam

```
{
    "Clusters": []
}
```

In AWS, your ability to perform actions is based on which *roles* you possess as a user. We won't delve into service access control here. For our purposes, you just need to create a set of roles that enable you to access EMR and to spin up, manage, and finally access clusters. You can create the necessary roles with one convenient built-in command:

```
$ aws emr create-default-roles
```

Once your HBase cluster is up and running in a little bit, you'll need to be able to access it remotely from your own machine. In AWS, direct access to remote processes is typically done over SSH. You'll need to create a new SSH *key pair*, upload it to AWS, and then specify that key pair by name when you create your cluster. Use these commands to create a key pair in your ~/.ssh directory and assign it restrictive permissions:

```
$ aws ec2 create-key-pair \
  --key-name HBaseShell \
  --query 'KeyMaterial' \
  --output text > ~/.ssh/hbase-shell-key.pem
$ chmod 400 ~/.ssh/hbase-shell-key.pem
```

Now you have a key pair stored in the hbase-shell-key.pem file that you can use later to SSH into your cluster. To ensure that it's been successfully created:

```
$ aws ec2 describe-key-pairs
{
    "KeyPairs": [
        {
            "KeyName": "HBaseShell",
            "KeyFingerprint": "1a:2b:3c:4d:1a:..."
        }
    ]
}
```

Creating the Cluster

Now that that initial configuration detour is out of the way, you can get your hands dirty and create your HBase cluster.

```
$ aws emr create-cluster \
  --name "Seven DBs example cluster" \
  --release-label emr-5.3.1 \
  --ec2-attributes KeyName=HBaseShell \
  --use-default-roles \
  --instance-type m1.large \
  --instance-count 3 \
  --applications Name=HBase
```

That's a pretty intricate shell command! Let's break down some of the non-obvious parts.

- --release-label specifies which release of EMR you're working with.

- --ec2-attributes specifies which key pair you want to use to create the cluster (which will enable you to have SSH access later).

- --instance-type specifies which type of machine you want your cluster to run on.

- --instance-count is the number of machines you want in the cluster (by default, 3 instances will mean one master node and two slave nodes).

- --use-default-roles means that you're using the default roles you created a minute ago.

- --applications determines which Hadoop application you'll install (just HBase for us).

If create-cluster is successful, you should get a JSON object back that displays the ID of the cluster. Here's an example ID:

```
{
    "ClusterId": "j-1MFV1QTNSBTD8"
}
```

For convenience, store the cluster ID in your environment so it's easier to use in later shell commands. This is always a good practice when working with AWS on the command line, as almost everything has a randomly generated identifier.

```
$ export CLUSTER_ID=j-1MFV1QTNSBTD8
```

You can verify that the cluster has been created by listing all of the clusters associated with your user account.

```
$ aws emr list-clusters
```

That command should now return a JSON object like this:

```
{
    "Clusters": [
        {
            "Status": {
                "Timeline": {
                    "CreationDateTime": 1487455208.825
                },
                "State": "STARTING",
                "StateChangeReason": {}
            },
```

```
        "NormalizedInstanceHours": 0,
        "Id": "j-1MFV1QTNSBTD8",
        "Name": "Seven DBs example cluster"
      }
    ]
}
```

At this point, your cluster has been *created* but it will take a while to actually start, usually several minutes. Run this command, which checks every five seconds for the current status of the cluster (you should see "STARTING" at first):

```
$ while true; do
    aws emr describe-cluster \
    --cluster-id ${CLUSTER_ID} \
    --query Cluster.Status.State
    sleep 5
  done
```

Again, this could take a while, so take a coffee break, read some EMR documentation, whatever you feel like. Once the the state of the cluster turns to "WAITING", it should be ready to go. You can now inspect all three machines running in the cluster (one master and two slave nodes):

```
$ aws emr list-instances \
  --cluster-id ${CLUSTER_ID}
```

Each instance has its own configuration object associated with it that tells you each instance's current status (RUNNING, TERMINATED, and so on), DNS name, ID, private IP address, and more.

Enabling Access to the Cluster

You have just one last step before you can access your HBase cluster via SSH. You need to authorize TCP *ingress* into the master node of the cluster. To do that, you need to get an identifier for the security group that it belongs to:

```
$ aws emr describe-cluster \
  --cluster-id ${CLUSTER_ID} \
  --query Cluster.Ec2InstanceAttributes.EmrManagedMasterSecurityGroup
```

That should return something like sg-bd63e1ab. Set the SECURITY_GROUP_ID environment variable to that value. Now, you need to run a command that instructs EC2 (which controls the machines running the cluster) to allow TCP ingress on port 22 (used for SSH) from the IP address of your current machine, which you can set as an environment variable.

```
$ export MY_CIDR=$(dig +short myip.opendns.com @resolver1.opendns.com.)/32
$ aws ec2 authorize-security-group-ingress \
  --group-id ${SECURITY_GROUP_ID} \
  --protocol tcp \
  --port 22 \
  --cidr $MY_CIDR
```

Finally, you can SSH into the cluster with the handy `emr ssh` command and point to your local SSH keys and the correct cluster:

```
$ aws emr ssh \
  --cluster-id ${CLUSTER_ID} \
  --key-pair-file ~/.ssh/hbase-shell-key.pem
```

Once the SSH connection is established, you should see a huge ASCII banner whiz by before you're dropped into a remote shell. Now you can open the HBase shell:

```
$ hbase shell
```

If you then see a shell prompt like `hbase(main):001:0>` pop up in your CLI, you've made it! You're now using your own machine as a portal into an HBase cluster running in a datacenter far away (or maybe close by; pretty cool either way). Run a couple other HBase commands from previous exercises for fun:

```
hbase(main):001:0> version
hbase(main):002:0> status
hbase(main):003:0> create 'messages', 'text'
hbase(main):004:0> put 'messages', 'arrival', 'text:', 'HBase: now on AWS!'
hbase(main):005:0> get 'messages', 'arrival'
```

As we mentioned before, always bear in mind that AWS costs money. The exercise that you went through today most likely cost less than a latté at the corner coffee shop. You're free to leave the cluster running, especially if you want to do the Day 3 homework in the next section. You can shut your cluster down at any time using the `terminate-clusters` command:

```
$ aws emr terminate-clusters \
  --cluster-ids ${CLUSTER_ID}
```

Day 3 Wrap-Up

Today you stepped outside of your own machine and installed an HBase cluster in an AWS datacenter, connected your local machine to the remote cluster, played with some of the HBase shell commands that you learned on Day 1, and learned a bit about interacting with AWS services via the command line. This will come in handy when you work with Amazon's DynamoDB and a variety of other AWS services.

Day 3 Homework

For today's homework, open up the AWS documentation for the Find section. For the Do section, leave your HBase cluster running on EMR with the HBase shell open. Just remember to terminate the cluster when you're done!

Find

1. Use the help interface aws for the CLI tool to see which commands are available for the emr subcommand. Read through the help material for some of these commands to get a sense of some of the capabilities offered by EMR that we didn't cover in today's cluster building exercise. Pay special attention to scaling-related commands.

2. Go to the EMR documentation at https://aws.amazon.com/documentation/emr and read up on how to use Simple Storage Service (S3) as a data store for HBase clusters.

Do

1. In your HBase shell that you're accessing via SSH, run some of the cluster metadata commands we explored on Day 2, such as scan 'hbase:meta'. Make note of anything that's fundamentally different from what you saw when running HBase locally in standalone mode.

2. Navigate around the EMR section of your AWS browser console[9] and find the console specific to your running HBase cluster. Resize your cluster down to just two machines by removing one of the slave nodes (known as core nodes). Then increase the cluster size back to three (with two slave/core nodes).

3. Resizing a cluster in the AWS console is nice, but that's not an automatable approach. The aws CLI tool enables you to resize a cluster programmatically. Consult the docs for the emr modify-instance-groups command by running aws emr modify-instance-groups help to find out how this works. Remove a machine from your cluster using that command.

Wrap-Up

HBase is a juxtaposition of simplicity and complexity. Its data storage model is pretty straightforward, with a lot of flexibility and just a few built-in schema constraints. A major barrier to understanding HBase, though, stems from the

---

9. https://console.aws.amazon.com/elasticmapreduce

fact that many terms are overloaded with baggage from the relational world (such as *table* and *column*). Schema design in HBase typically boils down to deciding on the performance characteristics that you want to apply to your tables and columns, which is pretty far afield from the relational world, where things usually hinge upon table design.

HBase's Strengths

Noteworthy features of HBase include a robust scale-out architecture and built-in versioning and compression capabilities. HBase's built-in versioning capability can be a compelling feature for certain use cases. Keeping the version history of wiki pages is a crucial feature for policing and maintenance, for instance. By choosing HBase, you don't have to take any special steps to implement page history—you get it for free. No other database in this book offers that out of the box.

On the performance front, HBase is meant to scale out. If you have huge amounts of data, measured in many terabytes or more, HBase may be for you. HBase is rack aware, replicating data within and between datacenter racks so that node failures can be handled gracefully and quickly.

The HBase community is pretty awesome. There's almost always somebody on the #hbase IRC channel,[10] on HBase's dedicated Slack channel,[11] or on the mailing list[12] ready to help with questions and get you pointed in the right direction.

HBase's Weaknesses

Although HBase is designed to scale out, it doesn't scale down. The HBase community seems to agree that five nodes is the minimum number you'll want to use. Because it's designed to be big, it can also be harder to administrate (though platforms like EMR, which you saw in Day 3, do provide some good managed options). Solving small problems isn't what HBase is about, and nonexpert documentation is tough to come by, which steepens the learning curve.

Additionally, HBase is almost never deployed alone. Instead, it is usually used in conjunction with other scale-ready infrastructure piece. These include

---

10. irc://irc.freenode.net/#hbase
11. https://apache-hbase.slack.com/
12. http://hbase.apache.org/mail-lists.html

Hadoop (an implementation of Google's MapReduce), the Hadoop distributed file system (HDFS), Zookeeper (a headless service that aids internode coordination), and Apache Spark (a popular cluster computing platform). This ecosystem is both a strength and a weakness; it simultaneously provides an ever-expanding set of powerful tools, but making them all work in conjunction with one another across many machines—sometimes in the thousands—can be quite cumbersome.

One noteworthy characteristic of HBase is that it doesn't offer any sorting or indexing capabilities aside from the row keys. Rows are kept in sorted order by their row keys, but no such sorting is done on any other field, such as column names and values. So, if you want to find rows by something other than their key, you need to either scan the table or maintain your own index (perhaps in a separate HBase table or in an external system).

Another missing concept is datatypes. All field values in HBase are treated as uninterpreted arrays of bytes. There is no distinction between, say, an integer value, a string, and a date. They're all bytes to HBase, so it's up to your application to interpret the bytes, which can be tricky, especially if you're used to relational access patterns like object-relational mappers (ORMs).

HBase on CAP

With respect to CAP, HBase is decidedly CP (for more information on the CAP theorem, see Appendix 2, *The CAP Theorem*, on page 315). HBase makes strong consistency guarantees. If a client succeeds in writing a value, other clients will receive the updated value on the next request. Some databases allow you to tweak the CAP equation on a per-operation basis. Not so with HBase. In the face of reasonable amounts of partitioning—for example, a node failing— HBase will remain available, shunting the responsibility off to other nodes in the cluster. However, in the pathological case, where only one node is left alive, HBase has no choice but to refuse requests.

The CAP discussion gets a little more complex when you introduce cluster-to-cluster replication, an advanced feature we didn't cover in this chapter. A typical multicluster setup could have clusters separated geographically by some distance. In this case, for a given column family, one cluster is the system of record, while the other clusters merely provide access to the replicated data. This system is *eventually consistent* because the replication clusters will serve up the most recent values they're aware of, which may not be the most recent values in the master cluster.

Parting Thoughts

HBase can be quite a challenge at first. The terminology is often deceptively reassuring, and the installation and configuration are not for the faint of heart. On the plus side, some of the features HBase offers, such as versioning and compression, are quite unique. These aspects can make HBase quite appealing for solving certain problems. And of course, it scales out to many nodes of commodity hardware quite well. All in all, HBase—like a nail gun— is a pretty big tool, so watch your thumbs.

## CHAPTER 4

MongoDB

MongoDB is in many ways like a power drill. Your ability to complete a task is framed largely by the components you choose to use (from drill bits of varying size to sander adapters). MongoDB's strength lies in its versatility, power, ease of use, and ability to handle jobs both large and small. Although it's a much newer invention than the hammer, it is a tool that builders reach for more and more often.

First publicly released in 2009, MongoDB (often just called *Mongo*) quickly became one of the most widely used NoSQL databases in existence, and remains somewhere very close to the top—if not right at the top—of that list today. MongoDB was designed as a scalable database—the name Mongo comes from "hu*mongo*us"—with performance and easy data access as core design goals. It is a document database, which allows you to store objects nested to whichever depth you'd like, and you can query that nested data in an ad hoc fashion. It enforces no schema (similar to HBase but unlike Postgres), so documents can contain fields or types that no other document in the collection contains (whether that's advisable is another matter).

But don't think that MongoDB's flexibility makes it a toy. There are some huge production MongoDB deployments out there, such as Foursquare, Comcast, Adobe, and CERN, where it's used to collect data from the Large Hadron Collider.

Hu(mongo)us

Mongo hits a sweet spot between the powerful queryability of a relational database and the distributed nature of other databases, like HBase. Project founder Dwight Merriman has said that MongoDB is the database he wishes he'd had at DoubleClick, where as the CTO he had to house large-scale data while still being able to satisfy ad hoc queries.

Mongo is a JSON document database (though technically data is stored in a binary form of JSON known as BSON). A Mongo document can be likened to a relational table row without a schema, whose values can nest to an arbitrary depth. To get an idea of what a JSON document is, check this out:

```
{
    "_id" : ObjectId("4d0b6da3bb30773266f39fea"),
    "country" : {
        "$ref" : "countries",
        "$id" : ObjectId("4d0e6074deb8995216a8309e")
    },
    "famous_for" : [
        "beer",
        "food"
    ],
    "last_census" : "Sun Jan 07 2018 00:00:00 GMT -0700 (PDT)",
    "mayor" : {
        "name" : "Ted Wheeler",
        "party" : "D"
    },
    "name" : "Portland",
    "population" : 582000,
    "state" : "OR"
}
```

JSON document

In some ways, document databases have an opposite workflow compared to relational databases. Relational databases such as PostgreSQL assume you know what data you wish to store without necessarily knowing how you want to use it; what's important is how you store it. The cost of query flexibility is paid upfront on storage. Document databases require you to make some assumptions on how you wish to use your data, but few assumptions on what exactly you wish to store. You can make fundamental "schema" changes on-the-fly, but you may have to pay for your design decisions later on.

Mongo is an excellent choice for an ever-growing class of web projects with large-scale data storage requirements but very little budget to buy big-iron hardware. Thanks to its lack of structured schema, Mongo can grow and change along with your data model. If you're in a web startup with dreams of enormity or are already large with the need to scale servers horizontally, consider MongoDB.

Day 1: CRUD and Nesting

We'll spend today working on some CRUD operations and finish up by performing nested queries in MongoDB. As usual, we won't walk you through the installation steps, but if you visit the Mongo website,[1] you can download a build for your OS or find instructions on how to build from source. If you have OS X, we recommend installing via Homebrew (brew install mongodb). If you use a Debian/Ubuntu variant, try MongoDB's own apt-get package.

---

1.   https://www.mongodb.com/download-center#community

Eric says:

On the Fence

I was on the fence about using a document database until I actually spent time on teams using document stores in production. Coming from the relational database world, I found Mongo to be an easy transition with its ad hoc queries, and its ability to scale out mirrored my own web-scale dreams in ways that many relational stores couldn't. But beyond the structure, I trusted Mongo's development team. They readily admitted that Mongo wasn't perfect, but their clear plans (and general adherence to those plans) were based on general web infrastructure use cases, rather than idyllic debates on scalability and replication. This pragmatic focus on usability should shine as you use MongoDB. A trade-off of this evolutionary behavior is that there are several paths to performing any given function in Mongo.

To prevent typos, Mongo requires you to first create the directory where mongod will store its data. A common location is /data/db. Ensure the user you run the server under has permission to read and write to this directory. If it's not already running, you can fire up the Mongo service by running mongod.

Command-Line Fun

To create a new database named book, first run this command in your terminal. It will connect to the MySQL-inspired command-line interface.

```
$ mongo book
```

Typing help in the console is a good start. We're currently in the book database, but you can view others via show dbs and switch databases with the use command.

Creating a collection in Mongo is as easy as adding an initial record to the collection. Because Mongo is schemaless, there is no need to define anything up front; merely using it is enough. What's more, our book database doesn't really exist until we first add values into it. The following code creates/inserts a towns collection:

```
> db.towns.insert({
  name: "New York",
  population: 22200000,
  lastCensus: ISODate("2016-07-01"),
  famousFor: [ "the MOMA", "food", "Derek Jeter" ],
  mayor : {
    name : "Bill de Blasio",
    party : "D"
  }
})
```

In the previous section, we said documents were JSON (well, really BSON under the hood), so we add new documents as JSON (as we will do later on with CouchDB and, to a lesser extent, DynamoDB).

With the show collections command, you can verify the collection now exists.

```
> show collections

towns
```

We just created the towns collection by storing an object in it. We can list the contents of a collection via find(). We formatted the output here for readability, but yours may just output as a single wrapped line.

```
> db.towns.find()

{
  "_id" : ObjectId("59093bc08c87e2ff4157bd9f"),
  "name" : "New York",
  "population" : 22200000,
  "lastCensus" : ISODate("2016-07-01T00:00:00Z"),
  "famousFor" : [ "the MOMA", "food", "Derek Jeter" ],
  "mayor" : {
    "name" : "Bill de Blasio",
    "party" : "I"
  }
}
```

Unlike a relational database, Mongo does not support server-side joins. A single JavaScript call will retrieve a document *and* all of its nested content, free of charge.

You may have noticed that the JSON output of your newly inserted town contains an _id field of type ObjectId. This is akin to SERIAL incrementing a numeric primary key in PostgreSQL. The ObjectId is always 12 bytes, composed of a timestamp, client machine ID, client process ID, and a 3-byte incremented counter. The figure on page 97 shows how bytes are laid out.

What's great about this autonumbering scheme is that each process on every machine can handle its own ID generation without colliding with other mongod instances. This design choice exhibits Mongo's generally distributed nature.

JavaScript

Mongo's native tongue is JavaScript. You'll use it when doing things as complex as mapreduce queries or as simple as asking for help.

```
> db.help()
> db.towns.help()
```

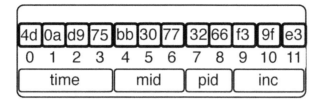

These commands will list available functions related to the given object. db is a JavaScript object that contains information about the current database. db.x is a JavaScript object representing a collection (named x). Commands are just JavaScript functions.

```
> typeof db
object
> typeof db.towns
object
> typeof db.towns.insert
function
```

If you want to inspect the source code for a function, call it without parameters or parentheses (think more Python than Ruby).

```
> db.towns.insert
function (obj, options, _allowDot) {
  if (!obj)
    throw Error("no object passed to insert!");

  var flags = 0;

  // etc.
}
```

Let's populate a few more documents into our towns collection by creating our own JavaScript function.

```
mongo/insertCity.js
function insertCity(
  name, population, lastCensus,
  famousFor, mayorInfo
) {
  db.towns.insert({
    name: name,
    population: population,
    lastCensus: ISODate(lastCensus),
    famousFor: famousFor,
    mayor : mayorInfo
  });
}
```

You can just paste the code for the function into the shell. Then we can call it.

```
> insertCity("Punxsutawney", 6200, '2016-01-31',
    ["Punxsutawney Phil"], { name : "Richard Alexander" }
)
> insertCity("Portland", 582000, '2016-09-20',
    ["beer", "food", "Portlandia"], { name : "Ted Wheeler", party : "D" }
)
```

We should now have three towns in our collection, which you can confirm by calling db.towns.find() as before.

Mongo Data Through a Visual Lens

All of the practical exercises for Mongo in this chapter will involve accessing it either through the Mongo shell or through JavaScript code. If you're more inclined to visual representations of data—and the systems around data—you may want to explore more UI-driven tools. One very notable Mongo-specific tool is Robo 3T,[a] previously known as Robomongo, which is a desktop app that enables you to visualize MongoDB datasets, monitor servers, engage in user management, edit data directly, and so on.

The authors themselves are largely disinclined toward UI-driven tools like this for databases, but Robo 3T is extremely well done, and if a nice UI brings you closer to grasping Mongo or any other database, we say go for it.

---

a.   https://robomongo.org/

Reading: More Fun in Mongo

Earlier, we called the find() function without params to get all documents. To access a specific one, you only need to set an _id property. _id is of type ObjectId, and so to query, you must convert a string by wrapping it in an ObjectId(str) function.

```
> db.towns.find({ "_id" : ObjectId("59094288afbc9350ada6b807") })
{
  "_id" : ObjectId("59094288afbc9350ada6b807"),
  "name" : "Punxsutawney",
  "population" : 6200,
  "lastCensus" : ISODate("2016-01-31T00:00:00Z"),
  "famousFor" : [ "Punxsutawney Phil" ],
  "mayor" : { "name" : "Richard Alexander" }
}
```

The find() function also accepts an optional second parameter: a fields object we can use to filter which fields are retrieved. If we want only the town name (along with _id), pass in name with a value resolving to 1 (or true).

```
> db.towns.find({ _id : ObjectId("59094288afbc9350ada6b807") }, { name : 1 })
{
  "_id" : ObjectId("59093e9eafbc9350ada6b803"),
  "name" : "Punxsutawney"
}
```

To retrieve all fields *except* name, set name to 0 (or false or null).

```
> db.towns.find({ _id : ObjectId("59094288afbc9350ada6b807") }, { name : 0 })
{
  "_id" : ObjectId("59093e9eafbc9350ada6b803"),
  "population" : 6200,
  "lastCensus" : ISODate("2016-01-31T00:00:00Z"),
  "famousFor" : [ "Punxsutawney Phil" ]
}
```

As in PostgreSQL, in Mongo you can construct ad hoc queries on the basis of field values, ranges, or a combination of criteria. To find all towns that begin with the letter *P* and have a population less than 10,000, you can use a Perl-compatible regular expression (PCRE)[2] and a range operator. This query should return the JSON object for Punxsutawney, but including only the name and population fields:

```
> db.towns.find(
  { name : /^P/, population : { $lt : 10000 } },
  { _id: 0, name : 1, population : 1 }
)
{ "name" : "Punxsutawney", "population" : 6200 }
```

Conditional operators in Mongo follow the format of field : { $op : value }, where $op is an operation like $ne (not equal to) or $gt (greater than). You may want a terser syntax, like field < value. But this is JavaScript code, not a domain-specific query language, so queries must comply with JavaScript syntax rules (later today you'll see how to use the shorter syntax in a certain case, but we'll skip that for now).

The good news about the querying language being JavaScript is that you can construct operations as you would objects. Here, we build criteria where the population must be between 10,000 and 1 million people.

```
> var population_range = {
  $lt: 1000000,
  $gt: 10000
}
> db.towns.find(
  { name : /^P/, population : population_range },
  { name: 1 }
)
{ "_id" : ObjectId("59094292afbc9350ada6b808"), "name" : "Portland" }
```

---

2.   http://www.pcre.org/

In addition to number ranges, we can also retrieve date ranges. For example, we can find all names with a *lastCensus* greater than or equal to June 1, 2016, like this:

```
> db.towns.find(
  { lastCensus : { $gte : ISODate('2016-06-01') } },
  { _id : 0, name: 1 }
)
{ "name" : "New York" }
{ "name" : "Portland" }
```

Notice how we again suppressed the _id field in the output explicitly by setting it to 0.

Digging Deep

Mongo loves nested array data. You can query by matching exact values:

```
> db.towns.find(
  { famousFor : 'food' },
  { _id : 0, name : 1, famousFor : 1 }
)
{ "name" : "New York", "famousFor" : [ "the MOMA", "food", "Derek Jeter" ] }
{ "name" : "Portland", "famousFor" : [ "beer", "food", "Portlandia" ] }
```

as well as matching partial values:

```
> db.towns.find(
  { famousFor : /moma/ },
  { _id : 0, name : 1, famousFor : 1 }
)
{ "name" : "New York", "famousFor" : [ "the MOMA", "food" ] }
```

or query by all matching values:

```
> db.towns.find(
  { famousFor : { $all : ['food', 'beer'] } },
  { _id : 0, name:1, famousFor:1 }
)
{ "name" : "Portland", "famousFor" : [ "beer", "food", "Portlandia" ] }
```

or the lack of matching values:

```
> db.towns.find(
  { famousFor : { $nin : ['food', 'beer'] } },
  { _id : 0, name : 1, famousFor : 1 }
)
{ "name" : "Punxsutawney", "famousFor" : [ "Punxsutawney Phil" ] }
```

But the true power of Mongo stems from its ability to dig down into a document and return the results of deeply nested subdocuments. To query a subdocument, your field name is a string separating nested layers with a dot. For instance, you can find towns with mayors from the Democratic Party:

```
> db.towns.find(
  { 'mayor.party' : 'D' },
  { _id : 0, name : 1, mayor : 1 }
)
{ "name" : "New York", "mayor" : { "name" : "Bill de Blasio", "party" : "D" } }
{ "name" : "Portland", "mayor" : { "name" : "Ted Wheeler", "party" : "D" } }
```

or those with mayors who don't have a party:

```
> db.towns.find(
  { 'mayor.party' : { $exists : false } },
  { _id : 0, name : 1, mayor : 1 }
)
{ "name" : "Punxsutawney", "mayor" : { "name" : "Richard Alexander" } }
```

The previous queries are great if you want to find documents with a single matching field, but what if you need to match several fields of a subdocument?

elemMatch

We'll round out our dig with the $elemMatch directive. Let's create another collection that stores countries. This time we'll override each _id to be a string of our choosing rather than an auto-generated identifier.

```
> db.countries.insert({
  _id : "us",
  name : "United States",
  exports : {
    foods : [
      { name : "bacon", tasty : true },
      { name : "burgers" }
    ]
  }
})
> db.countries.insert({
  _id : "ca",
  name : "Canada",
  exports : {
    foods : [
      { name : "bacon", tasty : false },
      { name : "syrup", tasty : true }
    ]
  }
})
```

```
> db.countries.insert({
  _id : "mx",
  name : "Mexico",
  exports : {
    foods : [{
      name : "salsa",
      tasty : true,
      condiment : true
    }]
  }
})
```

To validate the countries were added, we can execute the count function, expecting the number 3.

```
> db.countries.count()
3
```

Let's find a country that not only exports bacon but exports *tasty* bacon.

```
> db.countries.find(
  { 'exports.foods.name' : 'bacon',  'exports.foods.tasty' : true },
  { _id : 0, name : 1 }
)
{ "name" : "United States" }
{ "name" : "Canada" }
```

But this isn't what we wanted. Mongo returned *Canada* because it exports bacon and exports tasty syrup. $elemMatch helps us here. It specifies that if a document (or nested document) matches *all* of our criteria, the document counts as a match.

```
> db.countries.find(
  {
    'exports.foods' : {
      $elemMatch : {
        name : 'bacon',
        tasty : true
      }
    }
  },
  { _id : 0, name : 1 }
)
{ "name" : "United States" }
```

$elemMatch criteria can utilize advanced operators, too. You can find any country that exports a tasty food that also has a condiment label:

```
> db.countries.find(
    {
      'exports.foods' : {
        $elemMatch : {
          tasty : true,
          condiment : { $exists : true }
        }
      }
    },
    { _id : 0, name : 1 }
)
{ "name" : "Mexico" }
```

Mexico is just what we wanted.

Boolean Ops

So far, all of our criteria are implicitly *and* operations. If you try to find a country with the name *United States* and an _id of *mx*, Mongo will yield no results.

```
> db.countries.find(
    { _id : "mx", name : "United States" },
    { _id : 1 }
)
```

However, searching for one *or* the other with $or will return two results. Think of this layout like *prefix notation*: OR A B.

```
db.countries.find(
    {
      $or : [
        { _id : "mx" },
        { name : "United States" }
      ]
    },
    { _id:1 }
)
{ "_id" : "us" }
{ "_id" : "mx" }
```

There are so many operators in Mongo that we can't cover them all here, but we hope this has given you a taste of MongoDB's powerful querying capabilities. The table on page 104 is not a complete list of the commands but it does cover a good chunk of them.

Command	Description
$regex	Match by any PCRE-compliant regular expression string (or just use the // delimiters as shown earlier)
$ne	Not equal to
$lt	Less than
$lte	Less than or equal to
$gt	Greater than
$gte	Greater than or equal to
$exists	Check for the existence of a field
$all	Match all elements in an array
$in	Match any elements in an array
$nin	Does not match any elements in an array
$elemMatch	Match all fields in an array of nested documents
$or	or
$nor	Not or
$size	Match array of given size
$mod	Modulus
$type	Match if field is a given datatype
$not	Negate the given operator check

You can find all the commands on the MongoDB online documentation or grab a cheat sheet from the Mongo website. We will revisit querying in the days to come.

Updating

We have a problem. New York and Punxsutawney are unique enough, but did we add Portland, Oregon, or Portland, Maine (or Texas or the others)? Let's update our towns collection to add some U.S. states.

The update(criteria,operation) function requires two parameters. The first is a criteria query—the same sort of object you would pass to find(). The second parameter is either an object whose fields will replace the matched document(s) or a modifier operation. In this case, the modifier is to $set the field state with the string *OR*.

```
db.towns.update(
  { _id : ObjectId("4d0ada87bb30773266f39fe5") },
  { $set : { "state" : "OR" } }
);
```

You may wonder why the $set operation is even required. Mongo doesn't think in terms of attributes; it has only an internal, implicit understanding of attributes for optimization reasons. But nothing about the interface is *attribute*-oriented. Mongo is *document*-oriented. You will rarely want something like this (notice the lack of $set operation):

```
db.towns.update(
  { _id : ObjectId("4d0ada87bb30773266f39fe5") },
  { state : "OR" }
);
```

This would replace the *entire* matching document with the document you gave it ({ state : "OR" }). Because you didn't give it a command like $set, Mongo assumes you just want to switch them up, so be careful.

We can verify our update was successful by finding it (note our use of findOne() to retrieve only one matching object).

```
db.towns.findOne({ _id : ObjectId("4d0ada87bb30773266f39fe5") })

{
  "_id" : ObjectId("4d0ada87bb30773266f39fe5"),
  "famousFor" : [
    "beer",
    "food",
    "Portlandia"
  ],
  "lastCensus" : "Thu Sep 20 2017 00:00:00 GMT-0700 (PDT)",
  "mayor" : {
    "name" : "Sam Adams",
    "party" : "D"
  },
  "name" : "Portland",
  "population" : 582000,
  "state" : "OR"
}
```

You can do more than $set a value. $inc (increment a number) is a pretty useful one. Let's increment Portland's population by 1,000.

```
db.towns.update(
  { _id : ObjectId("4d0ada87bb30773266f39fe5") },
  { $inc : { population : 1000} }
)
```

There are more directives than this, such as the $ positional operator for arrays. New operations are added frequently and are updated in the online documentation. The list on page 106 includes the major directives.

Command	Description
$set	Sets the given field with the given value
$unset	Removes the field
$inc	Adds the given field by the given number
$pop	Removes the last (or first) element from an array
$push	Adds the value to an array
$pushAll	Adds all values to an array
$addToSet	Similar to push, but won't duplicate values
$pull	Removes matching values from an array
$pullAll	Removes all matching values from an array

References

As we mentioned previously, Mongo isn't built to perform joins. Because of its distributed nature, joins in Mongo would be pretty inefficient operations. Still, it's sometimes useful for documents to reference each other. In these cases, the Mongo community suggests that you use a construct like { $ref : "collection_name", $id : "reference_id" }. For example, we can update the towns collection to contain a reference to a document in countries.

```
> db.towns.update(
    { _id : ObjectId("59094292afbc9350ada6b808") },
    { $set : { country: { $ref: "countries", $id: "us" } } }
)
```

Now you can retrieve Portland from your towns collection.

```
> var portland = db.towns.findOne(
      { _id : ObjectId("59094292afbc9350ada6b808") }
    )
```

Then, to retrieve the town's country, you can query the countries collection using the stored $id.

```
> db.countries.findOne({ _id: portland.country.$id })
```

Better yet, in JavaScript, you can ask the town document the name of the collection stored in the fields reference.

```
> var portlandCountryRef = portland.country.$ref;
> db[portlandCountryRef].findOne({ _id: portland.country.$id })
```

The last two queries are equivalent; the second is just a bit more data-driven.

> **Spelling Bee Warning**
>
> Mongo, and schemaless databases in general, are not very friendly when it comes to misspellings. If you haven't run across this problem yet, you probably will at some point, so be warned. You can draw parallels between static and dynamic programming languages. You define static up front, while dynamic will accept values you may not have intended, even nonsensical types like person_name = 5.
>
> Documents are schemaless, so Mongo has no way of knowing if you intended to insert pipulation into your city or meant to query on lust_census; it will happily insert those fields or return no matching values. This can get you in trouble later on when you try to find a document that matches the condition population > 10000 and the result set is incomplete because Mongo doesn't even know that the object was intended to have a population field.
>
> This is less of a problem when you use Mongo in a more programmatic and less ad-hoc way, as we're doing here. But keep in mind that flexibility has its price. *Caveat emptor.*

Deleting

Removing documents from a collection is simple. Just replace the find() function with a call to remove(), and all documents that match given the criteria will be removed. It's important to note that the entire matching document will be removed, not just a matching element or a matching subdocument.

We recommend running find() to verify your criteria before running remove(). Mongo won't think twice before running your operation. Let's remove all countries that export bacon that isn't tasty.

```
> var badBacon = {
  'exports.foods' : {
    $elemMatch : {
      name : 'bacon',
      tasty : false
    }
  }
}
> db.countries.find(badBacon)
{
  "_id" : ObjectId("4d0b7b84bb30773266f39fef"),
  "name" : "Canada",
  "exports" : {
    "foods" : [
      {
        "name" : "bacon",
        "tasty" : false
      },
```

```
    {
      "name" : "syrup",
      "tasty" : true
    }
  ]
 }
}
```

Everything looks good. Let's remove it.

```
> db.countries.remove(badBacon)
> db.countries.count()
2
```

Now when you run count(), verify we are left with only two countries. If so, our parameter-targeted delete was successful!

Reading with Code

Let's close out this day with one more interesting query option: code. You can request that MongoDB run a decision function across your documents. We placed this last because it should always be a last resort. These queries run quite slowly, you can't index them, and Mongo can't optimize them. But sometimes it's hard to beat the power of custom code.

Let's say that we're looking for a city with a population between 6,000 and 600,000 people.

```
> db.towns.find(function() {
  return this.population > 6000 && this.population < 600000;
})
```

That should return Portland and Punxsutawney. Mongo even has a shortcut for simple decision functions.

```
> db.towns.find("this.population > 6000 && this.population < 600000")
```

You can run custom code with other criteria using the $where clause. In this example, the query also filters for towns famous for groundhogs named Phil.

```
db.towns.find({
  $where: "this.population > 6000 && this.population < 600000",
  famousFor: /Phil/
})
```

A word of warning: Mongo will blindly run this function against each document despite there being no guarantee that the given field exists in every document. For example, if you assume a *population* field exists and *population* is missing in even a *single* document, the entire query will fail because the JavaScript cannot properly execute. Be careful when you write custom JavaScript functions, be comfortable using JavaScript before attempting custom code, and in general avoid these sorts of operations in production.

Day 1 Wrap-Up

Today we took a peek at our first document database, MongoDB. We saw how we can store nested structured data as JSON objects and query that data to any depth. You learned that a *document* can be envisioned as a schemaless row in the relational model, keyed by a generated _id. A set of documents is called a *collection* in Mongo, similar to a *table* in PostgreSQL but also quite different.

Unlike the previous styles we've encountered, with collections of sets of simple datatypes, Mongo stores complex, denormalized documents, stored and retrieved as collections of arbitrary JSON structures. Mongo tops off this flexible storage strategy with a powerful query mechanism unconstrained by any predefined schema.

Its denormalized nature makes a document database a superb choice for storing data with unknown qualities, while other styles (such as relational or columnar) prefer, or sometimes even demand, that you know your data models in advance and require schema migrations to add or edit fields.

Day 1 Homework

Find

1. Bookmark the online MongoDB documentation and read up on something you found intriguing today.

2. Look up how to construct regular expressions in Mongo.

3. Acquaint yourself with command-line db.help() and db.collections.help() output.

4. Find a Mongo driver in your programming language of choice (Ruby, Java, PHP, Go, Elixir, and so on).

Do

1. Print a JSON document containing { "hello" : "world" }.

2. Select a town via a case-insensitive regular expression containing the word *new*.

3. Find all cities whose names contain an *e* and are famous for food or beer.

4. Create a new database named *blogger* with a collection named *articles*. Insert a new article with an author name and email, creation date, and text.

5. Update the article with an array of comments, containing a comment with an author and text.

6. Run a query from an external JavaScript file that you create yourself.

Day 2: Indexing, Aggregating, Mapreduce

Increasing MongoDB's query performance is the first item on today's docket, followed by some more powerful and complex grouped queries. Finally, we'll round out the day with some data analysis using mapreduce.

Indexing: When Fast Isn't Fast Enough

One of Mongo's useful built-in features is indexing in the name of enhanced query performance—something, as you've seen, that's not available on all NoSQL databases. MongoDB provides several of the best data structures for indexing, such as the classic B-tree as well as other additions, such as two-dimensional and spherical GeoSpatial indexes.

For now, we're going to do a little experiment to see the power of MongoDB's B-tree index by populating a series of phone numbers with a random country prefix (feel free to replace this code with your own country code). Enter the following code into your console. This will generate 100,000 phone numbers (it may take a while), between *1-800-555-0000* and *1-800-565-0000*.

```
mongo/populatePhones.js
populatePhones = function(area, start, stop) {
  for(var i = start; i < stop; i++) {
    var country = 1 + ((Math.random() * 8) << 0);
    var num = (country * 1e10) + (area * 1e7) + i;
    var fullNumber = "+" + country + " " + area + "-" + i;
    db.phones.insert({
      _id: num,
      components: {
        country: country,
        area: area,
        prefix: (i * 1e-4) << 0,
        number: i
      },
      display: fullNumber
    });
    print("Inserted number " + fullNumber);
  }
  print("Done!");
}
```

Run the function with a three-digit area code (like 800) and a range of seven-digit numbers (5,550,000 to 5,650,000—please verify your zeros when typing).

```
> populatePhones(800, 5550000, 5650000) // This could take a minute
> db.phones.find().limit(2)

{ "_id" : 18005550000, "components" : { "country" : 1, "area" : 800,
  "prefix" : 555, "number" : 5550000 }, "display" : "+1 800-5550000" }
{ "_id" : 88005550001, "components" : { "country" : 8, "area" : 800,
  "prefix" : 555, "number" : 5550001 }, "display" : "+8 800-5550001" }
```

Whenever a new collection is created, Mongo automatically creates an index by the _id. These indexes can be found in the system.indexes collection. The following query shows all indexes in the database:

```
> db.getCollectionNames().forEach(function(collection) {
 print("Indexes for the " + collection + " collection:");
 printjson(db[collection].getIndexes());
});
```

Most queries will include more fields than just the _id, so we need to make indexes on those fields.

We're going to create a B-tree index on the display field. But first, let's verify that the index will improve speed. To do this, we'll first check a query without an index. The explain() method is used to output details of a given operation.

```
> db.phones.find({display: "+1 800-5650001"}).
    explain("executionStats").executionStats
{
  "executionTimeMillis": 52,
  "executionStages": {
    "executionTimeMillisEstimate": 58,
  }
}
```

Your output will differ from ours here and only a few fields from the output are shown here, but note the executionTimeMillisEstimate field—milliseconds to complete the query—will likely be double digits.

We create an index by calling ensureIndex(fields,options) on the collection. The fields parameter is an object containing the fields to be indexed against. The options parameter describes the type of index to make. In this case, we're building a unique index on display that should just drop duplicate entries.

```
> db.phones.ensureIndex(
  { display : 1 },
  { unique : true, dropDups : true }
)
```

Now try find() again, and check explain() to see whether the situation improves.

```
> db.phones.find({ display: "+1 800-5650001" }).
    explain("executionStats").executionStats
{
  "executionTimeMillis" : 0,
  "executionStages": {
    "executionTimeMillisEstimate": 0,
  }
}
```

The executionTimeMillisEstimate changed from 52 to 0—an infinite improvement (52 / 0)! Just kidding, but the query is now orders of magnitude faster. Mongo is no longer doing a full collection scan but instead walking the tree to retrieve the value. Importantly, scanned objects dropped from 109999 to 1—since it has become a single unique lookup.

explain() is a useful function, but you'll use it only when testing specific query calls. If you need to profile in a normal test or production environment, you'll need the *system profiler*.

Let's set the profiling level to 2 (level 2 stores all queries; profiling level 1 stores only slower queries greater than 100 milliseconds) and then run find() as normal.

```
> db.setProfilingLevel(2)
> db.phones.find({ display : "+1 800-5650001" })
```

This will create a new object in the system.profile collection, which you can read as any other table to get information about the query, such as a timestamp for when it took place and performance information (such as executionTimeMillis-Estimate as shown). You can fetch documents from that collection like any other:

```
> db.system.profile.find()
```

This will return a list of objects representing past queries. This query, for example, would return stats about execution times from the first query in the list:

```
> db.system.profile.find()[0].execStats
{
  "stage" : "EOF",
  "nReturned" : 0,
  "executionTimeMillisEstimate" : 0,
  "works" : 0,
  "advanced" : 0,
  "needTime" : 0,
```

```
  "needYield" : 0,
  "saveState" : 0,
  "restoreState" : 0,
  "isEOF" : 1,
  "invalidates" : 0
}
```

Like yesterday's nested queries, Mongo can build your index on nested values. If you wanted to index on all area codes, use the dot-notated field representation: components.area. In production, you should always build indexes in the background using the { background : 1 } option.

```
> db.phones.ensureIndex({ "components.area": 1 }, { background : 1 })
```

If we find() all of the system indexes for our phones collection, the new one should appear last. The first index is always automatically created to quickly look up by _id, and the other two we added ourselves.

```
> db.phones.getIndexes()
[
  {
    "v" : 2,
    "key" : {
      "_id" : 1
    },
    "name" : "_id_",
    "ns" : "book.phones"
  },
  {
    "v" : 2,
    "unique" : true,
    "key" : {
      "display" : 1
    },
    "name" : "display_1",
    "ns" : "book.phones"
  },
  {
    "v" : 2,
    "key" : {
      "components.area" : 1
    },
    "name" : "components.area_1",
    "ns" : "book.phones",
    "background" : 1
  }
]
```

Our book.phones indexes have rounded out quite nicely.

We should close this section by noting that creating an index on a large collection can be slow and resource-intensive. Indexes simply "cost" more in Mongo than in a relational database like Postgres due to Mongo's schemaless nature. You should always consider these impacts when building an index by creating indexes at off-peak times, running index creation in the background, and running them manually rather than using automated index creation. There are plenty more indexing tricks and tips online, but these are the basics that may come in handy the most often.

Mongo's Many Useful CLI Tools

Before we move on to aggregation in Mongo, we want to briefly tell you about the other shell goodies that Mongo provides out-of-the-box in addition to mongod and mongo. We won't cover them in this book but we do strongly recommend checking them out, as they together make up one of the most amply equipped CLI toolbelts in the NoSQL universe.

Command	Description
mongodump	Exports data from Mongo into .bson files. That can mean entire collections or databases, filtered results based on a supplied query, and more.
mongofiles	Manipulates large GridFS data files (GridFS is a specification for BSON files exceeding 16 MB).
mongooplog	Polls operation logs from MongoDB replication operations.
mongorestore	Restores MongoDB databases and collections from backups created using mongodump.
mongostat	Displays basic MongoDB server stats.
mongoexport	Exports data from Mongo into CSV (comma-separated value) and JSON files. As with mongodump, that can mean entire databases and collections or just some data chosen on the basis of query parameters.
mongoimport	Imports data into Mongo from JSON, CSV, or TSV (term-separated value) files. We'll use this tool on Day 3.
mongoperf	Performs user-defined performance tests against a MongoDB server.
mongos	Short for "MongoDB shard," this tool provides a service for properly routing data into a sharded MongoDB cluster (which we will not cover in this chapter).
mongotop	Displays usage stats for each collection stored in a Mongo database.
bsondump	Converts BSON files into other formats, such as JSON.

For more in-depth info, see the MongoDB reference documentation.[a]

---

a. https://docs.mongodb.com/manual/reference/program

Aggregated Queries

MongoDB includes a handful of single-purpose *aggregators*: count() provides the number of documents included in a result set (which we saw earlier), distinct() collects the result set into an array of unique results, and aggregate() returns documents according to a logic that you provide.

The queries we investigated yesterday were useful for basic data extraction, but any post-processing would be up to you to handle. For example, say you wanted to count the phone numbers greater than 5599999 or provide nuanced data about phone number distribution in different countries—in other words, to produce aggregate results using many documents. As in PostgreSQL, count() is the most basic aggregator. It takes a query and returns a number (of matching documents).

```
> db.phones.count({'components.number': { $gt : 5599999 } })
50000
```

The distinct() method returns each matching value (not a full document) where one or more exists. We can get the distinct component numbers that are less than 5,550,005 in this way:

```
> db.phones.distinct('components.number',
  {'components.number': { $lt : 5550005 } })
[ 5550000, 5550001, 5550002, 5550003, 5550004 ]
```

The aggregate() method is more complex but also much more powerful. It enables you to specify a pipeline-style logic consisting of *stages* such as: $match filters that return specific sets of documents; $group functions that group based on some attribute; a $sort() logic that orders the documents by a sort key; and many others.[3]

You can chain together as many stages as you'd like, mixing and matching at will. Think of aggregate() as a combination of WHERE, GROUP BY, and ORDER BY clauses in SQL. The analogy isn't perfect, but the aggregation API does a lot of the same things.

Let's load some city data into Mongo. There's an included mongoCities100000.js file containing insert statements for data about nearly 100,000 cities. Here's how you can execute that file in the Mongo shell: c

```
> load('mongoCities100000.js')
> db.cities.count()
99838
```

---

3. https://docs.mongodb.com/manual/reference/operator/aggregation-pipeline/

Here's an example document for a city:

```
{
  "_id" : ObjectId("5913ec4c059c950f9b799895"),
  "name" : "Sant Julià de Lòria",
  "country" : "AD",
  "timezone" : "Europe/Andorra",
  "population" : 8022,
  "location" : {
    "longitude" : 42.46372,
    "latitude" : 1.49129
  }
}
```

We could use aggregate() to, for example, find the average population for all cities in the Europe/London timezone. To do so, we could $match all documents where timezone equals Europe/London, and then add a $group stage that produces one document with an _id field with a value of averagePopulation and an avgPop field that displays the average value across all population values in the collection:

```
> db.cities.aggregate([
  {
    $match: {
      'timezone': {
        $eq: 'Europe/London'
      }
    }
  },
  {
    $group: {
      _id: 'averagePopulation',
      avgPop: {
        $avg: '$population'
      }
    }
  }
])
{ "_id" : "averagePopulation", "avgPop" : 23226.22149712092 }
```

We could also match all documents in that same timezone, sort them in descending order by population, and then $project documents that only contain the population field:

```
> db.cities.aggregate([
  {
    // same $match statement the previous aggregation operation
  },
```

```
  {
    $sort: {
      population: -1
    }
  },
  {
    $project: {
      _id: 0,
      name: 1,
      population: 1
    }
  }
])
```

You should see results like this:

```
{ "name" : "City of London", "population" : 7556900 }
{ "name" : "London", "population" : 7556900 }
{ "name" : "Birmingham", "population" : 984333 }
// many others
```

Experiment with it a bit—try combining some of the stage types we've already covered in new ways—and then delete the collection when you're done, as we'll add the same data back into the database using a different method on Day 3.

```
> db.cities.drop()
```

This provides a very small taste of Mongo's aggregation capabilities. The possibilities are really endless, and we encourage you to explore other stage types. Be forewarned that aggregations *can* be quite slow if you add a lot of stages and/or perform them on very large collections. There are limits to how well Mongo, as a schemaless database, can optimize these sorts of operations. But if you're careful to keep your collections reasonably sized and, even better, structure your data to not require bold transformations to get the outputs you want, then aggregate() can be a powerful and even speedy tool.

Server-Side Commands

In addition to evaluating JavaScript functions, there are several pre-built commands in Mongo, most of which are executed on the server, although some require executing only under the admin database (which you can access by entering use admin). The top command, for example, will output access details about all collections on the server.

```
> use admin
> db.runCommand("top")
{
  "totals" : {
    "note" : "all times in microseconds",
    "admin.system.roles" : {
      "total" : {
      "time" : 3666,
      "count" : 1
    },
  // etc
  }
}
```

You can also list all commands that are currently available (let's switch back to the book database first because the admin database provides a different set of commands):

```
> use book
> db.listCommands()
```

When you run listCommands(), you may notice a lot of commands we've used already. In fact, you can execute many common commands through the runCommand() method, such as counting the number of phones. However, you may notice a slightly different output.

```
> db.runCommand({ "find" : "someCollection" })
{
  "cursor" : {
    "id" : NumberLong(0),
    "ns" : "book.someCollection",
    "firstBatch" : [ ]
  },
  "ok" : 1
}
```

Here, we see that this function returns an object containing a cursor and an *ok* field. That's because db.phones.find() is a wrapper function created for our convenience by the shell's JavaScript interface, whereas runCommand() is an operation executed on the server. Remember that we can play detective on how a function such as find() works by leaving off the calling parentheses.

```
> db.phones.find
function (query, fields, limit, skip, batchSize, options) {
  var cursor = new DBQuery(this._mongo,
                            // other query parameters
                            options || this.getQueryOptions());

  // some cursor-building logic

  return cursor;
}
```

So what about the DBQuery object? How much more can we find out about it?

```
> DBQuery
function DBQuery() {
    [native code]
}
```

Okay, looks like Mongo isn't going to reveal too much about that. No matter: this way of diving into function definitions is a great way to both explore Mongo conceptually and to get a better sense of what's happening inside of your queries and operations.

> ### Diversion
>
> We took this quick diversion into function definitions for two reasons:
>
> • To drive home the idea that most of the magic you execute in the mongo console is executed on the server, not the client, which just provides some convenient wrapper functions.
>
> • We can leverage the concept of executing server-side code for our own purposes to create something in MongoDB that's similar to the *stored procedures* we saw in PostgreSQL.
>
> Any JavaScript function can be stored in a special collection named system.js. This is just a normal collection; you save the function by setting the name as the _id and a function object as the value.
>
> ```
> > db.system.js.save({
>     _id: 'getLast',
>     value: function(collection) {
>       return collection.find({}).sort({'_id':1}).limit(1)[0];
>     }
> })
> ```
>
> Now you can use that function by loading it into the current namespace:
>
> ```
> > use book
> > db.loadServerScripts()
> > getLast(db.phones).display
> +1 800-5550010
> ```

Mapreduce (and Finalize)

Mapreduce operations are designed for performing computations over large datasets. Every mapreduce operation is split into two basic steps. First, a *map* step performs some series of filtering and/or sorting operation, winnowing the original dataset down into some subset. Then, a *reduce* step performs some kind of operation on that subset. An example mapreduce operation would be finding all baseball players in Major League history with the first name Dave (the map step) and then finding the cumulative batting average for all of those Daves (the reduce step).

In MongoDB, the map step involves creating a mapper function that calls an emit() function. The benefit of this approach is you can emit more than once per document. The reduce() function accepts a single key and a list of values that were emitted to that key. Finally, Mongo provides an optional third step called finalize(), which is executed only once per mapped value after the reducers are run. This allows you to perform any final calculations or cleanup you may need.

Because we already know the basics of mapreduce, we'll skip the intro wading-pool example and go right to the high-dive. Let's generate a report that counts all phone numbers that contain the same digits for each country. First, we'll store a helper function that extracts an array of all distinct numbers (understanding how this helper works is not imperative to understanding the overall mapreduce).

```
mongo/distinctDigits.js
distinctDigits = function(phone){
  var number = phone.components.number + '',
      seen = [],
      result = [],
      i = number.length;

  while(i--) {
    seen[+number[i]] = 1;
  }

  for (var i = 0; i < 10; i++) {
    if (seen[i]) {
      result[result.length] = i;
    }
  }

  return result;
}

db.system.js.save({_id: 'distinctDigits', value: distinctDigits})
```

Load the file in the mongo command line. If the file exists in the same directory you launched mongo from, you need only the filename; otherwise, a full path is required.

```
> load('distinctDigits.js')
```

Now we can get to work on the mapper. As with any mapreduce function, deciding what fields to map by is a crucial decision because it dictates the aggregated values that you return. Because our report is finding distinct numbers, the array of distinct values is one field. But because we also need to query by country, that is another field. We add both values as a compound key: {digits : X, country : Y}.

Our goal is to simply count these values, so we emit the value 1 (each document represents one item to count). The reducer's job is to sum all those 1s together.

```
mongo/map1.js
map = function() {
  var digits = distinctDigits(this);
  emit({
    digits: digits,
    country: this.components.country
  }, {
    count : 1
  });
}
```

```
mongo/reduce1.js
reduce = function(key, values) {
  var total = 0;
  for (var i = 0; i < values.length; i++) {
    total += values[i].count;
  }
  return { count : total };
}

results = db.runCommand({
  mapReduce: 'phones',
  map:       map,
  reduce:    reduce,
  out:       'phones.report'
})
```

Because we set the collection name via the out parameter (out: 'phones.report'), you can query the results like any other. It's a materialized view that you can see in the show tables list.

```
> db.phones.report.find({'_id.country' : 8})
{
  "_id" : { "digits" : [ 0, 1, 2, 3, 4, 5, 6 ], "country" : 8 },
  "value" : { "count" : 19 }
}
{
  "_id" : { "digits" : [ 0, 1, 2, 3, 5 ], "country" : 8 },
  "value" : { "count" : 3 }
}
{
  "_id" : { "digits" : [ 0, 1, 2, 3, 5, 6 ], "country" : 8 },
  "value" : { "count" : 48 }
}
```

```
{
  "_id" : { "digits" : [ 0, 1, 2, 3, 5, 6, 7 ], "country" : 8 },
  "value" : { "count" : 12 }
}
has more
```

Type it to continue iterating through the results. Note that the unique emitted keys are under the field _ids, and all of the data returned from the reducers is under the field value.

If you prefer that the mapreducer just output the results, rather than outputting to a collection, you can set the out value to { inline : 1 }, but bear in mind that there is a limit to the size of a result you can output. As of Mongo 2.0, that limit is 16 MB.

Reducers can have either mapped (emitted) results or other reducer results as inputs. Why would the output of one reducer feed into the input of another if they are mapped to the same key? Think of how this would look if run on separate servers, as shown in the figure that follows.

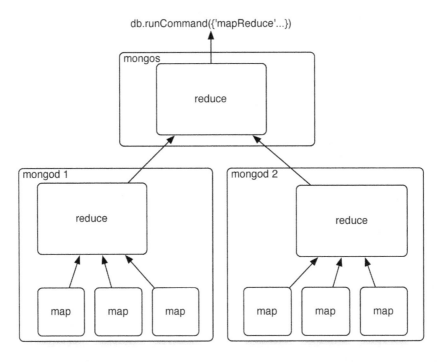

Each server must run its own map() and reduce() functions and then push those results to be merged with the service that initiated the call, gathering them up. Classic divide and conquer. If we had renamed the output of the reducer to total instead of count, we would have needed to handle both cases in the loop, as shown here:

```
mongo/reduce2.js
reduce = function(key, values) {
  var total = 0;
  for(var i = 0; i < values.length; i++) {
    var data = values[i];
    if('total' in data) {
      total += data.total;
    } else {
      total += data.count;
    }
  }
  return { total : total };
}
```

However, Mongo predicted that you might need to perform some final changes, such as renaming a field or some other calculations. If you really need the output field to be total, you can implement a finalize() function, which works the same way as the finalize function under group().

Day 2 Wrap-Up

On Day 2, we've expanded our query power by including several aggregate queries: count(), distinct(), and topped off by aggregate(). To speed up the response time of these queries, we used MongoDB's indexing options. When more power is required, the ever-present mapReduce() is available.

Day 2 Homework

Find

1. Find a shortcut for admin commands.

2. Find the online documentation for queries and cursors.

3. Find the MongoDB documentation for mapreduce.

4. Through the JavaScript interface, investigate the code for three collections functions: help(), findOne(), and stats().

Do

1. Implement a finalize method to output the count as the total.

2. Install a Mongo driver for a language of your choice, and connect to the database. Populate a collection through it, and index one of the fields.

Day 3: Replica Sets, Sharding, GeoSpatial, and GridFS

Mongo has a powerful ability to store and query data in a variety of ways. But then again, other databases can do those things, too. What makes document databases unique is their ability to efficiently handle arbitrarily nested, schemaless data documents. Thus far, we've run Mongo as a single server. But if you were to run Mongo in production, you'd want to run it as a cluster of machines, which would provide for much higher availability and enable you to replicate data across servers, shard collections into many pieces, and perform queries in parallel.

Replica Sets

Mongo was meant to scale out, not to run in standalone mode. It was built for data consistency and partition tolerance, but sharding data has a cost: If one part of a collection is lost, the whole thing is compromised. What good is querying against a collection of countries that contains only the Western Hemisphere or only Asia? Mongo deals with this implicit sharding weakness in a simple manner: duplication. You should rarely run a single Mongo instance in production and instead replicate the stored data across multiple services.

Rather than muck with our existing database, today we'll start from scratch and spawn a few new servers. Mongo's default port is 27017, so we'll start up each server on other ports. Remember that you must create the data directories first, so create three of them:

```
$ mkdir ./mongo1 ./mongo2 ./mongo3
```

Next, we'll fire up the Mongo servers. This time we'll add the replSet flag with the name *book* and specify the ports.

```
$ mongod --replSet book --dbpath ./mongo1 --port 27011
```

Open another terminal window and run the next command, which launches another server, pointing to a different directory, available on another port. Then open a third terminal to start the third server.

```
$ mongod --replSet book --dbpath ./mongo2 --port 27012
$ mongod --replSet book --dbpath ./mongo3 --port 27013
```

Notice that you get lots of this noise on the output, with error messages like this:

```
[initandlisten] Did not find local voted for document at startup
```

That's a good thing because we haven't yet initialized our replica set and Mongo is letting us know that. Fire up a mongo shell to one of the servers, and execute the rs.initiate() function.

```
$ mongo localhost:27011
> rs.initiate({
  _id: 'book',
  members: [
    {_id: 1, host: 'localhost:27011'},
    {_id: 2, host: 'localhost:27012'},
    {_id: 3, host: 'localhost:27013'}
  ]
})
> rs.status().ok
1
```

Notice we're using a new object called rs (replica set) instead of db (database). Like other objects, it has a help() method you can call. Running the status() command will let us know when our replica set is running, so just keep checking the status for completion before continuing. If you watch the three server outputs, you should see that one server outputs this line:

```
Member ... is now in state PRIMARY
```

And two servers will have the following output:

```
Member ... is now in state SECONDARY
```

PRIMARY will be the master server. Chances are, this will be the server on port 27011 (because it started first); however, if it's not, go ahead and fire up a console to the primary. Just insert any old thing on the command line, and we'll try an experiment.

```
> db.echo.insert({ say : 'HELLO!' })
```

After the insert, exit the console, and then let's test that our change has been replicated by shutting down the master node; pressing Ctrl+C is sufficient. If you watch the logs of the remaining two servers, you should see that one of the two has now been promoted to master (it will output the Member ... is now in state PRIMARY line). Open a console into that machine (for us it was *local-host:27012*), and db.echo.find()() should contain your value.

We'll play one more round of our console-shuffle game. Open a console into the remaining SECONDARY server by running mongo localhost:27013. Just to be sure, run the isMaster() function. Ours looked like this:

```
> db.isMaster().ismaster
false
> db.isMaster().primary
localhost:27012
```

In this shell, let's attempt to insert another value.

```
> db.echo.insert({ say : 'is this thing on?' })
WriteResult({ "writeError" : { "code" : 10107, "errmsg" : "not master" } })
```

This message is letting us know that we can neither write to a secondary node nor read directly from it. There is only one master per replica set, and you must interact with it. It is the gatekeeper to the set.

Replicating data has its own issues not found in single-source databases. In the Mongo setup, one problem is deciding who gets promoted when a master node goes down. Mongo deals with this by giving each mongod service a vote, and the one with the freshest data is elected the new master. Right now, you should still have two mongod services running. Go ahead and shut down the current master (aka primary node). Remember, when we did this with three nodes, one of the others just got promoted to be the new master. Now the last remaining node is implicitly the master.

Go ahead and relaunch the other servers and watch the logs. When the nodes are brought back up, they go into a recovery state and attempt to resync their data with the new master node. "Wait a minute!?" we hear you cry. "So, what if the original master had data that did not yet propagate?" Those operations are dropped. A write in a Mongo replica set isn't considered successful until most nodes have a copy of the data.

The Problem with Even Nodes

The concept of replication is easy enough to grasp: You write to one MongoDB server, and that data is duplicated across others within the replica set. If one server is unavailable, then one of the others can be promoted and serve requests. But a server can be unavailable in more ways than a server crash. Sometimes, the network connection between nodes is down (such as a network *partition*, thinking back to the P in CAP). In that case, Mongo dictates that *the majority of nodes that can still communicate now constitute the network.*

MongoDB expects an odd number of total nodes in the replica set. Consider a five-node network, for example. If connection issues split it into a three-node fragment and a two-node fragment, the larger fragment has a clear majority and can elect a master and continue servicing requests. With no clear majority, a quorum couldn't be reached.

To see why an odd number of nodes is preferred, consider what might happen to a four-node replica set. Say a network partition causes two of the servers to lose connectivity from the other two. One set will have the original master, but because it can't see a *clear majority* of the network, the master steps down. The other set will similarly be unable to elect a master because it, too, can't communicate with a clear majority of nodes. Both sets are now unable to process requests and the system is effectively down. Having an odd number of total nodes would have made this particular scenario—a fragmented network where each fragment has less than a clear majority—less likely to occur.

Some databases (such as CouchDB) are built to allow multiple masters, but Mongo is not, and so it isn't prepared to resolve data updates between them. MongoDB deals with conflicts between multiple masters by simply not allowing them.

Because it's a CP system, Mongo always knows the most recent value; the client needn't decide. Mongo's concern is strong consistency on writes, and preventing a multimaster scenario is not a bad method for achieving it.

> ## Voting and Arbiters
>
> You may not always want to have an odd number of servers replicating data. In that case, you can either launch an arbiter (generally recommended) or increase voting rights on your servers (generally not recommended). In Mongo, an arbiter is a voting but nonreplicating server in the replica set. You launch it just like any other server but on configuration set a flag, like this: {_id: 3, host: 'localhost:27013', arbiterOnly : true}. Arbiters are useful for breaking ties, like the U.S. Vice President in the Senate. By default, each mongod instance has a single vote.

Sharding

One of the core goals of Mongo is to provide safe and quick handling of very large datasets. The clearest method of achieving this is through horizontal sharding by value ranges—or just *sharding* for brevity. Rather than a single server hosting all values in a collection, some range of values is split, or *sharded*, onto other servers. For example, in our phone numbers collection, we may put all phone numbers less than 1-500-000-0000 onto Mongo server

A and put numbers greater than or equal to 1-500-000-0001 onto server B. Mongo makes this easier by autosharding, managing this division for you.

Let's launch a couple of (nonreplicating) mongod servers. Like replica sets, there's a special parameter necessary to be considered a shard server (which just means this server is capable of sharding).

```
$ mkdir ./mongo4 ./mongo5
$ mongod --shardsvr --dbpath ./mongo4 --port 27014
$ mongod --shardsvr --dbpath ./mongo5 --port 27015
```

Now you need a server to actually keep track of your keys. Imagine you created a table to store city names alphabetically. You need some way to know that, for example, cities starting with A through N go to server mongo4 and O through Z go to server mongo5. In Mongo, you create a *config server* (which is just a regular mongod) that keeps track of which server (mongo4 or mongo5) owns what values. You'll need to create and initialize a second replica set for the cluster's configuration (let's call it configSet).

```
$ mkdir ./mongoconfig
$ mongod --configsvr --replSet configSet --dbpath ./mongoconfig --port 27016
```

Now enter the Mongo shell for the config server by running mongo localhost:27016 and initiate the config server cluster (with just one member for this example):

```
> rs.initiate({
  _id: 'configSet',
  configsvr: true,
  members: [
    {
      _id: 0,
      host: 'localhost:27016'
    }
  ]
})
{ "ok" : 1}
> rs.status().ok
1
```

Finally, you need to run yet another server called mongos, which is the single point of entry for our clients. The mongos server will connect to the mongoconfig config server to keep track of the sharding information stored there. You point mongos to the replSet/server:port with the --configdb flag.

```
$ mongos --configdb configSet/localhost:27016 --port 27020
```

A neat thing about mongos is that it is a lightweight clone of a full mongod server. Nearly any command you can throw at a mongod you can throw at a mongos, which makes it the perfect go-between for clients to connect to multiple sharded servers. The following picture of our server setup may help.

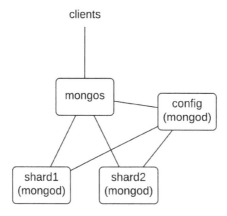

Now let's jump into the mongos server console in the admin database by running mongo localhost:27020/admin. We're going to configure some sharding.

```
> sh.addShard('localhost:27014')
{ "shardAdded" : "shard0000", "ok" : 1 }
> sh.addShard('localhost:27015')
{ "shardAdded" : "shard0001", "ok" : 1 }
```

With that setup, now we have to give it the database and collection to shard and the field to shard by (in our case, the city name).

```
> db.runCommand({ enablesharding : "test" })
{ "ok" : 1 }
> db.runCommand({ shardcollection : "test.cities", key : {name : 1} })
{ "collectionsharded" : "test.cities", "ok" : 1 }
```

mongos vs. mongoconfig

You may wonder why Mongo separates the config server and the mongos *point of entry* into two different servers. In production environments, they will generally live on different physical servers. The config server (which can itself be replicated across multiple servers) manages the sharded information for other sharded servers, while mongos will likely live on your local application server where clients can easily connect (without needing to manage which shards to connect to).

With all that setup out of the way, let's load some data. If you download the book code, you'll find a 12 MB data file named mongoCities100000.json that contains data for every city in the world with a population of more than 1,000 people. Download that file, and run the following import script that imports the data into your mongos server:

```
$ mongoimport \
  --host localhost:27020 \
  --db test \
  --collection cities \
  --type json \
  mongoCities100000.json
```

If the import is successful, you should see imported 99838 documents in the output (not quite 100,000 cities as the filename would suggest, but pretty close).

GeoSpatial Queries

Mongo has a neat trick built into it. Although we've focused on server setups today, no day would be complete without a little bit of razzle-dazzle, and that's Mongo's ability to quickly perform geospatial queries. First, connect to the mongos sharded server.

```
$ mongo localhost:27020
```

The core of the geospatial secret lies in indexing. It's a special form of indexing geographic data called *geohash* that not only finds values of a specific value or range quickly but finds nearby values quickly in ad hoc queries. Conveniently, at the end of our previous section, we installed a lot of geographic data. So to query it, step 1 is to index the data on the location field. The *2d* index must be set on any two value fields, in our case a hash (for example, { longitude:1.48453, latitude:42.57205 }), but it could easily have been an array (for example [1.48453, 42.57205]).

```
> db.cities.ensureIndex({ location : "2d" })
```

Now, we can use an aggregation pipeline (think back to Day 2) to assemble a list of all cities close to Portland, OR sorted in descending order by population (displaying the name of the city, the population, and the distance from the 45.52/-122.67 latitude/longitude point).

```
> db.cities.aggregate([
  {
    $geoNear: {
      near: [45.52, -122.67],
      distanceField: 'dist'
    }
  },
  {
    $sort: {
      population: -1
    }
  },
  {
```

```
    $project: {
      _id: 0,
      name: 1,
      population: 1,
      dist: 1
    }
  }
])
{ "name" : "Portland", "population" : 540513, "dist" : 0.007103984797274343 }
{ "name" : "Vancouver", "population" : 157517, "dist" : 0.11903458741054997 }
{ "name" : "Salem", "population" : 146922, "dist" : 0.6828926855663344 }
{ "name" : "Gresham", "population" : 98851, "dist" : 0.2395159760851125 }
// many others
```

As you can see, Mongo's aggregation API provides a very nice interface for working with schemaless geospatial data. We've only scratched the surface here (no pun intended), but if you're interested in exploring the full potential of MongoDB, we strongly encourage you to dig more deeply.[4]

GridFS

One downside of a distributed system can be the lack of a single coherent filesystem. Say you operate a website where users can upload images of themselves. If you run several web servers on several different nodes, you must manually replicate the uploaded image to each web server's disk or create some alternative central system. Mongo handles this scenario using a distributed filesystem called GridFS.

Mongo comes bundled with a command-line tool for interacting with GridFS. The great thing is that you don't have to set up anything special to use it. If you list the files in the mongos managed shards using the command mongofiles, you get an empty list.

```
$ mongofiles -h localhost:27020 list

connected to: localhost:27020
```

But upload any file...

```
$ echo "here's some file data" > just-some-data.txt
$ mongofiles -h localhost:27020 put just-some-data.txt
2017-05-11T20:03:32.272-0700    connected to: localhost:27020
added file: my-file.txt
```

...and *voilà!* If you list the contents of mongofiles, you'll find the uploaded name.

```
$ mongofiles -h localhost:27020 list

2017-05-11T20:04:39.019-0700    connected to: localhost:27020
just-some-data.txt     22
```

---

4. https://docs.mongodb.com/manual/core/2dsphere

Back in your mongo console, you can see the collections Mongo stores the data in.

```
> show collections
cities
fs.chunks
fs.files
```

Because they're just plain old collections, they can be replicated or queried like any other. Here we'll look up the filename of the text file we imported.

```
> db.fs.files.find()[0].filename
just-some-data.txt
```

Day 3 Wrap-Up

This wraps up our investigation of MongoDB. Today we focused on how Mongo enhances data durability with replica sets and supports horizontal scaling with sharding. We looked at good server configurations and how Mongo provides the mongos server to act as a relay for handling autosharding between multiple nodes. Finally, we toyed with some of Mongo's built-in tools, such as geospatial queries and GridFS.

Day 3 Homework

Find

1. Read the full replica set configuration options in the online docs.

2. Find out how to create a spherical geo index.

Do

1. Mongo has support for bounding shapes (namely, squares and circles). Find all cities within a 50-mile radius around the center of London.[5]

2. Run six servers: three servers in a replica set, and each replica set is one of two shards. Run a config server and mongos. Run GridFS across them (this is the final exam).

Wrap-Up

We hope this taste of MongoDB has piqued your fancy and showed you how it earns the moniker of the "humongous" database. We covered a lot in a single chapter, but as usual, we only clawed at the surface.

---

5. https://docs.mongodb.com/manual/reference/operator/query/geoWithin/

Mongo's Strengths

Mongo's primary strength lies in its ability to handle huge amounts of data (and huge amounts of requests) by replication and horizontal scaling. But it also has an added benefit of a very flexible data model. You don't ever need to conform to a schema and can simply nest any values you would generally join using SQL in an RDBMS.

Finally, MongoDB was built to be easy to use. You may have noticed the similarity between Mongo commands and SQL database concepts (minus the server-side joins). This is not by accident and is one reason Mongo has so much mind share amongst people who have defected from the relational database camp. It's different enough to scratch a lot of developer itches but not so different that it becomes a weird and scary monster.

Mongo's Weaknesses

Mongo encourages denormalization of schemas (by not having any) and that can be a bit too much for some to swallow. Some developers find the cold, hard constraints of a relational database reassuring. It can be dangerous to insert any old value of any type into any collection. A single typo can cause hours of headache if you don't think to look at field names and collection names as a possible culprit. Mongo's flexibility is generally not important if your data model is already fairly mature and locked down.

Because Mongo is focused on large datasets, it works best in large clusters, which can require some effort to design and manage. Unlike some clustered databases where adding new nodes is a transparent and relatively painless process, setting up a Mongo cluster requires a little more forethought.

Parting Thoughts

Mongo is an excellent choice if you are currently using a relational database to store your data using ORM-style patterns. We often recommend it to developers steeped in frameworks such as Ruby on Rails and Django because they can then perform validations and field management through the models at the application layer and because schema migrations become a thing of the past (for the most part). Adding new fields to a document is as easy as adding a new field to your data model, and Mongo will happily accept the new terms. We find Mongo to be a much more natural answer to many common problem scopes for application-driven datasets than relational databases.

## CHAPTER 5

CouchDB

Ratchet wrenches are light and convenient tools you carry around for a range of jobs, big and small. As with power drills, you can swap out variously sized bits like sockets or screws. Unlike a power drill that needs to be plugged into 120 volts of AC power, however, a wrench is happy to rest in your pocket and run on elbow grease. Apache CouchDB is like that. Able to scale down as well as up, it fits problem spaces of varying size and complexity with ease.

CouchDB is the quintessential JSON- and REST-based document-oriented database. First released all the way back in 2005, CouchDB was designed with the web in mind and all the innumerable flaws, faults, failures, and glitches that come with it. Consequently, CouchDB offers a robustness unmatched by most other databases. Whereas other systems tolerate occasional network drops, CouchDB thrives even when connectivity is only rarely available.

Like MongoDB, CouchDB stores *documents*—JSON objects consisting of key-value pairs where values may be any of several types, including other objects nested to any depth. What you don't get, though, is ad hoc querying. Instead, indexed *views* produced by incremental *mapreduce* operations are the principal way you discover documents.

Relaxing on the Couch

CouchDB lives up to its tag line: relax. Instead of focusing on working well only in massive clusters running on hundreds of nodes, CouchDB aims to support a variety of deployment scenarios from the datacenter down to the smartphone. You can run CouchDB on your Android phone, on your MacBook, and in your datacenter. Written in Erlang, CouchDB is built tough—the only way to shut it down is to kill the process! With its append-only storage model, your data is virtually incorruptible and easy to replicate, back up, and restore.

CouchDB is document oriented, using JSON as its storage and communication language. All calls to CouchDB happen through its REST interface. Replication can be one way (from one database to another) or bidirectional (back and forth between databases), and ad hoc (triggered at will) or continuous (triggered at periodic intervals). CouchDB gives you a lot of flexibility to decide how to structure, protect, and distribute your data.

Frontend-to-Backend Syncing with PouchDB

The past few years have seen a dramatic increase in interest in web apps that remain usable even when the user is offline. One of the core difficulties behind building such offline-friendly applications is the data synchronization problem. If a user uses an app offline for an hour and makes a wide variety of changes, what happens when their connection comes back and the discrepancy between client and server state needs to be resolved?

PouchDB is a very interesting tool that has emerged from the CouchDB ecosystem to address this problem. PouchDB is an open source database created in JavaScript that acts as a client-side, in-browser data store that automatically synchronizes data with CouchDB on the backend.

We won't cover PouchDB in this book, but we do find it to be a compelling solution to a problem that's widely encountered but has very few ready-made solutions. If you're looking to use CouchDB as a backend for web apps, you'd be remiss not to take a look.

Comparing CouchDB and MongoDB

One of the big questions we wanted to address in this book is "What's the difference between CouchDB and MongoDB?" On the surface, CouchDB and MongoDB—which we covered in Chapter 4, *MongoDB*, on page 93—can seem quite similar. They're both document-oriented databases with an affinity for JavaScript that use JSON for data transport. There are many differences, though, ranging from project philosophy to implementation to scalability characteristics. We'll cover many of these as we explore the beautiful simplicity of CouchDB.

During our three-day tour, we'll explore many of CouchDB's compelling features and design choices. We'll start, as always, with individual CRUD commands and then move on to indexing through mapreduce views. As we've done with other databases, we'll import some structured data and then use it to explore some advanced concepts. Finally, we'll develop some simple event-driven client-side applications using Node.js and learn how CouchDB's master-master replication strategy deals with conflicting updates. Let's get to it!

Day 1: CRUD, Fauxton, and cURL Redux

Today we're going to kick-start our CouchDB exploration by using CouchDB's friendly Fauxton web interface to perform basic CRUD operations. After that, we'll revisit cURL to make REST calls. All libraries and drivers for CouchDB end up sending REST requests under the hood, so it makes sense to start by understanding how they work.

Settling into CouchDB with Fauxton

CouchDB comes with a useful web interface called Fauxton (it was called Futon in pre-2.0 releases). Once you have CouchDB installed and running, open a web browser to http://localhost:5984/_utils/. This will open the landing page shown in the figure that follows.

Before we can start working with documents, we need to create a database to house them. We're going to create a database to store data about musicians along with album and track data from those artists' discographies. Click the Create Database button. In the pop-up, enter *music* and click Create. This will redirect you automatically to the database's page. From here, we can create new documents or open existing ones.

Welcome to the Admin Party!

In Fauxton, you may notice the Admin Party! button on the left-hand sidebar navigation panel. You can use this interface to create admin users with specified usernames and passwords. Until you do this, *all* users of your database are admins, which means they can do just about whatever they want, including deleting databases and running expensive replication operations. We won't create an admin user in this chapter, but if you were running CouchDB in production, you would be well advised to do so.

On the music database's page, click the plus sign next to All Documents and then New Doc. This will take you to a new page, as you can see in the figure that follows.

Just as in MongoDB, a document consists of a JSON object containing key-value pairs called *fields*. All documents in CouchDB have an _id field, which must be unique and can never be changed. You can specify an _id explicitly, but if you don't, CouchDB will generate one for you. In our case, the default is fine, so click Create Document to finish.

Immediately after saving the document, CouchDB will assign it an additional field called _rev. The _rev field will get a new value every time the document changes. The format for the revision string consists of an integer followed by a dash and then a pseudorandom unique string. The integer at the beginning denotes the numerical revision, in this case 1.

The _id and _rev fields names are reserved in CouchDB. To update or delete an existing document, you must provide *both* an _id and the matching _rev. If either of these do not match, CouchDB will reject the operation. This is how it prevents conflicts—by ensuring that only the most recent document revisions are modified.

There are no transactions or locking in CouchDB. To modify an existing record, you first read it out, taking note of the _id and _rev. Then you request an update by providing the full document, including the _id and _rev. All operations are first come, first served. By requiring a matching _rev, CouchDB ensures that the document you think you're modifying hasn't been altered behind your back while you weren't looking.

With the document page still open, modify the JSON object, which should have just one _id. Enter a key/value pair with a key of *name* and a value of *The Beatles*. Then click the Save Changes button. Your JSON object should look like this:

```
{
  "_id": "2ac58771c197f70461056f7c7e00c0f9",
  "name": "The Beatles"
}
```

CouchDB is not limited to storing string values. It can handle any JSON structure nested to any depth. Modify the JSON again, setting the value of a new *albums* key to the following (this is not an exhaustive list of the Beatles' albums):

```
[
  "Help!",
  "Sgt. Pepper's Lonely Hearts Club Band",
  "Abbey Road"
]
```

After you click Create Document, it should look like the figure that follows.

There's more relevant information about an album than just its name, so let's add some. Modify the albums field and replace the value you just set with this:

```
[{
  "title": "Help!",
  "year": 1965
},{
  "title": "Sgt. Pepper's Lonely Hearts Club Band",
  "year": 1967
},{
  "title": "Abbey Road",
  "year": 1969
}]
```

After you save the document, this time you should be able to expand the albums value to expose the nested documents underneath. It should resemble the figure on page 140.

Clicking the Delete Document button would do what you might expect; it would remove the document from the music database. But don't do it just yet. Instead, let's drop down to the command line and take a look at how to communicate with CouchDB over REST.

Performing RESTful CRUD Operations with cURL

All communication with CouchDB is REST-based, and this means issuing commands over HTTP. Here we'll perform some basic CRUD operations before moving on to the topic of views. To start, open a command prompt and run the following (which includes setting the root URL for CouchDB as an environment variable for the sake of convenience):

```
$ export COUCH_ROOT_URL=http://localhost:5984
$ curl ${COUCH_ROOT_URL}
{
  "couchdb": "Welcome",
  "version": "2.0.0",
  "vendor": {
    "name": "The Apache Software Foundation"
  }
}
```

Issuing GET requests (cURL's default) retrieves information about the thing indicated in the URL. Accessing the root as you just did merely informs you that CouchDB is up and running and what version is installed. Next, let's get some information about the music database we created earlier (output formatted here for readability):

```
$ curl "${COUCH_ROOT_URL}/music/"
{
  "db_name": "music",
  "update_seq": "4-g1AA...aZxxw",
  "sizes": {
    "file": 24907,
    "external": 193,
    "active": 968
  },
  "purge_seq": 0,
  "other": {
    "data_size": 193
  },
  "doc_del_count": 0,
  "doc_count": 1,
  "disk_size": 24907,
  "disk_format_version": 6,
  "data_size": 968,
  "compact_running": false,
  "instance_start_time": "0"
}
```

This returns some information about how many documents are in the database, how long the server has been up, how many operations have been performed, disk size, and more.

Reading a Document with GET

To retrieve a specific document, append its _id to the database URL like so:

```
$ curl "${COUCH_ROOT_URL}/music/2ac58771c197f70461056f7c7e0001f9"
{
  "_id": "2ac58771c197f70461056f7c7e0001f9",
  "_rev": "8-e1b7281f6adcd82910c6473be2d4e2ec",
  "name": "The Beatles",
  "albums": [
    {
      "title": "Help!",
      "year": 1965
    },
    {
      "title": "Sgt. Pepper's Lonely Hearts Club Band",
      "year": 1967
    },
    {
      "title": "Abbey Road",
      "year": 1969
    }
  ]
}
```

In CouchDB, issuing GET requests is always safe. CouchDB won't make any changes to documents as the result of a GET. To make changes, you have to use other HTTP commands such as PUT, POST, and DELETE.

Creating a Document with POST

To create a new document, use POST. Make sure to specify a Content-Type header with the value application/json; otherwise, CouchDB will refuse the request.

```
$ curl -i -XPOST "${COUCH_ROOT_URL}/music/" \
 -H "Content-Type: application/json" \
 -d '{ "name": "Wings" }'
HTTP/1.1 201 Created
Cache-Control: must-revalidate
Content-Length: 95
Content-Type: application/json
Date: Sun, 30 Apr 2017 23:15:42 GMT
Location: http://localhost:5984/music/2ac58771c197f70461056f7c7e002eda
Server: CouchDB/2.0.0 (Erlang OTP/19)
X-Couch-Request-ID: 92885ae1d3
X-CouchDB-Body-Time: 0

{
  "ok": true,
  "id": "2ac58771c197f70461056f7c7e002eda",
  "rev": "1-2fe1dd1911153eb9df8460747dfe75a0"
}
```

The HTTP response code 201 Created tells us that our creation request was successful. The body of the response contains a JSON object with useful information, such as the _id and _rev values.

Updating a Document with PUT

The PUT command is used to update an existing document or create a new one with a specific _id. Just like GET, the URL for a PUT URL consists of the database URL followed by the document's _id.

```
$ curl -i -XPUT \
  "${COUCH_ROOT_URL}/music/2ac58771c197f70461056f7c7e002eda" \
  -H "Content-Type: application/json" \
  -d '{
    "_id": "74c7a8d2a8548c8b97da748f43000f1b",
    "_rev": "1-2fe1dd1911153eb9df8460747dfe75a0",
    "name": "Wings",
    "albums": ["Wild Life", "Band on the Run", "London Town"]
  }'
HTTP/1.1 201 Created
Cache-Control: must-revalidate
Content-Length: 95
```

```
Content-Type: application/json
Date: Sun, 30 Apr 2017 23:25:13 GMT
ETag: "2-17e4ce41cd33d6a38f04a8452d5a860b"
Location: http://localhost:5984/music/2ac58771c197f70461056f7c7e002eda
Server: CouchDB/2.0.0 (Erlang OTP/19)
X-Couch-Request-ID: 6c0bdfffa5
X-CouchDB-Body-Time: 0
{
  "ok": true,
  "id": "2ac58771c197f70461056f7c7e002eda",
  "rev": "2-17e4ce41cd33d6a38f04a8452d5a860b"
}
```

Unlike MongoDB, in which you modify documents *in place*, with CouchDB you always overwrite the entire document to make any change. The Fauxton web interface you saw earlier may have made it look like you could modify a single field in isolation, but behind the scenes it was rerecording the whole document when you hit Save Changes.

As we mentioned earlier, both the _id and _rev fields must exactly match the document being updated, or the operation will fail. To see how, try executing the same PUT operation again.

```
HTTP/1.1 409 Conflict
Cache-Control: must-revalidate
Content-Length: 58
Content-Type: application/json
Date: Sun, 30 Apr 2017 23:25:52 GMT
Server: CouchDB/2.0.0 (Erlang OTP/19)
X-Couch-Request-ID: 5b626b9060
X-CouchDB-Body-Time: 0

{"error":"conflict","reason":"Document update conflict."}
```

You'll get an HTTP 409 Conflict response with a JSON object describing the problem. This is how CouchDB enforces consistency.

Removing a Document with DELETE

Finally, you can use the DELETE operation to remove a document from the database.

```
$ curl -i -XDELETE \
  "${COUCH_ROOT_URL}/music/2ac58771c197f70461056f7c7e002eda" \
  -H "If-Match: 2-17e4ce41cd33d6a38f04a8452d5a860b"
HTTP/1.1 200 OK
Cache-Control: must-revalidate
Content-Length: 95
Content-Type: application/json
Date: Sun, 30 Apr 2017 23:26:40 GMT
```

```
ETag: "3-42aafb7411c092614ce7c9f4ab79dc8b"
Server: CouchDB/2.0.0 (Erlang OTP/19)
X-Couch-Request-ID: c4dcb91db2
X-CouchDB-Body-Time: 0
{
  "ok": true,
  "id": "2ac58771c197f70461056f7c7e002eda",
  "rev": "3-42aafb7411c092614ce7c9f4ab79dc8b"
}
```

The DELETE operation will supply a new revision number, even though the document is gone. It's worth noting that the document wasn't really removed from disk, but rather a new empty document was appended, flagging the document as deleted. Just like with an update, CouchDB does not modify documents in place. But for all intents and purposes, it's deleted.

Day 1 Wrap-Up

Now that you've learned how to do basic CRUD operations in Fauxton and cURL, you're ready to move on to more advanced topics. On Day 2, we'll dig into creating indexed *views*, which will provide other avenues for retrieving documents than just specifying them by their _id values.

Day 1 Homework

Find

1. Find the CouchDB HTTP API reference documentation online.

2. We've already used GET, POST, PUT, and DELETE. What other HTTP methods are supported?

Do

1. Use cURL to PUT a new document into the music database with a specific _id of your choice.

2. Use cURL to create a new database with a name of your choice, and then delete that database also via cURL.

3. CouchDB supports *attachments*, which are arbitrary files that you can save with documents (similar to email attachments). Again using cURL, create a new document that contains a text document as an attachment. Lastly, craft and execute a cURL request that will return just that document's attachment.

Day 2: Creating and Querying Views

In CouchDB, a *view* is a window into the documents contained in a database. Views are the principal way that documents are accessed in all but trivial cases, such as those individual CRUD operations you saw on Day 1. Today, you'll discover how to create the functions that make up a view. You'll also learn how to perform ad hoc queries against views using cURL. Finally, you'll import music data, which will make the views more salient and demonstrate how to use couchrest, a popular Ruby library for working with CouchDB.

Accessing Documents Through Views

A view consists of mapper and reducer functions that are used to generate an ordered list of key-value pairs. Both keys and values can be any valid JSON. The simplest view is called _all_docs. It is provided out-of-the-box for all databases and contains an entry for each document in the database, keyed by its string _id.

To retrieve all of the things in the database, issue a GET request for the _all_docs view.

```
$ curl "${COUCH_ROOT_URL}/music/_all_docs"
{
  "total_rows": 1,
  "offset": 0,
  "rows": [
    {
      "id": "2ac58771c197f70461056f7c7e0001f9",
      "key": "2ac58771c197f70461056f7c7e0001f9",
      "value": {
        "rev": "7-d37c47883f4d30913c6a38644410685d"
      }
    }
  ]
}
```

You can see in the previous output the one document we've created so far. The response is a JSON object that contains an array of rows. Each row is an object with three fields:

- id is the document's _id.
- key is the JSON key produced by the mapreduce functions.
- value is the associated JSON value, also produced through mapreduce.

In the case of _all_docs, the id and key fields match, but for custom views this will almost never be the case.

By default, views will include only metadata for documents in the value field rather than each document's content. To retrieve all of the document's fields, add the include_docs=true URL parameter.

```
$ curl "${COUCH_ROOT_URL}/music/_all_docs?include_docs=true"
{
  "total_rows": 1,
  "offset": 0,
  "rows": [
    {
      "id": "2ac58771c197f70461056f7c7e0001f9",
      "key": "2ac58771c197f70461056f7c7e0001f9",
      "value": {
        "rev": "7-d37c47883f4d30913c6a38644410685d"
      },
      "doc": {
        "_id": "2ac58771c197f70461056f7c7e0001f9",
        "_rev": "7-d37c47883f4d30913c6a38644410685d",
        "name": "The Beatles",
        "albums": [
          {
            "title": "Help!",
            "year": 1965
          },
          {
            "title": "Sgt. Pepper's Lonely Hearts Club Band",
            "year": 1967
          },
          {
            "title": "Abbey Road",
            "year": 1969
          }
        ]
      }
    }
  ]
}
```

Here you can see that the other properties, name and albums, have been added to the value object in the output. With this basic structure in mind, let's make our own views.

Writing Your First View

Now that we've gotten a rough overview of how views work, let's try creating our own views. To start, we'll reproduce the behavior of the _all_docs view, and after that, we'll make increasingly complex views to extract deeper information from our documents for indexing.

To create a view, open a browser to Fauxton[1] as we did in Day 1. Next, open the music database by clicking the link. Click the plus symbol next to Design Documents and then click New View. That should bring you to a page that resembles the figure that follows.

The code in the Map Function box on the right should look like this:

```
function(doc) {
  emit(_doc.id, 1);
}
```

Change the emitter function to emit(null, doc). If you click the Options button in the upper right and then click Run Query, CouchDB will execute this function once for each document in the database, passing in that document as the doc parameter each time. This will generate a result that looks like the figure on page 148.

The secret to this output, and all views, is the emit() function (this works just like the MongoDB function of the same name). emit takes two arguments: the key and the value. A given map function may call emit one time, many times, or no times for a given document. In the previous case, the map function emits the key-value pair null/doc. As you see in the output table, the key is indeed null, and the value is the same object you saw on Day 1 when we requested it directly from cURL.

To make a mapper that achieves the same thing as _all_docs, we need to emit something a little different. Recall that _all_docs emits the document's _id field for the key and a simple object containing only the _rev field for the value.

With that in mind, change the Map Function code to the following, and then click Run.

```
function(doc) {
  emit(doc._id, { rev: doc._rev });
}
```

The output table should now resemble the following JSON payload, echoing the same key-value pair we saw earlier when enumerating records via _all_docs:

```
{
 "id": "2ac58771c197f70461056f7c7e0001f9",
 "key": "2ac58771c197f70461056f7c7e0001f9",
 "value": {
  "rev": "8-e1b7281f6adcd82910c6473be2d4e2ec"
 },
 "_id": "2ac58771c197f70461056f7c7e0001f9"
}
```

Saving a View as a Design Document

When using CouchDB in production, you should store your views in *design documents*. A design document is a real document in the database, just like the Beatles document we created earlier. As such, it can show up in views and be replicated to other CouchDB servers in the usual fashion. To save a design document in Fauxton, click the Create Document and Build Index button, and then fill in the Design Document and Index name fields.

Design documents always have IDs that start with _design/ and contain one or more views. The index name distinguishes this view from others housed in the same design document. Deciding which views belong in which design documents is largely application-specific and subject to taste. As a general rule, you should group views based on what they do relative to your data. You'll see examples of this as we create more interesting views.

Finding Artists by Name

Now that we've covered the basics of view creation, let's develop an application-specific view. Recall that our music database stores artist information, including a name field that contains the band's name. Using the normal GET access pattern or the _all_docs view, we can access documents by their _id values, but we're more interested in looking up bands by name.

In other words, today we can look up the document with _id equal to 2ac58771c197f70461056f7c7e0001f9, but how do we find the document with name equal to *The Beatles*? For this, we need a view. In Fauxton, head back to the New View page, enter *artists* as the name of the design document and *by_ name* as the name of the view. Then enter the following Map Function code and click Create Document and Build Index.

```
couchdb/artistsByNameMapper.js
function(doc) {
  if ('name' in doc) {
    emit(doc.name, doc._id);
  }
}
```

This function checks whether the current document has a name field and, if so, emits the name and document _id as the relevant key-value pair. This should produce a table like this:

Key	Value
"The Beatles"	"2ac58771c197f70461056f7c7e0001f9"

Finding Albums by Name

Finding artists by name is pretty useful, but we can do more. This time, let's make a view that lets us find albums. This will be the first example where the map function will emit more than one result per document.

Return to the New View page once again (by clicking the plus sign next to Design Documents). Set the design doc name to *albums* and the index name to *by_name*; then enter the following mapper and click Create Document and Build Index:

```
couchdb/albumsByNameMapper.js
function(doc) {
  if ('name' in doc && 'albums' in doc) {
    doc.albums.forEach(function(album){
      var
        key = album.title || album.name,
        value = { by: doc.name, album: album };
      emit(key, value);
    });
  }
}
```

This function checks whether the current document has a name field and an albums field. If so, it emits a key-value pair for each album where the key is the album's title or name and the value is a compound object containing the artist's name and the original album object. The row field should contain an array with these key/value pairs:

Key	Value
"Abbey Road"	{by: "The Beatles", album: {title: "Abbey Road", year: 1969}}
"Help!"	{by: "The Beatles", album: {title: "Help!", year: 1965}}
"Sgt. Pepper's Lonely Hearts Club Band"	{by: "The Beatles", album: {title: "Sgt. Pepper's Lonely Hearts Club Band", year: 1967}}

Just as we did with the Artists By Name view, click the Create Document and Build Index button. This time, for Design Document, enter *albums*, and for the index name enter *by_name*. Click Save to persist the change. Now let's see how to query these documents.

Querying Our Custom Artist and Album Views

Now that we have a couple of custom design documents saved, let's jump back to the command line and query them with the curl command. We'll start with the Artists By Name view. On the command line, execute the following:

```
$ curl "${COUCH_ROOT_URL}/music/_design/artists/_view/by_name"
{
  "total_rows": 1,
  "offset": 0,
  "rows": [
    {
      "id": "2ac58771c197f70461056f7c7e0001f9",
      "key": "The Beatles",
      "value": "2ac58771c197f70461056f7c7e0001f9"
    }
  ]
}
```

To query a view, construct the path /<database_name>/_design/<design_doc>/_view/
<view_name>, replacing the parts as appropriate. In our case, we're querying
the by_name view in the artists design document of the music database. No surprise
here that the output includes our one document, keyed by the band name.

Next, let's try to find albums by name:

```
$ curl "${COUCH_ROOT_URL}/music/_design/albums/_view/by_name"
{
  "total_rows": 3,
  "offset": 0,
  "rows": [
    {
      "id": "2ac58771c197f70461056f7c7e0001f9",
      "key": "Abbey Road",
      "value": {
        "by": "The Beatles",
        "album": {
          "title": "Abbey Road",
          "year": 1969
        }
      }
    },
    {
      "id": "2ac58771c197f70461056f7c7e0001f9",
      "key": "Help!",
      "value": {
        "by": "The Beatles",
        "album": {
          "title": "Help!",
          "year": 1965
        }
      }
    },
    {
      "id": "2ac58771c197f70461056f7c7e0001f9",
      "key": "Sgt. Pepper's Lonely Hearts Club Band",
```

```
      "value": {
        "by": "The Beatles",
        "album": {
          "title": "Sgt. Pepper's Lonely Hearts Club Band",
          "year": 1967
        }
      }
    }
  ]
}
```

CouchDB will ensure that the records are presented in alphanumerical order by the emitted keys. In effect, this is the indexing that CouchDB offers. When designing your views, it's important to pick emitted keys that will make sense when ordered. Requesting a view in this fashion returns the whole set, but what if you want just a subset? One way to do that is to use the key URL parameter. When you specify a key, only rows with that exact key are returned.

```
$ curl '${COUCH_ROOT_URL}/music/_design/albums/_view/by_name?key="Help!"'
{
  "total_rows": 3,
  "offset": 1,
  "rows": [
    {
      "id": "2ac58771c197f70461056f7c7e0001f9",
      "key": "Help!",
      "value": {
        "by": "The Beatles",
        "album": {
          "title": "Help!",
          "year": 1965
        }
      }
    }
  ]
}
```

Notice the total_rows and offset fields in the response. The total_rows field counts the total number of records in the view, not just the subset returned for this request. The offset field tells us how far into that full set the first record presented appears. Based on these two numbers and the length of the rows, we can calculate how many more records there are in the view on both sides. Requests for views can be sliced a few other ways beyond the keys parameter, but to really see them in action, we're going to need more data.

Importing Data Into CouchDB Using Ruby

Importing data is a recurring problem that you'll face no matter what database you end up using. CouchDB is no exception here. In this section, we'll use

Ruby to import structured data into our music database. Through this, you'll see how to perform bulk imports into CouchDB, and it will also give us a nice pool of data to work with when we create more advanced views.

We'll use music data from Jamendo.com,[2] a site devoted to hosting freely licensed music. Jamendo provides all their artist, album, and track data in a structured XML format, making it ideal for importing into a document-oriented database such as CouchDB. Download a GZIPped version of the XML:

```
$ curl -O https://imgjam.com/data/dbdump_artistalbumtrack.xml.gz
```

The XML file is over 200 MB. To parse Jamendo's XML file, we'll use the libxml-ruby gem.

Rather than writing our own Ruby-CouchDB driver or issuing HTTP requests directly, we'll use a popular Ruby gem called couchrest that wraps these calls into a convenient Ruby API. We'll be using only a few methods from the API, but if you want to continue using this driver for your own projects, you can check out the documentation.[3] On the command line, install the necessary gems:

```
$ gem install libxml-ruby couchrest
```

Just as we did for Wikipedia data in Chapter 3, *HBase*, on page 53, we'll use a streaming XML parser to process documents sequentially for insert as they're streamed in through standard input. Here's the code:

couchdb/import_from_jamendo.rb
```ruby
require 'libxml'
require 'couchrest'

include LibXML

class JamendoCallbacks
  include XML::SaxParser::Callbacks

  def initialize
    @db = CouchRest.database!("http://localhost:5984/music")
    @count = 0
    @max = 10000 # maximum number to insert
    @stack = []
    @artist = nil
    @album = nil
    @track = nil
    @tag = nil
    @buffer = nil
  end
```

---

2. http://www.jamendo.com/
3. http://rdoc.info/github/couchrest/couchrest/master/

```ruby
  def on_start_element(element, attributes)
    case element
    when 'artist'
      @artist = { :albums => [] }
      @stack.push @artist
    when 'album'
      @album = { :tracks => [] }
      @artist[:albums].push @album
      @stack.push @album
    when 'track'
      @track = { :tags => [] }
      @album[:tracks].push @track
      @stack.push @track
    when 'tag'
      @tag = {}
      @track[:tags].push @tag
      @stack.push @tag
    when 'Artists', 'Albums', 'Tracks', 'Tags'
      # ignore
    else
      @buffer = []
    end
  end

  def on_characters(chars)
    @buffer << chars unless @buffer.nil?
  end

  def on_end_element(element)
    case element
    when 'artist'
      @stack.pop
      @artist['_id'] = @artist['id'] # reuse Jamendo's artist id for doc _id
      @artist[:random] = rand
      @db.save_doc(@artist, false, true)
      @count += 1
      if !@max.nil? && @count >= @max
        on_end_document
      end
      if @count % 500 == 0
        puts "  #{@count} records inserted"
      end
    when 'album', 'track', 'tag'
      top = @stack.pop
      top[:random] = rand
    when 'Artists', 'Albums', 'Tracks', 'Tags'
      # ignore
    else
      if @stack[-1] && @buffer
        @stack[-1][element] = @buffer.join.force_encoding('utf-8')
        @buffer = nil
```

```
      end
    end
  end

  def on_end_document
    puts "TOTAL: #{@count} records inserted"
    exit(0)
  end
end
parser = XML::SaxParser.io(ARGF)
parser.callbacks = JamendoCallbacks.new
parser.parse
```

A few things that you should make note of:

1. At the very beginning of the script, we bring in all of the gems we need.

2. The standard way to use LibXML is by defining a callbacks class. Here we define a JamendoCallbacks class to encapsulate our SAX handlers for various events.

3. The first thing our class does during initialization is connect to our local CouchDB server using the couchrest API and then create the music database (if it doesn't exist already). After that, it sets up some instance variables for storing state information during the parse. Note that if you set the @max parameter to nil, all documents will be imported, not just the first 100.

4. Once parsing has started, the on_start_element() method will handle any opening tags. Here we watch for certain especially interesting tags, such as <artist>, <album>, <track>, and <tag>. We specifically ignore certain container elements—<Artists>, <Albums>, <Tracks>, and <Tags>—and treat all others as properties to be set on the nearest container items.

5. Whenever the parser encounters character data, we buffer it to be added as a property to the current container element (the end of @stack).

6. Much of the interesting stuff happens in the on_end_element() method. Here, we close out the current container element by popping it off the stack. If the tag closes an <artist> element, we take the opportunity to save off the document in CouchDB with the @db.save_doc() method. For any container element, we also add a random property containing a freshly generated random number. We'll use this later when selecting a random track, album, or artist.

7. Ruby's ARGF stream combines standard input and any files specified on the command line. We feed this into LibXML and specify an instance of our JamendoCallbacks class to handle the tokens—start tags, end tags, and character data—as they're encountered.

To run the script, pipe the unzipped XML content into the import script:

```
$ zcat < dbdump_artistalbumtrack.xml.gz | ruby import_from_jamendo.rb
TOTAL: 10000 records inserted
```

The script will begin importing 10,000 records (you can adjust the limit by changing the value of the @max variable in the script). When the import has finished, drop back down to the command line and we'll see how our views look. First, let's pull up a few artists. The limit URL parameter specifies that we want only that number of documents in the response (or less).

```
$ curl "${COUCH_ROOT_URL}/music/_design/artists/_view/by_name?limit=5"
{"total_rows":10001,"offset":0,"rows":[
{"id":"5385","key":" A.n.K.h // ","value":"5385"},
{"id":"354581","key":" E2U","value":"354581"},
{"id":"457184","key":" EL VECINO","value":"457184"},
{"id":"338059","key":" ENIGMA63","value":"338059"},
{"id":"378976","key":" John Ov3rblast","value":"378976"}
]}
```

The previous request started at the very beginning of the list of artists. To jump to the middle, we can use the startkey parameter:

```
$ curl "${COUCH_ROOT_URL}/music/_design/artists/_view/by_name?\
limit=5&startkey=%22C%22"
{"total_rows":10001,"offset":1320,"rows":[
{"id":"363267","key":"C-74","value":"363267"},
{"id":"357962","key":"c-dio","value":"357962"},
{"id":"350911","key":"C-Jay L'infidel J.B","value":"350911"},
{"id":"1188","key":"c-nergy","value":"1188"},
{"id":"832","key":"C. Glen Williams","value":"832"}
]}
```

Previously, we started with artists whose names began with *C*. Specifying an endkey provides another way to limit the returned content. Here we specify that we want artists only between *C* and *D*:

```
$ curl "${COUCH_ROOT_URL}/music/_design/artists/_view/by_name?\
startkey=%22C%22&endkey=%22D%22&limit=5"
{"total_rows":10001,"offset":1320,"rows":[
{"id":"363267","key":"C-74","value":"363267"},
{"id":"357962","key":"c-dio","value":"357962"},
{"id":"350911","key":"C-Jay L'infidel J.B","value":"350911"},
{"id":"1188","key":"c-nergy","value":"1188"},
{"id":"832","key":"C. Glen Williams","value":"832"}
]}
```

To get the rows in reverse order, use the descending URL parameter. Be sure to reverse your startkey and endkey as well.

```
$ curl "${COUCH_ROOT_URL}/music/_design/artists/_view/by_name?\
startkey=%22D%22&endkey=%22C%22&limit=5&descending=true"
{"total_rows":10001,"offset":8174,"rows":[
{"id":"1689","key":"czskamaarù","value":"1689"},
{"id":"341426","key":"CZAQU","value":"341426"},
{"id":"360640","key":"Cystoflo","value":"360640"},
{"id":"355941","key":"CYRUS DA VIRUS","value":"355941"},
{"id":"427004","key":"Cyrix Project","value":"427004"}
]}
```

A number of other URL parameters are available for modifying view requests, but these are the most common and are the ones you'll reach for the most often. Some of the URL parameters have to do with grouping, which comes from the reducer part of CouchDB mapreduce views. You'll explore these tomorrow.

Day 2 Wrap-Up

Today we covered some good ground. You learned how to create basic views in CouchDB and save them into design documents. You explored different ways of querying views to get subsets of the indexed content. Using Ruby and a popular gem called couchrest, we imported structured data and used it to support our views. Tomorrow, we'll expand on these ideas by creating more advanced views by adding reducers then move on to other APIs that CouchDB supports.

Day 2 Homework

Find

1. We've seen that the emit() method can output keys that are strings. What other types of values does it support? What happens when you emit an array of values as a key?

2. Find a list of available URL parameters (like limit and startkey) that can be appended to view requests and what they do.

Do

1. The import script import_from_jamendo.rb assigned a random number to each artist by adding a property called random. Create a mapper function that will emit key-value pairs where the key is the random number and the value is the band's name. Save this in a new design document named _design/random with the index name artist.

2. Craft a cURL request that will retrieve a random artist.

   Hint: You'll need to use the startkey parameter, and you can produce a random number on the command line using `ruby -e 'puts rand'`.

3. The import script also added a random property for each album, track, and tag. Create three additional views in the _design/random design document with the index names album, track, and tag to match the earlier artist view.

Day 3: Advanced Views, Changes API, and Replicating Data

In Days 1 and 2, you learned how to perform basic CRUD operations and interact with views for finding data. Building on this experience, today we'll take a closer look at views, dissecting the reduce part of the mapreduce equation. After that, we'll develop some Node.js applications in JavaScript to leverage CouchDB's unique Changes API. Lastly, we'll discuss replication and how CouchDB handles conflicting data.

Creating Advanced Views with Reducers

Mapreduce-based views provide the means by which we can harness CouchDB's indexing and aggregation facilities. In Day 2, all our views consisted solely of mappers. Now we're going to add reducers to the mix, developing new capabilities against the data we imported from Jamendo in Day 2.

One great thing about the Jamendo data is its depth. Artists have albums, which have tracks; tracks, in turn, have attributes, including tags. We'll now turn our attention to tags to see whether we can write a view to collect and count them. First, return to the New View page, set the design doc name to *tags* and the index name to *by_name*, and then enter the following map function:

```
couchdb/tagsByNameMapper.js
function(doc) {
  (doc.albums || []).forEach(function(album){
    (album.tracks || []).forEach(function(track){
      (track.tags || []).forEach(function(tag){
        emit(tag.idstr, 1);
      });
    });
  });
}
```

This function digs into the artist document and then down into each album, each track, and finally each tag. For each tag, it emits a key-value pair consisting of the tag's idstr property (a string representation of the tag, like "rock") and the number 1.

With the map function in place, click on the Reduce selector and choose CUSTOM. Enter the following in the text field:

couchdb/simpleCountReducer.js
```
function(key, values, rereduce) {
  return sum(values);
}
```

This code merely sums the numbers in the values list—which we'll talk about momentarily once we've run the view. The output should be a series of JSON objects containing key/value pairs like this:

Key	Value
"17sonsrecords"	1
"17sonsrecords"	1
"17sonsrecords"	1
"17sonsrecords"	1
"17sonsrecords"	1
"acid"	1
"acousticguitar"	1
"acousticguitar"	1
"action"	1
"action"	1

This shouldn't be too surprising. The value is always 1 as we indicated in the mapper, and the Key fields exhibit as much repetition as there is in the tracks themselves. Notice, however, the Options button in the upper-right corner. Check the Reduce box, click Run Query, and then look at the table again. It should now look something like this:

Key	Value
"17sonsrecords"	5
"acid"	1
"acousticguitar"	2
"action"	2
"adventure"	3
"aksband"	1
"alternativ"	1
"alternativ"	3
"ambient"	28
"autodidacta"	17

What happened? In short, the reducer *reduced* the output by combining like mapper rows in accordance with our Reducer Function. The CouchDB mapreduce engine works conceptually like the other mapreducers we've seen before (like MongoDB's *Mapreduce (and Finalize)*, on page 119). Specifically, here's a high-level outline of the steps CouchDB takes to build a view:

1. Send documents off to the mapper function.

2. Collect all the emitted values.

3. Sort emitted rows by their keys.

4. Send chunks of rows with the same keys to the reduce function.

5. If there was too much data to handle all reductions in a single call, call the reduce function again but with previously reduced values.

6. Repeat recursive calls to the reduce function as necessary until no duplicate keys remain.

Reduce functions in CouchDB take three arguments: key, values, and rereduce. The first argument, key, is an array of tuples—two element arrays containing the key emitted by the mapper and the _id of the document that produced it. The second argument, values, is an array of values corresponding to the keys.

The third argument, rereduce, is a Boolean value that will be true if this invocation is a *rereduction*. That is, rather than being sent keys and values that were emitted from mapper calls, this call is sent the products of previous reducer calls. In this case, the key parameter will be null.

Stepping Through Reducer Calls

Let's work through an example based on the output we just saw. Consider documents (artists) with tracks that have been tagged as "ambient." The mappers run on the documents and emit key-value pairs of the form "ambient"/1. At some point, enough of these have been emitted that CouchDB invokes a reducer. That call might look like this:

```
reduce(
  [["ambient", id1], ["ambient", id2], ...],    // keys are the same
  [1, 1, ...],                                   // values are all 1
  false                                          // rereduce is false
)
```

Recall that in our reducer function we take the sum() of values. Because they're all 1, the sum will simply be the length—effectively a count of how many tracks have the "ambient" tag. CouchDB keeps this return value for later processing. For the sake of this example, let's call that number 10.

Some time later, after CouchDB has run these kinds of calls several times, it decides to combine the intermediate reducer results by executing a rereduce:

```
reduce(
  null,              // key array is null
  [10, 10, 8],       // values are outputs from previous reducer calls
  true               // reduce is true
)
```

Our reducer function again takes the sum() of values. This time, the values add up to 28. Rereduce calls may be recursive. They go on as long as there is reduction to be done, which means until all the intermediate values have been combined into one.

Most mapreduce systems, including the ones used by other databases we've covered in this book such as MongoDB, throw away the output of mappers and reducers after the work is done. In those systems, mapreduce is seen as a means to an end—something to be executed whenever the need arises, each time starting from scratch. Not so with CouchDB.

Once a view is codified into a design document, CouchDB will keep the intermediate mapper and reducer values until a change to a document would invalidate the data. At that time, CouchDB will incrementally run mappers and reducers to correct for the updated data. It won't start from scratch, recalculating everything each time. This is the genius of CouchDB views. CouchDB is able to use mapreduce as its primary indexing mechanism by not tossing away intermediate data values.

Watching CouchDB for Changes

CouchDB's incremental approach to mapreduce is an innovative feature, to be sure; it's one of many that set CouchDB apart from other databases. The next feature we will investigate is the Changes API. This interface provides mechanisms for watching a database for changes and getting updates instantly.

The Changes API makes CouchDB a perfect candidate for a system of record. Imagine a multidatabase system where data is streaming in from several directions and other systems need to be kept up-to-date. Examples might include a search engine backed by Lucene or ElasticSeach or a caching layer implemented using memcached or Redis. You could have different maintenance scripts kick off in response to changes too—performing tasks such as database compaction and remote backups. In short, this simple API opens up a world of possibilities. Today we'll learn how to harness it.

To make use of the API, we're going to develop some simple client applications using Node.js.[4] Because Node.js is event-driven and code for it is written in JavaScript, it's a natural fit for integrating with CouchDB. If you don't already have Node.js, head over to the Node.js site and install the latest stable version (we use version 7.4.0).

The three flavors of the Changes API are polling, long-polling, and continuous. We'll talk about each of these in turn. As always, we'll start with cURL to get close to the bare metal and then follow up with a programmatic approach.

cURLing for Changes

The first and simplest way to access the Changes API is through the polling interface. Head to the command line, and try the following (the output is truncated for brevity; yours will differ):

```
$ curl "${COUCH_ROOT_URL}/music/_changes"
{
  "results":[{
    "seq":"10057-g1.....FqzAI2DMmw",
    "id":"370255",
    "changes":[{"rev":"1-a7b7cc38d4130f0a5f3eae5d2c963d85"}]
  },{
    "seq":"10057-g1.....A0Y9NEs7RUb",
    "id":"370254",
    "changes":[{"rev":"1-2c7e0deec3ffca959ba0169b0e8bfcef"}]
  },{
    ... many more records ...
  },{
    "seq":"10057-g1.....U9OzMnILy7J",
    "id":"357995",
    "changes":[{"rev":"1-aa649aa53f2858cb609684320c235aee"}]
  }],
  "last_seq":100
}
```

When you send a GET request for _changes with no other parameters, CouchDB will respond with everything it has. Just like accessing views, you can specify a limit parameter to request just a subset of the data, and adding include_docs=true will cause full documents to be returned.

Typically you won't want all the changes from the beginning of time. You're more likely to want the changes that have occurred since you last checked. For this, use the since parameter, specifying a sequence ID (pull one from the output of the last cURL command):

---

4.   http://nodejs.org/

```
$ curl "${COUCH_ROOT_URL}/music/_changes?since=10057-g1.....FqzAI2DMmw"
{
  "results":[{
    "seq":"10057-g1.....U9OzMnILy7J",
    "id":"357995",
    "changes":[{"rev":"1-aa649aa53f2858cb609684320c235aee"}]
  }],
  "last_seq":100
}
```

Using this method, the client application would check back periodically to find out whether any new changes have occurred, taking application-specific actions accordingly.

Polling is a fine solution if you can cope with long delays between updates. If updates are relatively rare, then you can use polling without encountering any serious drawbacks. For example, if you were pulling blog entries, polling every five minutes might be just fine.

If you want updates quicker, without incurring the overhead of reopening connections, then long polling is a better option. When you specify the URL parameter feed=longpoll, CouchDB will leave the connection open for some time, waiting for changes to happen before finishing the response. Try this:

```
$ curl "${COUCH_ROOT_URL}/music/_changes?feed=longpoll&\
since=10057-g1.....FqzAI2DMmw"
{"results":[
```

You should see the beginning of a JSON response but nothing else. If you leave the terminal open long enough, CouchDB will eventually close the connection by finishing it:

```
],
"last_seq":9000}
```

From a development perspective, writing a driver that watches CouchDB for changes using polling is equivalent to writing one for long polling. The difference is essentially just how long CouchDB is willing to leave the connection open. Now let's turn our attention to writing a Node.js application that watches and uses the change feed.

Polling for Changes with Node.js

Node.js is a strongly event-driven system, so our CouchDB watcher will adhere to this principle as well. Our driver will watch the changes feed and emit change events whenever CouchDB reports changed documents. To get started, we'll look at a skeletal outline of our driver, talk about the major pieces, and then fill in the feed-specific details.

Without further ado, here's the outline of our watcher program, as well as a brief discussion of what it does:

```
couchdb/watchChangesSkeleton.js
var http = require('http'),
    events = require('events');

/**
 * create a CouchDB watcher based on connection criteria;
 * follows the Node.js EventEmitter pattern, emits 'change' events.
 */
exports.createWatcher = function(options) {

  var watcher = new events.EventEmitter();

  watcher.host = options.host || 'localhost';
  watcher.port = options.port || 5984;
  watcher.last_seq = options.last_seq || 0;
  watcher.db = options.db || '_users';

  watcher.start = function() {
    // ... feed-specific implementation ...
  };

  return watcher;

};

// start watching CouchDB for changes if running as main script
if (!module.parent) {
  exports.createWatcher({
    db: process.argv[2],
    last_seq: process.argv[3]
  })
  .on('change', console.log)
  .on('error', console.error)
  .start();
}
```

So what's happening in this watcher? A few things to pay attention to:

- exports is a standard object provided by the CommonJS Module API that Node.js implements. Adding the createWatcher() method to exports makes it available to other Node.js scripts that might want to use this as a library. The options argument allows the caller to specify which database to watch as well as override other connection settings.

- createWatcher() produces an EventEmitter object that the caller can use to listen for change events. With an EventEmitter, you can listen to events by calling its on() method and trigger events by calling its emit() method.

- watcher.start() is responsible for issuing HTTP requests to watch CouchDB for changes. When changes to documents happen, watcher should emit

them as change events. All of the feed-specific implementation details will
be in here.

- The last chunk of code at the bottom specifies what the script should do if
  it's called directly from the command line. In this case, the script will invoke
  the createWatcher() method then set up listeners on the returned object that
  dump results to standard output. Which database to connect to and what
  sequence ID number to start from can be set via command-line arguments.

So far, there's nothing specific to CouchDB at all in this code. It's all just
Node.js's way of doing things. With the skeleton in place, let's add the code
to connect to CouchDB via long polling and emit events. The following is just
the code that goes inside the watcher.start() method. Written inside the previous
outline (where the comment says *feed-specific implementation*), the new
complete file should be called watchChangesLongpolling.js.

couchdb/watchChangesLongpollingImpl.js

```
var httpOptions = {
  host: watcher.host,
  port: watcher.port,
  path: '/' +
        watcher.db +
        '/_changes' +
        '?feed=longpoll&include_docs=true&since=' +
        watcher.last_seq
};

http.get(httpOptions, function(res) {
  var buffer = '';

  res.on('data', function (chunk) {
    buffer += chunk;
  });
  res.on('end', function() {
    var output = JSON.parse(buffer);
    if (output.results) {
      watcher.last_seq = output.last_seq;
      output.results.forEach(function(change){
        watcher.emit('change', change);
      });
      watcher.start();
    } else {
      watcher.emit('error', output);
    }
  })
})
.on('error', function(err) {
  watcher.emit('error', err);
});
```

Here are some things to look out for in the long polling script:

- The first thing this script does is set up the httpOptions configuration object in preparation for the request. The path points to the same _changes URL we've been using, with feed set to longpoll and include_docs=true.

- After that, the script calls http.get(), a Node.js library method that fires off a GET request according to our settings. The second parameter to http.get is a callback that will receive an HTTPResponse. The response object emits data events as the content is streamed back, which we add to the buffer.

- Finally, when the response object emits an end event, we parse the buffer (which should contain JSON). From this we learn the new last_seq value, emit a change event, and then reinvoke watcher.start() to wait for the next change.

To run this script in command-line mode, execute it like this (output truncated for brevity):

```
$ node watchChangesLongpolling.js music
{ seq: '...',
  id: '370255',
  changes: [ { rev: '1-a7b7cc38d4130f0a5f3eae5d2c963d85' } ],
  doc:
   { _id: '370255',
     _rev: '1-a7b7cc38d4130f0a5f3eae5d2c963d85',
     albums: [ [Object] ],
     id: '370255',
     name: '""ATTIC""',
     url: 'http://www.jamendo.com/artist/ATTIC_(3)',
     mbgid: '',
     random: 0.4121620435325435 } }
{ seq: '...',
  id: '370254',
  changes: [ { rev: '1-2c7e0deec3ffca959ba0169b0e8bfcef' } ],
  doc:
   { _id: '370254',
     _rev: '1-2c7e0deec3ffca959ba0169b0e8bfcef',
  ... many more entries ...
```

Hurrah, our app works! After outputting a record for each document, the process will keep running, polling CouchDB for future changes.

Feel free to modify a document in Fauxton directly or increase the @max value on import_from_jamendo.rb and run it again. You'll see those changes reflected on the command line. Next you'll see how to go full steam ahead and use the continuous feed to get even snappier updates.

Watching for Changes Continuously

The polling and long polling feeds produced by the _changes service both produce proper JSON results. The *continuous* feed does things a little differently. Instead of combining all available changes into a results array and closing the stream afterward, it sends each change separately and keeps the connection open. This way, it's ready to return more JSON-serialized change notification objects as changes become available.

To see how this works, try the following, supplying a value for since (output truncated for readability):

```
$ curl "${COUCH_ROOT_URL}/music/_changes?since=...feed=continuous"
{"seq":"...","id":"357999","changes":[{"rev":"1-0329f5c885...87b39beab0"}]}
{"seq":"...","id":"357998","changes":[{"rev":"1-79c3fd2fe6...1e45e4e35f"}]}
{"seq":"...","id":"357995","changes":[{"rev":"1-aa649aa53f...320c235aee"}]}
```

Eventually, if no changes have happened for a while, CouchDB will close the connection after outputting a line like this:

```
{"last_seq":100}
```

The benefit of this method over polling or long polling is the reduced overhead that accompanies leaving the connection open. There's no time lost reestablishing the HTTP connections. On the other hand, the output isn't straight JSON, which means it's a bit more of a chore to parse. Also, it's not a good fit if your client is a web browser. A browser downloading the feed asynchronously might not receive any of the data until the entire connection finishes (better to use long polling in this case).

Filtering Changes

As you've just seen, the Changes API provides a unique window into the goings-on of a CouchDB database. On the plus side, it provides all the changes in a single stream. However, sometimes you may want just a subset of changes, rather than the fire hose of everything that has ever changed. For example, you may be interested only in document deletions or maybe only in documents that have a particular quality. This is where *filter functions* come in.

A filter is a function that takes in a document (and request information) and makes a decision about whether that document ought to be allowed through the filter. This is gated by the return value. Let's explore how this works. Most artist documents we've been inserting into the music database have a country property that contains a three-letter code. Say you're interested only in bands from Russia (RUS). Your filter function might look like the following:

```
function(doc) {
  return doc.country === "RUS";
}
```

If we added this to a design document under the key filters, we'd be able to specify it when issuing requests for _changes. But before we do, let's expand the example. Rather than always wanting Russian bands, it'd be better if we could parameterize the input so the country could be specified in the URL.

Here's a parameterized country-based filter function:

```
function(doc, req) {
  return doc.country === req.query.country;
}
```

Notice this time how we're comparing the document's country property to a parameter of the same name passed in the request's query string. To see this in action, let's create a new design document just for geography-based filters and add it:

```
$ curl -XPUT "${COUCH_ROOT_URL}/music/_design/wherabouts" \
  -H "Content-Type: application/json" \
  -d '{"language":"javascript","filters":{"by_country":
    "function(doc,req){return doc.country === req.query.country;}"
  }}'
{
  "ok":true,
  "id":"_design/wherabouts",
  "rev":"1-c08b557d676ab861957eaeb85b628d74"
}
```

Now we can make a country-filtered changes request:

```
$ curl "${COUCH_ROOT_URL}/music/_changes?\
filter=wherabouts/by_country&\
country=RUS"
{"results":[
{"seq":10,"id":"5987","changes":[{"rev":"1-2221be...a3b254"}]},
{"seq":57,"id":"349359","changes":[{"rev":"1-548bde...888a83"}]},
{"seq":73,"id":"364718","changes":[{"rev":"1-158d2e...5a7219"}]},
...
```

Because filter functions may contain arbitrary JavaScript, more sophisticated logic can be put into them. Testing for deeply nested fields would be similar to what we did for creating views. You could also use regular expressions for testing properties or compare them mathematically (for example, filtering by a date range). There's even a user context property on the request object (req.userCtx) that you can use to find out more about the credentials provided with the request.

We'll revisit Node.js and the CouchDB Changes API in Chapter 8, *Redis*, on page 259 when we build a multidatabase application. For now, though, it's time to move on to the last distinguishing feature of CouchDB we're going to cover: replication.

Replicating Data in CouchDB

CouchDB is all about asynchronous environments and data durability. According to CouchDB, the safest place to store your data is on many nodes in your cluster (you can configure how many), and CouchDB provides the tools to do so. Some other databases we've looked at maintain a single master node to guarantee consistency. Still others ensure it with a quorum of agreeing nodes. CouchDB does neither of these; instead, it supports something called multi-master or master-master replication.

Each CouchDB server is equally able to receive updates, respond to requests, and delete data, regardless of whether it's able to connect to any other server. In this model, changes are selectively replicated in one direction, and all data is subject to replication in the same way.

Replication is the last major topic in CouchDB that we'll be discussing. First you'll see how to set up ad hoc and continuous replication between databases. Then you'll work through the implications of conflicting data and how to make applications capable of handling these cases gracefully.

To begin, click the Replication link on the left side of the page. It should open a page that looks like the figure that follows.

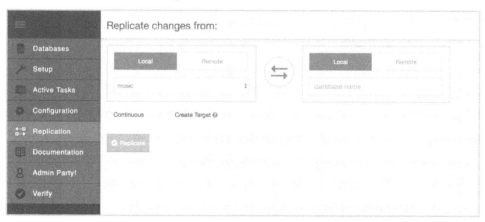

In the "Replicate changes from" dialog, choose *music* from the left drop-down menu and enter *music-repl* in the right-side slot. Leave the Continuous checkbox unchecked, check the Create Target box, and then click Replicate. This should produce an event message in the event log below the form followed by a big green banner at the top of the page saying that the replication operation has begun.

To confirm that the replication request worked, go back to the Fauxton Databases page. There should now be a new database called music-repl with the same number of documents as the music database. If it has fewer, give it some time and refresh the page—CouchDB may be in the process of catching up. Don't be concerned if the Update Seq values don't match. That's because the original music database had deletions and updates to documents, whereas the music-repl database had only insertions to bring it up to speed.

Creating Conflicts

Next, we'll create a conflict and then explore how to deal with it. Keep the Replicator page handy because we're going to be triggering ad hoc replication between music and music-repl frequently. Drop back to the command line, and enter this to create a document in the music database:

```
$ curl -XPUT "${COUCH_ROOT_URL}/music/theconflicts" \
 -H "Content-Type: application/json" \
 -d '{ "name": "The Conflicts" }'
{
  "ok":true,
  "id":"theconflicts",
  "rev":"1-e007498c59e95d23912be35545049174"
}
```

On the Replication page, click Replicate to trigger another synchronization. We can confirm that the document was successfully replicated by retrieving it from the music-repl database.

```
$ curl "${COUCH_ROOT_URL}/music-repl/theconflicts"
{
  "_id":"theconflicts",
  "_rev":"1-e007498c59e95d23912be35545049174",
  "name":"The Conflicts"
}
```

Next, let's update it in music-repl by adding an album called *Conflicts of Interest*.

```
$ curl -XPUT "${COUCH_ROOT_URL}/music-repl/theconflicts" \
  -H "Content-Type: application/json" \
  -d '{
    "_id": "theconflicts",
    "_rev": "1-e007498c59e95d23912be35545049174",
    "name": "The Conflicts",
    "albums": ["Conflicts of Interest"]
  }'
```

```
{
  "ok":true,
  "id":"theconflicts",
  "rev":"2-0c969fbfa76eb7fcdf6412ef219fcac5"
}
```

And create a conflicting update in music proper by adding a different album: *Conflicting Opinions*.

```
$ curl -XPUT "${COUCH_ROOT_URL}/music/theconflicts" \
  -H "Content-Type: application/json" \
  -d '{
    "_id": "theconflicts",
    "_rev": "1-e007498c59e95d23912be35545049174",
    "name": "The Conflicts",
    "albums": ["Conflicting Opinions"]
  }'
{
  "ok":true,
  "id":"theconflicts",
  "rev":"2-cab47bf4444a20d6a2d2204330fdce2a"
}
```

At this point, both the music and music-repl databases have a document with an _id value of theconflicts. Both documents are at version 2 and derived from the same base revision (1-e007498c59e95d23912be35545049174). Now the question is, what happens when we try to replicate between them?

> ## Fine-Grained Data Replication in CouchDB 2.0
>
> With early versions of CouchDB, if you set up a multi-node CouchDB cluster, *all* documents were stored on all nodes in the cluster. CouchDB 2.0 brought a native clustering capability that enables you to store documents on only *some* nodes in the cluster and to determine, at write time, how many nodes should store the document, enabling you to choose a *replication factor* for data.
>
> We won't cover this or related issues such as sharding, but if you plan on using CouchDB in production, you should check out some theoretical documentation[a] to see how it works and receive guidance in making intelligent decisions about replication.
>
> _____
> a.   http://docs.couchdb.org/en/latest/cluster/theory.html

Resolving Conflicts

With our document now in a conflicting state between the two databases, head back to the Replication page and kick off another replication. If you were expecting this to fail, you may be shocked to learn that the operation succeeds just fine. So how did CouchDB deal with the discrepancy?

It turns out that CouchDB basically just picks one and calls that one the winner. Using a deterministic algorithm, all CouchDB nodes will pick the same winner when a conflict is detected. However, the story doesn't end there. CouchDB stores the unselected "loser" documents as well so that a client application can review the situation and resolve it at a later date.

To find out which version of our document won during the last replication, we can request it using the normal GET request channel. By adding the conflicts= true URL parameter, CouchDB will also include information about the conflicting revisions.

```
$ curl "${COUCH_ROOT_URL}/music-repl/theconflicts?conflicts=true"
{
  "_id":"theconflicts",
  "_rev":"2-cab47bf4444a20d6a2d2204330fdce2a",
  "name":"The Conflicts",
  "albums":["Conflicting Opinions"],
  "_conflicts":[
    "2-0c969fbfa76eb7fcdf6412ef219fcac5"
  ]
}
```

So, we see that the second update won. Notice the _conflicts field in the response. It contains a list of other revisions that conflicted with the chosen one. By adding a rev parameter to a GET request, we can pull down those conflicting revisions and decide what to do about them.

```
$ curl "${COUCH_ROOT_URL}/music-repl/theconflicts?rev=2-0c969f..."
{
  "_id":"theconflicts",
  "_rev":"2-0c969fbfa76eb7fcdf6412ef219fcac5",
  "name":"The Conflicts",
  "albums":["Conflicts of Interest"]
}
```

The takeaway here is that CouchDB does not try to intelligently merge conflicting changes. How you should merge two documents is highly application specific, and a general solution isn't practical. In our case, combining the two albums arrays by concatenating them makes sense, but one could easily think of scenarios where the appropriate action is not obvious.

For example, imagine you're maintaining a database of calendar events. One copy is on your smartphone; another is on your laptop. You get a text message from a party planner specifying the venue for the party you're hosting, so you update your phone database accordingly. Later, back at the office, you receive another email from the planner specifying a *different* venue. So you update your laptop database and then replicate between them.

CouchDB has no way of knowing which of the two venues is "correct." The best it can do is make them consistent, keeping the old value around so you can verify which of the conflicting values should be kept. It would be up to the application to determine the right user interface for presenting this situation and asking for a decision.

Day 3 Wrap-Up

And so ends our tour of CouchDB. Here in Day 3, you started out by learning how to add reducer functions to your mapreduce-generated views. After that, we took a deep dive into the Changes API, including a jaunt into the world of event-driven server-side JavaScript development with Node.js. Lastly, we took a brief look at how you can trigger replication between databases and how client applications can detect and correct for conflicts.

Day 3 Homework

Find

1. What native reducers are available in CouchDB? What are the benefits of using native reducers over custom JavaScript reducers?

2. How can you filter the changes coming out of the _changes API on the server side?

3. Like everything in CouchDB, the tasks of initializing and canceling replication are controlled by HTTP commands under the hood. What are the REST commands to set up and remove replication relationships between servers?

4. How can you use the _replicator database to persist replication relationships?

Do

1. Create a new module called watchChangesContinuous.js based on the skeletal Node.js module described in the section *Polling for Changes with Node.js*, on page 163.

2. Implement watcher.start() such that it monitors the continuous _changes feed. Confirm that it produces the same output as watchChangesLongpolling.js.

   Hint: If you get stuck, you can find an example implementation in the downloads that accompany this book.

3. Documents with conflicting revisions have a _conflicts property. Create a view that emits conflicting revisions and maps them to the doc _id.

Wrap-Up

Throughout this chapter, you've seen how to do a pretty wide range of tasks with CouchDB, from performing basic CRUD operations to building views out of mapreduce functions. You saw how to watch for changes, and you explored how to develop nonblocking event-driven client applications. Finally, you learned how to perform ad-hoc replication between databases and how to detect and resolve conflicts. Despite all of this content, there's still a lot we didn't cover, but now it's time to wrap things up before heading off to our next database.

CouchDB's Strengths

CouchDB is a robust and stable member of the NoSQL community. Built on the philosophy that networks are unreliable and hardware failure is imminent, CouchDB offers a heartily decentralized approach to data storage. Small enough to live in your smartphone and big enough to support the enterprise, CouchDB affords a variety of deployment situations.

CouchDB's Weaknesses

Of course, CouchDB isn't well suited for everything. CouchDB's mapreduce-based views, while novel, can't perform all the fancy data slicing you'd expect from a relational database. In fact, you shouldn't be running ad-hoc queries *at all* in production. As with many other NoSQL databases, CouchDB always works best when you have a very good sense of what you're going to need in advance. In some databases, that means knowing the key or "address" of an object; in CouchDB, that means knowing all of your queries in advance. If your use case doesn't allow for that kind of foreknowledge, then you may want to look elsewhere.

Parting Thoughts

CouchDB's attention to robustness in the face of uncertainty makes it a great choice if your system must stand up to the harsh realities of the wild Internet. By leveraging standard "webisms" like HTTP/REST and JSON, CouchDB fits in easily wherever web technologies are prevalent, which is increasingly everywhere. Inside the walled garden of a datacenter, CouchDB can still make sense if you commit to managing conflicts when they arise or if you utilize some more recently added clustering features.

There are plenty of other features that make CouchDB unique and special that we didn't have time to cover. A short list would include ease of backups, binary attachments to documents, and CouchApps, a system for developing and deploying web apps directly through CouchDB with no other middleware. Having said that, we hope we've provided enough of an overview to whet your appetite for more. Try CouchDB for your next data-driven web app; you won't be disappointed!

## CHAPTER 6

Neo4J

A bungee cord is a helpful tool because you can use it to tie together the most disparate of things, no matter how awkwardly shaped or ill fitting they may be. In a lot of ways, Neo4j is the bungee cord of databases, a system intended not so much to store information about things as to *tie them together and record their connections with each other.*

Neo4j is a member of a family of databases known as *graph databases* because it stores data as a graph (in the mathematical sense). Neo4j is known for being "whiteboard friendly" because virtually any diagram that you can draw using boxes and lines on a whiteboard can be stored in Neo4j.

Neo4j focuses more on the *relationships between* values than on the *commonalities among sets of* values (such as collections of documents or tables of rows). In this way, it can store highly variable data in a natural and straightforward way.

On one side of the scale spectrum, Neo4j is small enough to be embedded into nearly any application; on the other side of the spectrum, Neo4j can run in large clusters of servers using master-slave replication and store tens of billions of nodes and as many relationships. In other words, Neo4j can handle just about any size problem that you can throw at it.

Neo4j Is Whiteboard Friendly

Imagine you need to create a wine suggestion engine in which wines are categorized by different varieties, regions, wineries, vintages, and designations. Imagine that you also need to keep track of things like articles describing those wines written by various authors and to enable users to track their favorite wines.

If you were using a relational model, you might create a category table and a many-to-many relationship between a single winery's wine and some combination of categories and other data. But this isn't quite how humans mentally model data. In the following figure, compare this wine suggestion schema in relational UML:

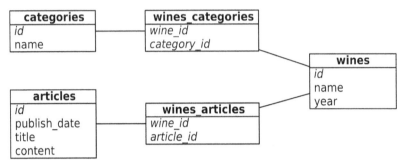

to this wine suggestion data on a whiteboard:

There's an old saying in the relational database world: *on a long enough timeline, all fields become optional.* Neo4j handles this implicitly by providing values and structure only where necessary. If a wine blend has no vintage, add a bottle year and point the vintages to the blend node instead. In graph databases such as Neo4j there is simply no schema to adjust.

Over the next three days you'll learn how to interact with Neo4j through a web console, using a querying language called Cypher, then via a REST interface, and finally through search indexes. You'll work with some simple graphs as well as some larger graphs with graph algorithms. Finally, on Day 3, you'll take a peek at the enterprise tools that Neo4j provides for mission-critical applications, from full ACID-compliant transactions to high-availability clustering and incremental backups.

In this chapter, we'll use the Neo4j 3.1.4 Enterprise Edition. Most of the actions you perform on Days 1 and 2 can actually use the GPL Community edition, but we'll require some enterprise functionality for Day 3: Distributed High Availability. You can download a free trial version of the Enterprise Edition from the Neo4j website.

Day 1: Graphs, Cypher, and CRUD

Today we're really going to jump in with both feet. In addition to exploring the Neo4j web interface, we'll get deep into graph database terminology and CRUD. Much of today will be learning how to query a graph using a querying language called *Cypher*. The concepts here differ significantly from other databases we've looked at so far, which have largely taken a document- or record-based view of the world. In Neo4j, nodes inside of graphs act like documents because they store properties, but what makes Neo4j special is that the *relationship* between those nodes takes center stage.

But before we get to all that, let's start with the web interface to see how Neo4j represents data in graph form and how to navigate that graph. After you've downloaded and unzipped the Neo4j package, cd into the Neo4j directory and start up the server like this:

```
$ bin/neo4j start
```

To make sure you're up and running, try curling this URL:

```
$ curl http://localhost:7474/db/data/
```

Like CouchDB, the default Neo4j package comes equipped with a fully featured web administration tool and data browser, which is excellent for experimentation. Even better, it has one of the coolest graph data browsers we've ever seen. This is perfect for getting started because graph traversal can feel very awkward at first try.

Neo4j's Web Interface

Launch a web browser and navigate to the administration page.[1]

You'll be greeted by a colorful dashboard like the one in the figure on page 180.

In the Connect to Neo4j component, sign in using the default username and password (enter neo4j for both). That will open up a command-line-style interface at the top of the page (distinguished by the $ on the far left). Type in :server connect to connect to the database.

You can enter :help commands at any time for an in-depth explanation of the existing commands. :help cypher will bring up a help page with instructions for specific Cypher commands (more on Cypher, the querying language we'll be using through this web interface, in a moment).

---

1. http://localhost:7474/browser/

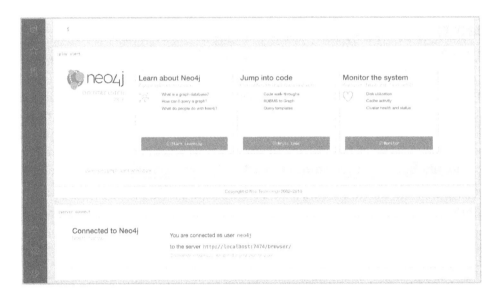

Nodes and Relationships: A Note on Terminology

A *node* in a graph database is not entirely unlike the nodes we talked about in prior chapters. Previously, when we spoke of a node, we meant a physical server in a network. If you viewed the entire network as a huge interconnected graph, a server node was a point, or *vertex*, between the server *relationships*, or *edges*.

In Neo4j, a node is conceptually similar: It's a vertex between edges that may hold data. That data is stored as a set of key-value pairs (as in many other non-relational databases we've talked about).

Neo4j via Cypher

There are several ways that you can interact with Neo4j. In addition to client libraries in a wide variety of programming languages (as with the other databases in this book), you can also interact with Neo4j via a REST API (more on this in Day 2), and via two querying languages created with Neo4j exclusively in mind: *Gremlin* and *Cypher*. While Gremlin has some interesting properties, Cypher is now considered standard.

Cypher is a rich, Neo4j-specific graph traversal language. In Cypher, as in mathematical graph theory, graph data points are called *nodes*. Unlike in graph theory, however, graphs in Cypher consist of *nodes* rather than *vertices* (as they are called in graph theory) and connections between nodes are called *relationships* (rather than *edges*). Statements used to query Neo4j graphs in Cypher typically look something like this:

```
$ MATCH [some set of nodes and/or relationships]
  WHERE [some set of properties holds]
  RETURN [some set of results captured by the MATCH and WHERE clauses]
```

In addition to querying the graph using MATCH, you can create new nodes and relationships using CREATE, update the values associated with nodes and relationships using UPDATE, and much more. That's fairly abstract, but don't worry —you'll get the hang of it via examples over the course of the next few sections.

At the moment, our not-so-exciting Neo4j graph consists of no nodes and no relationships. Let's get our hands dirty and change that by adding a node for a specific wine to our graph. That node will have a few properties: a name property with a value of Prancing Wolf, a style property of ice wine, and a vintage property of 2015. To create this node, enter this Cypher statement into the console:

```
$ CREATE (w:Wine {name:"Prancing Wolf", style: "ice wine", vintage: 2015})
```

In the section of the web UI immediately below the console, you should see output like that in the figure that follows.

At the top, you'll see the Cypher statement you just ran. The Rows tile shows you the nodes and/or relationships that you created in the last Cypher statement, and the Code tile provides in-depth information about the action you just completed (mostly info about the transaction that was made via Neo4j's REST API).

At any time, we can access all nodes in the graph, kind of like a SELECT * FROM entire_graph statement:

```
$ MATCH (n)
  RETURN n;
```

At this point, that will return just one solitary node. Let's add some others. Remember that we also want to keep track of wine-reviewing publications in our graph. So let's create a node representing the publication *Wine Expert Monthly*:

```
$ CREATE (p:Publication {name: "Wine Expert Monthly"})
```

In the last two statements, Wine and Publication were *labels* applied to the nodes, not types. We could create a node with the label Wine that had a completely different set of properties. Labels are extremely useful for querying purposes, as you'll see in a bit, but Neo4j doesn't require you to have predefined types. If you *do* want to enforce types, you'll have to do that at the application level.

So now we have a graph containing two nodes but they currently have no relationship with one another. Because *Wine Expert Monthly reports on* this Prancing Wolf wine, let's create a reported_on relationship that connects the two nodes:

```
$ MATCH (p:Publication {name: "Wine Expert Monthly"}),
    (w:Wine {name: "Prancing Wolf", vintage: 2015})
  CREATE (p)-[r:reported_on]->(w)
```

In this statement, we've MATCHed the two nodes that we want to connect via their labels (Wine and Publication) and their name property, created a reported_on relationship and stored that in the variable r, and finally RETURNed that relationship. You can see the end result in the figure that follows.

If you click on the relationship between the nodes in the web UI, you can see the ID of the relationship is 0. You can use Neo4j's REST interface to access information about the relationship at http://localhost:7474/db/data/relationship/0 or via Cypher by running:

```
$ MATCH ()-[r]-()
  WHERE id(r) = 0
  RETURN r
```

Relationships, like nodes, can contain properties and can be thought of as objects in their own right. After all, we don't want to know simply *that* a relationship exists; we want to know *what* constitutes that relationship. Let's say that we want to specify which score *Wine Expert Monthly* gave the Prancing Wolf wine. We can do that by adding a rating property to the relationship that we just created.

```
$ MATCH ()-[r]-()
  WHERE id(r) = 0
  SET r.rating = 97
  RETURN r
```

We also could've specified the rating when creating the relationship, like this:

```
$ MATCH (p:Publication {name: "Wine Expert Monthly"}),
    (w:Wine {name: "Prancing Wolf"})
  CREATE (p)-[r:reported_on {rating: 97}]->(w)
```

At this point, if you display the entire graph again using MATCH (n) RETURN n; and click on the relationship, you'll see that rating: 97 is now a property of the reported_on relationship. Another bit of info that we want to note is that the Prancing Wolf wine is made from the *Riesling* grape. We *could* insert this info by adding a grape_type: Riesling property to the Prancing Wolf node, but let's do things in a more Neo4j-native fashion instead by creating a new node for the Riesling grape type and adding relationships to wines of that type:

```
$ CREATE (g:GrapeType {name: "Riesling"})
```

Let's add a relationship between the Riesling node and the Prancing Wolf node using the same method:

```
$ MATCH (w:Wine {name: "Prancing Wolf"}),(g:GrapeType {name: "Riesling"})
  CREATE (w)-[r:grape_type]->(g)
```

Now we have a three-node graph: a wine, a type of grape, and a publication.

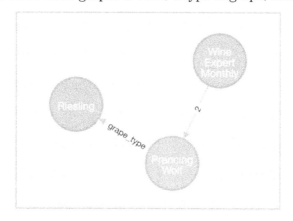

So far, we've created and updated both nodes and relationships. You can also delete both from a graph. The following are three Cypher statements that will create a new node, establish a relationship between that node and one of our existing nodes, delete the relationship, and then delete the node (you can't delete a node that still has relationships associated with it):

```
$ CREATE (e: EphemeralNode {name: "short lived"})
$ MATCH (w:Wine {name: "Prancing Wolf"}),
    (e:EphemeralNode {name: "short lived"})
  CREATE (w)-[r:short_lived_relationship]->(e)
$ MATCH ()-[r:short_lived_relationship]-()
  DELETE r
$ MATCH (e:EphemeralNode)
  DELETE e
```

Our wine graph is now back to where it was before creating the short lived node. Speaking of deletion, if you ever want to burn it all down and start from scratch with an empty graph, you can use the following command at any time to delete all nodes and relationships. But beware! This command will delete the entire graph that you're working with, so run it only if you're sure that you're ready to move on from a graph's worth of data for good.

```
$ MATCH (n)
  OPTIONAL MATCH (n)-[r]-()
  DELETE n, r
```

Now that you know how to start from scratch, let's continue building out our wine graph. Wineries typically produce more than one wine. To express that relationship in an RDBMS, we might create a separate table for each winery and store wines that they produce as rows. The most natural way to express this in Neo4j would be—you guessed it—to represent wineries as nodes in the graph and create relationships between wineries and wines. Let's create a node for Prancing Wolf Winery and add a relationship with the Prancing Wolf wine node that we created earlier:

```
$ CREATE (wr:Winery {name: "Prancing Wolf Winery"})
$ MATCH (w:Wine {name: "Prancing Wolf"}),
    (wr:Winery {name: "Prancing Wolf Winery"})
  CREATE (wr)-[r:produced]->(w)
```

We'll also add two more wines produced by Prancing Wolf Winery—a Kabinett and a Spätlese—and also create produced relationships and specify that all of the Prancing Wolf wines are Rieslings.

```
$ CREATE (w:Wine {name:"Prancing Wolf", style: "Kabinett", vintage: 2002})
$ CREATE (w:Wine {name: "Prancing Wolf", style: "Spätlese", vintage: 2010})
$ MATCH (wr:Winery {name: "Prancing Wolf"}),(w:Wine {name: "Prancing Wolf"})
  CREATE (wr)-[r:produced]->(w)
$ MATCH (w:Wine),(g:GrapeType {name: "Riesling"})
  CREATE (w)-[r:grape_type]->(g)
```

This will result in a graph that's fully fleshed out, like the one shown in the figure that follows.

Schemaless Social

In addition to knowing about wines, wineries, and publications, we want our wine graph to have a social component—that is, we want to know about the *people* affiliated with these wines and their relationships with one another. To do that, we just need to add more nodes. Suppose that you want to add three people, two who know each other and one stranger, each with their own wine preferences.

Alice has a bit of a sweet tooth so she's a big fan of ice wine.

```
$ CREATE (p:Person {name: "Alice"})
$ MATCH (p:Person {name: "Alice"}),
    (w:Wine {name: "Prancing Wolf", style: "ice wine"})
  CREATE (p)-[r:likes]->(w)
```

Tom likes Kabinett and ice wine and trusts anything written by *Wine Expert Monthly*.

```
$ CREATE (p: Person {name: "Tom"})
$ MATCH (p:Person {name: "Tom"}),
    (w:Wine {name: "Prancing Wolf", style: "ice wine"})
  CREATE (p)-[r:likes]->(w)
$ MATCH (p:Person {name: "Tom"}),
    (pub:Publication {name: "Wine Expert Monthly"})
  CREATE (p)-[r:trusts]->(pub)
```

Patty is friends with both Tom and Alice but is new to wine and has yet to choose any favorites.

```
$ CREATE (p:Person {name: "Patty"})
$ MATCH (p1:Person {name: "Patty"}),
    (p2:Person {name: "Tom"})
  CREATE (p1)-[r:friends]->(p2)
$ MATCH (p1:Person {name: "Patty"}),
    (p2:Person {name: "Alice"})
  CREATE (p1)-[r:friends]->(p2)
```

Note that without changing any fundamental structure of our existing graph, we were able to superimpose behavior beyond our original intent. The new nodes are related, as you can see in the following figure.

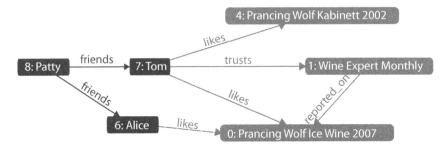

Stepping Stones

Thus far, we've mostly been performing simple, almost CRUD-like operations using Cypher. You can do *a lot* with these simple commands, but let's dive in and see what else Cypher has to offer. First, let's explore Cypher's syntax for querying all relationships that a node has with a specific type of node. The --> operator lets us do that. First, let's see all nodes associated with Alice:

```
$ MATCH (p:Person {name: "Alice"})-->(n)
  RETURN n;
```

Now let's see all of the people that Alice is friends with, except let's return only the name property of those nodes:

```
$ MATCH (p:Person {name: "Alice"})-->(other: Person)
  RETURN other.name;
```

That should result in two returned values: Patty and Tom. Now let's say that we want to see which nodes with the label Person are in the graph, but excluding Patty (boo, Patty!). Note the <> operator, which is used instead of != in Cypher:

```
$ MATCH (p:Person)
  WHERE p.name <> 'Patty'
  RETURN p;
```

Thus far, all of our queries have sought out nodes adjacent to one another. But we also said at the beginning of the chapter that Neo4j is an extremely scalable database capable of storing tons of nodes and relationships. Cypher is absolutely up to the task of dealing with far more complex relationships than the ones we've seen thus far. Let's add some nodes that aren't directly related to Patty (for Alice's friend Ahmed and Tom's friend Kofi) and then query for a relationship.

```
$ CREATE (p1:Person {name: "Ahmed"}), (p2:Person {name: "Kofi"});
$ MATCH (p1:Person {name: "Ahmed"}),(p2:Person {name: "Alice"})
  CREATE (p1)-[r:friends]->(p2);
$ MATCH (p1:Person {name: "Kofi"}),(p2:Person {name: "Tom"});
  CREATE (p1)-[r:friends]->(p2);
```

Cypher lets us query for friends of friends of Alice like this:

```
$ MATCH
    (fof:Person)-[:friends]-(f:Person)-[:friends]-(p:Person {name: "Patty"})
  RETURN fof.name;
```

As expected, this returns two values: Ahmed and Kofi.

Indexes, Constraints, and "Schemas" in Cypher

Neo4j doesn't enable you to enforce hard schemas the way that relational databases do, but it does enable you to provide *some* structure to nodes in your graphs by creating indexes and constraints for specified labels.

As with many other databases in this book, you can provide a nice speed-up for computationally expensive queries by creating indexes on labels and properties associated with that label. Remember that each Wine in our graph has a name property. You can create an index on that type/property combination like this:

```
$ CREATE INDEX ON :Wine(name);
```

You can easily remove indexes at any time:

```
$ DROP INDEX ON :Wine(name);
```

Indexes are super easy to use in Neo4j because you don't really have to *do* much to use them. Once you've established an index for nodes with a specific label and property, you can continue to query those nodes as you did before, and Neo4j will figure out the rest. This query, which returns all nodes with the label Wine, would look exactly the same before and after creating an index on Wine/name:

```
$ MATCH (w:Wine {name: 'Some Name'})
  RETURN w;
```

While indexes can help speed up queries, *constraints* can help you sanitize your data inputs by preventing writes that don't satisfy criteria that you specify. If you wanted to ensure that every Wine node in your graph had a unique name, for example, you could create this constraint:

```
$ CREATE CONSTRAINT ON (w:Wine) ASSERT w.name IS UNIQUE;
```

Functions in Cypher

In the Postgres chapter, we covered stored procedures, which enable you to write functions *in Postgres*—and highly complex ones at that—that can be used to process data. Stored procedures shift responsibility for data processing to the database rather than keeping it in the application, which is sometimes a good idea, sometimes not.

Neo4j offers a wide variety of Cypher *functions* that work just liked stored procedures. These built-in functions can be used to manipulate strings and other types, calculate spatial distances, perform mathematical calculations, and much more. Using these functions can help you maintain a nice balance between in-database and application-side data crunching.

Check out the Cypher documentation for a full listing.[a] You'll find functions such as filter() for applying complex filtering operations, abs() for calculating the absolute value of integers, range() for generating a range of integers, and more. You can also write your own functions in Java and call those functions from Cypher, but that won't be covered in this book.

---

a. http://neo4j.com/docs/developer-manual/current/cypher/functions/

Now, if you try to create two Wine nodes with the same name, you'll get an error:

```
$ CREATE (w:Wine {name: "Daring Goat", style: "Spätlese", vintage: 2008});
$ CREATE (w:Wine {name: "Daring Goat", style: "Riesling", vintage: 2006});
WARNING: Node 219904 already exists...
```

Even better, when you create a constraint, Neo4j will automatically check your existing data to make sure that all nodes with the given label conform to the constraint. Like indexes, constraints can be removed using a DROP statement, though make sure to include the entire constraint statement:

```
$ DROP CONSTRAINT ON (w:Wine) ASSERT w.name IS UNIQUE;
```

Keep in mind that you cannot apply a constraint to a label that already has an index, and if you do create a constraint on a specific label/property pair, an index will be created automatically. So *usually* you'll only need to explicitly create a constraint *or* an index.

If you want to see the status of a label's "schema," you can see that information in the shell:

```
$ schema ls -l :Wine
Indexes
  ON :Wine(name) ONLINE (for uniqueness constraint)

Constraints
  ON (wine:Wine) ASSERT wine.name IS UNIQUE
```

Although Neo4j isn't fundamentally schema-driven the way that relational databases are, indexes and constraints will help keep your queries nice and fast and your graph sane. They are an absolute must if you want to run Neo4j in production.

Day 1 Wrap-Up

Today we began digging into the graph database Neo4j and the Cyper querying language—and what a different beast we've encountered! Although we didn't cover specific design patterns per se, our brains are now buzzing with the strange and beautiful possibilities opened up by the graph database worldview. Remember that if you can draw it on a whiteboard, you can store it in a graph database.

Day 1 Homework

Find

1. Browse through the Neo4j docs at https://neo4j.com/docs and read more about Cypher syntax. Find some Cypher features mentioned in those docs that we didn't have a chance to use here and pick your favorite.

2. Experiment with an example graph consisting of movie-related data by going back to the browser console at http://localhost:7474/browser, typing :play movie-graph into the web console, and following the instructions.

Do

1. Create a simple graph describing some of your closest friends, your relationships with them, and even some relationships between your friends. Start with three nodes, including one for yourself, and create five relationships.

Day 2: REST, Indexes, and Algorithms

Today we'll start with Neo4j's REST interface. First, we'll use the REST interface to create and index nodes and relationships, and to execute full-text search. Then we'll look at a plugin that lets us execute Cypher queries on the server via REST, freeing our code from the confines of the web console.

Taking a REST

Just like HBase, Mongo, and CouchDB, Neo4j ships with a REST interface. One reason all of these databases support REST is that it allows language-agnostic interactions in a standard connection interface. You can connect to

Neo4j—which requires Java to work—from a separate machine that isn't running Java at all.

Before beginning today's exercises, check to make sure that the REST server is running by issuing a curl command to the base URL. It runs on the same port as the web admin tool you used yesterday, at the /db/data/ path (note the slash at the end).

```
$ curl http://localhost:7474/db/data/
{
  "extensions" : { },
  "node" : "http://localhost:7474/db/data/node",
  "relationship" : "http://localhost:7474/db/data/relationship",
  "node_index" : "http://localhost:7474/db/data/index/node",
  "relationship_index" : "http://localhost:7474/db/data/index/relationship",
  "extensions_info" : "http://localhost:7474/db/data/ext",
  "relationship_types" : "http://localhost:7474/db/data/relationship/types",
  "batch" : "http://localhost:7474/db/data/batch",
  "cypher" : "http://localhost:7474/db/data/cypher",
  "indexes" : "http://localhost:7474/db/data/schema/index",
  "constraints" : "http://localhost:7474/db/data/schema/constraint",
  "transaction" : "http://localhost:7474/db/data/transaction",
  "node_labels" : "http://localhost:7474/db/data/labels",
  "neo4j_version" : "3.0.7"
}
```

If the server is running, this request will return a nice JSON object describing the URLs that you can use for other commands, such as node-, relationship-, and index-related actions.

Creating Nodes and Relationships Using REST

It's as easy to create nodes and relationships over REST in Neo4j as in CouchDB or Mongo. Creating a node requires a POST to the /db/data/node path with JSON data. As a matter of convention, it pays to give each node a name property. This makes viewing any node's information easy: just call name.

```
$ curl -i -XPOST http://localhost:7474/db/data/node \
  -H "Content-Type: application/json" \
  -d '{
    "name": "P.G. Wodehouse"
    "genre": "British Humour"
  }'
```

When posted, you'll get the node path in the header and a body of metadata about the node (both are truncated here for brevity). All of this data is retrievable by calling GET on the given header Location value (or the self property in the metadata).

```
HTTP/1.1 201 Created
Location: http://localhost:7474/db/data/node/341
Content-Type: application/json; charset=UTF-8

{
  "extensions" : { },
  "metadata" : {
    "id" : 341,
    "labels" : [ ]
  },
  "paged_traverse" : "...",
  "outgoing_relationships": "...",
  "data" : {
    "name" : "P.G. Wodehouse",
    "genre" : "British Humour"
  }
}
```

If you just want to fetch the node properties (not the metadata), you can GET that by appending /properties to the node URL or even an individual property by further appending the property name.

```
$
$ curl http://localhost:7474/db/data/node/9/properties/genre
"British Humour"
```

One node doesn't do us much good, so go ahead and create another one with these properties: ["name" : "Jeeves Takes Charge", "style" : "short story"].

Because P. G. Wodehouse wrote the short story "Jeeves Takes Charge," we can make a relationship between them.

```
$ curl -i -XPOST http://localhost:7474/db/data/node/9/relationships \
  -H "Content-Type: application/json" \
  -d '{
    "to": "http://localhost:7474/db/data/node/10",
    "type": "WROTE",
    "data": {"published": "November 28, 1916"}
  }'
```

A nice thing about the REST interface is that it actually reported on how to create a relationship early in the body metadata's create_relationship property. In this way, the REST interfaces tend to be mutually discoverable.

Finding Your Path

Through the REST interface, you can find the path between two nodes by posting the request data to the starting node's /paths URL. The POST request data must be a JSON string denoting the node you want the path to, the type of relationships you want to follow, and the path-finding algorithm to use.

For example, we're looking for a path following relationships of the type WROTE from node 1 using the shortestPath algorithm and capping out at a depth of 10.

```
$ curl -X POST http://localhost:7474/db/data/node/9/paths \
  -H "Content-Type: application/json" \
  -d '{
    "to": "http://localhost:7474/db/data/node/10",
    "relationships": {"type": "WROTE"},
    "algorithm": "shortestPath",
    "max_depth": 10
  }'
[ {
  "start" : "http://localhost:7474/db/data/node/9",
  "nodes" : [
    "http://localhost:7474/db/data/node/9",
    "http://localhost:7474/db/data/node/10"
  ],
  "length" : 1,
  "relationships" : [ "http://localhost:7474/db/data/relationship/14" ],
  "end" : "http://localhost:7474/db/data/node/10"
} ]
```

The other path algorithm choices are allPaths, allSimplePaths, and dijkstra. You can find information on these algorithms in the online documentation,[2] but detailed coverage is outside the scope of this book.

Indexing

Like other databases we've seen, Neo4j supports fast data lookups by constructing indexes. We briefly mentioned indexing toward the end of Day 1. There is a twist, though. Unlike other database indexes where you perform queries in much the same way as without one, Neo4j indexes have a different path because the indexing service is actually a separate service.

The simplest index is the key-value or hash style. You key the index by some node data, and the value is a REST URL, which points to the node in the graph. You can have as many indexes as you like, so we'll name this one authors. The end of the URL will contain the author name we want to index and pass in node 1 as the value (or whatever your Wodehouse node was).

```
$ curl -X POST http://localhost:7474/db/data/index/node/authors \
  -H "Content-Type: application/json" \
  -d '{
    "uri": "http://localhost:7474/db/data/node/9",
    "key": "name",
    "value": "P.G.+Wodehouse"
  }'
```

---

2. https://neo4j.com/blog/graph-search-algorithm-basics/

Retrieving the node is simply a call to the index, which you'll notice doesn't return the URL we specified but rather the actual node data.

```
$ curl http://localhost:7474/db/data/index/node/authors/name/P.G.+Wodehouse
```

Besides key-value, Neo4j provides a full-text search inverted index, so you can perform queries like this: "Give me all books that have names beginning with Jeeves." To build this index, you need to build it against the entire dataset, rather than our one-offs earlier. Neo4j incorporates Lucene to build our inverted index.

```
$ curl -X POST http://localhost:7474/db/data/index/node \
  -H "Content-Type: application/json" \
  -d '{
    "name": "fulltext",
    "config": {"type": "fulltext", "provider": "lucene"}
    }'
```

The POST will return a JSON response containing information about the newly added index.

```
{
  "template": "http://localhost:7474/db/data/index/...",
  "provider": "lucene",
  "type": "fulltext"
}
```

Now if you add Wodehouse to the full-text index, you get this:

```
$ curl -X POST http://localhost:7474/db/data/index/node/fulltext \
  -H "Content-Type: application/json" \
  -d '{
    "uri": "http://localhost:7474/db/data/node/9",
    "key": "name",
    "value" : "P.G.+Wodehouse"
  }'
```

Then a search is as easy as a Lucene syntax query on the index URL.

```
$ curl http://localhost:7474/db/data/index/node/fulltext?query=name:P*
```

Indexes can also be built on edges like we did previously; you just have to replace the instances of *node* in the URLs with *relationship*—for example, http://localhost:7474/db/data/index/relationship/published/date/1916-11-28.

REST and Cypher

We spent much of Day 1 using Cypher and the first half of today using the REST interface. If you wondered which you should use, fear not. The Neo4j REST interface has a Cypher plugin (which is installed by default in the version of Neo4j we're using).[3] You can send through REST any commands you could in the Cypher console. This allows you the power and flexibility of both tools in production. This is a great combination because Cypher is better geared toward powerful queries, where REST is geared toward deployment and language flexibility.

The following code will return the names of all relationships. You only need to send the data to the plugin URL as a JSON string value, under the field query.

```
$ curl -X POST \
  http://localhost:7474/db/data/cypher \
  -H "Content-Type: application/json" \
  -d '{
    "query": "MATCH ()-[r]-() RETURN r;"
  }'
{
  "columns" : [ "n.name" ],
  "data" : [ [ "Prancing Wolf" ], [ "P.G. Wodehouse" ] ]
}
```

From here on out, code samples will use Cypher (as on Day 1) because it has a much more clean and compact syntax. The REST interface is a good thing to bear in mind, though, for use cases in which it would be beneficial to set up an HTTP client to fetch information from Neo4j.

Big Data

Up until now, we've dealt with very small datasets, so now it's time to see what Neo4j can do with some big data. We'll explore a dataset covering information about over 12,000 movies and over 40,000 actors, 6,000 directors, and others involved in those movies.

This dataset has been made available[4] by the good folks at Neo4j, who have conveniently made the data directly digestible by Neo4j; thus, we don't need to convert it from CSV, XML, or some other format.

First, let's download the dataset as a Zip file, unzip it, and add it to the /data folder in our Neo4j directory:

```
$ cd /path/to/neo4j
$ curl -O <copy URL from footnote 4>
$ unzip cineasts_12k_movies_50k_actors_2.1.6.zip
$ mv cineasts_12k_movies_50k_actors.db data/movies.db
```

---

3. http://neo4j.com/docs/developer-manual/3.0/http-api/#http-api-transactional
4. http://example-data.neo4j.org/files/cineasts_12k_movies_50k_actors_2.1.6.zip

That dataset was generated to work with version 2.1.6 of Neo4j, but we're using a much later version (3.0.7). We'll need to make one small configuration change to enable it to work with our version. In the /conf folder there's a file called neo4j.conf, and inside that file there's a line that looks like this:

```
#dbms.allow_format_migrations=true
```

Delete the # at the beginning of the line. That will instruct Neo4j to automatically migrate the format to fit our version. Now, fire up the Neo4j shell, specifying our movies.db database and the config file we just modified:

```
$ bin/neo4j-shell -path data/movies.db -config conf/neo4j.conf
```

This is our first encounter with the Neo4j shell. It's somewhat like the web console we used earlier in this chapter, but with the crucial difference that it returns raw values rather than pretty charts. It is a more direct and no-frills way to interact with Neo4j and better to use once you have gotten the hang of the database. When the shell fires up, you should see a shell prompt like this:

```
neo4j-sh (?)$
```

You can enter help to get a list of available shell commands. At any time in the shell, you can either enter one of those commands *or* a Cypher query.

Our shell session is already pointing to our movie database, so let's see what nodes are there:

```
neo4j> MATCH (n) RETURN n;
```

Whoa! That's a lot of nodes, 63,042 to be exact (you can obtain that result by returning count(n) instead of just n). We warned you that this is a Big Data section! Let's make some more specific queries now. First, let's see what types of relationships exist:

```
neo4j> MATCH ()-[r]-() RETURN DISTINCT type(r);
+------------+
| type(r)    |
+------------+
| "ACTS_IN"  |
| "DIRECTED" |
| "RATED"    |
| "FRIEND"   |
+------------+
4 rows
```

Here, the ()-[r]-() expresses that we don't care what the nodes look like; we just want to know about the relationship between them, which we're storing in the variable r. You can also see that in Cypher you use type(r) instead of, say, r.type to get the relationship type (because types are a special attribute of relationships). As you can see, there are four types of relationships present in the database. Now, let's look at all the nodes and see both which labels are applied to them and how many nodes are characterized by that label:

```
$ MATCH (n) RETURN DISTINCT labels(n), count(n);
+---------------------------------------------+
| labels(n)                       | count(*) |
+---------------------------------------------+
| ["Person","Actor","Director"]   | 846      |
| ["Person","User"]               | 45       |
| ["Person","Actor"]              | 44097    |
| ["Person","Director"]           | 5191     |
| []                              | 1        |
| ["Movie"]                       | 12862    |
+---------------------------------------------+
6 rows
```

As you can see, all nodes that aren't movies have the Person label (or no label); of those, all Persons are either Actors, Directors, Users (the folks who put the dataset together), or a Director and Actor (we're looking at you, Clint Eastwood). Let's perform some other queries to explore the database.

Let's see everyone who's both an actor and a director, and then get the count of people who share that distinction:

```
> MATCH (p:Actor:Director) RETURN p.name;
> MATCH (p:Actor:Director) RETURN count(p.name);
```

Now let's see who directed the immortal *Top Gun*:

```
> MATCH (d:Director)-[:DIRECTED]-(m:Movie {title: "Top Gun"}) RETURN d.name;
```

Let's see how many movies the legendary Meryl Streep has acted in:

```
> MATCH (a:Actor {name: "Meryl Streep"})-[:ACTS_IN]-(m:Movie)
  RETURN count(m);
```

Finally, let's get a list of actors who have appeared in over fifty movies:

```
> MATCH (a: Actor)-[:ACTS_IN]->(m:Movie)
  WITH a, count(m) AS movie_count
  WHERE movie_count > 50
  RETURN a.name; # only 6 actors!
```

Now that we've played with this specific dataset a little bit, let's solve a more challenging algorithmic problem that uses Neo4j more like the high-powered graph database that it really is. What's the most common algorithmic problem in showbiz? You may have guessed already...

Six Degrees of...

...you guessed it: Kevin Bacon. We're going to solve the six degrees of Kevin Bacon problem here so that you can memorize some of the key results and be a big hit at your next dinner party. More specifically, we want to know how many actors are within six degrees of Mr. Bacon, what percentage of the actors in the database have that distinction, what the shortest "path" from an actor to Kevin Bacon happens to be, and so on. You'll find some similar Neo4j exercises online but this one utilizes a very large dataset that can generate more true-to-life results.

What you may find in this exercise is that Cypher has *a lot* already baked into the language. To get the results we're after, we won't need to write a sophisticated algorithm on the client side or traverse a node tree or anything like that. We just need to learn a little bit more about how Cypher works.

In the last section, you saw that you can make very specific queries about nodes and relationships. Let's find out which Movies nodes Kevin Bacon has the relationship ACTED_IN with (let's see the number of movies first and then list the titles):

```
> MATCH (Actor {name:"Kevin Bacon"})-[:ACTS_IN]-(m:Movie) RETURN count(m);
> MATCH (Actor {name:"Kevin Bacon"})-[:ACTS_IN]-(m:Movie) RETURN m.title;
```

Only thirty movies in our database! Amazing that such a not-exceedingly prolific actor is so well connected in Hollywood. But remember, the magic of Kevin Bacon is not the *number* of movies he's been in; it's the *variety* of actors he's shared the screen with. Let's find out how many actors share this distinction (this query will make more sense later):

```
> MATCH (Actor {name: "Kevin Bacon"})-[:ACTS_IN]->(Movie)
    <-[:ACTS_IN]-(other:Actor)
  RETURN count(DISTINCT other);
+----------+
| count(a) |
+----------+
| 304      |
+----------+
```

Still not a *huge* number, but remember this is only one degree of Kevin Bacon. Here, we can see that you can actually *reverse* the direction of the relationship arrow in a query, which is quite useful in more complex queries like this.

Now let's find out how many actors are *two* degrees from Kevin Bacon. From the previous expression, it's not entirely clear *how* to write that query because we'd need to make that relationship chain much more complex, resulting in

Be Wary of Repetition

You may have noticed the DISTINCT expression in many of these Cypher queries. This is *extremely* important in Cypher queries because it enables you to exclude redundant results. Running the previous query without using DISTINCT results in a count of 313, which suggests that there are a few actors who are within two degrees of Kevin Bacon more than once. Quite the distinction (no pun intended)!

For some datasets, these discrepancies may be much larger, skewing the results beyond recognition and usefulness. When dealing with graphs, this is something that can really bite you, so if your results ever seem off, checking for redundancy is a good place to start.

a mess of arrows and brackets. Fortunately, Cypher provides us with some syntactical sugar for this using star notation (*).

```
> MATCH (Actor {name: "Kevin Bacon"})-[:ACTS_IN*1..2]-(other:Actor)
  RETURN count(DISTINCT other);
+-----------+
| count(a)  |
+-----------+
| 304       |
+-----------+
```

Two things to be aware of. First, there's no Movie label anywhere here. That's because Actors can only have ACTS_IN relationships with Movies, so we can safely leave that part out. Second, note that that's the same result as before (a count of 313), so something is not quite right. It turns out that this Cypher star notation is a bit tricky because each "jump" between nodes counts. So you'll need to think of this query in terms of a four-jump chain (actor-movie-actor-movie-actor) and rewrite the query:

```
> MATCH (Actor {name: "Kevin Bacon"})-[:ACTS_IN*1..4]-(other:Actor)
  RETURN count(DISTINCT other);
+----------------------+
| count(DISTINCT other) |
+----------------------+
| 9096                 |
+----------------------+
```

If you use 5 instead of 4 in that query, you'll get the same result and for the same reason. You need to make an actor-to-movie jump to include more actors in the result set.

As you can see, the quotient between 2 degrees and 1 degree is about 79, so the web of relationships fans out very quickly. Calculating 3 degrees yields 31,323. Counting 4 degrees takes *minutes* and might even time out on your machine, so we don't recommend running that query unless you need a (long) hot chocolate break.

Thus far, we've only really been counting nodes that share some trait, though our ability to describe those traits has been enhanced. We're still not equipped to answer any of our initial questions, such as how many degrees lie between Kevin Bacon and other actors, what percentage of actors lie within N degrees, and so on.

To get traction into those questions, we need to begin querying for path data, as we did in the REST exercises. Once again, Cypher comes through in the clutch for us with its shortestPath function, which enables you to easily calculate the distance between two nodes. You can specify the relationship type you're interested in specifically or just use * if the relationship type doesn't matter.

We can use the shortestPath function to find the number of degrees separating Kevin Bacon and another dashing actor, Sean Penn, using this query:

```
> MATCH (
    bacon:Actor {name: "Kevin Bacon"}),
    (penn:Actor {name: "Sean Penn"}
  ),
  p=shortestPath((bacon)-[:ACTS_IN*]-(penn))
  RETURN length(p);
+---------------+
| length(p) / 2 |
+---------------+
| 2             |
+---------------+
```

But wait a second. According to IMDB, Messieurs Bacon and Penn starred together in *Mystic River*. So why does it take 2 degrees to connect these two when it should be one? Well, it turns out that *Mystic River* isn't in our database.

```
> MATCH (m:Movie {name: "Mystic River"})
  RETURN count(DISTINCT m);
+-------------------+
| count(DISTINCT m) |
+-------------------+
| 0                 |
+-------------------+
```

Looks like our database is lacking some crucial bits of cinema. So maybe don't use these results to show off at your next dinner party just yet; you might want to find a more complete database for that. But for now, you know how to calculate shortest paths, so that's a good start. Try finding the number of degrees between some of your favorite actors.

Another thing we're interested in beyond the shortest path between any two actors is the percentage of actors that lie within N degrees. We can do that by using a generic other node with the Actor label and counting the *number* of shortest paths that are found within a number of degrees. We'll start with 2 degrees and divide the result by the total number of actors, making sure to specify that we don't include the original Kevin Bacon node in the shortest path calculation (or we'll get a nasty and long-winded error message).

```
> MATCH p=shortestPath(
    (bacon:Actor {name: "Kevin Bacon"})-[:ACTS_IN*1..2]-(other:Actor)
  )
  WHERE bacon <> other
  RETURN count(p);
+----------+
| count(p) |
+----------+
| 304      |
+----------+
```

Just as expected, the same result as before. What happened there is that Neo4j traversed every relationship within 1 degree of Kevin Bacon and found the number that had shortest paths. So in this case, p returns a list of many shortest paths between Kevin Bacon and many actors rather than just a single shortest path to one actor. Now let's divide by the total number of actors (44,943) and add an extra decimal place to make sure we get a float:

```
> MATCH p=shortestPath(
    (bacon:Actor {name: "Kevin Bacon"})-[:ACTS_IN*1..2]-(other:Actor)
  )
  WHERE bacon <> other
  RETURN count(p) / 44943.0;
+----------------------+
| count(p) / 44943.0   |
+----------------------+
| 0.006764123445252876 |
+----------------------+
```

That's a pretty small percentage of actors. But now re-run that query using 4 instead of 2 (to symbolize 2 degrees rather than 1):

```
> MATCH p=shortestPath(
    (bacon:Actor {name: "Kevin Bacon"})-[:ACTS_IN*1..4]-(other:Actor)
  )
  WHERE bacon <> other
  RETURN count(p) / 44943.0;
+--------------------+
| count(p) / 44943.0 |
+--------------------+
| 0.2023674432058385 |
+--------------------+
```

Already up to 20 percent within just 1 extra degree. Running the same query gets you almost 70 percent for 3 degrees, a little over 90 percent for 4 degrees, 93 percent for 5, and about 93.4 percent for a full 6 degrees. So how many actors have *no* relationship with Kevin Bacon whatsoever in our database? We can find that out by not specifying an N for degrees and just using any degree:

```
> MATCH p=shortestPath(
    (bacon:Actor {name: "Kevin Bacon"})-[:ACTS_IN*]-(other:Actor)
  )
  WHERE bacon <> other
  RETURN count(p) / 44943.0;
+--------------------+
| count(p) / 44943.0 |
+--------------------+
| 0.9354960728033287 |
+--------------------+
```

Just a little bit higher than the percentage of actors within 6 degrees, so if you're related to Kevin Bacon *at all* in our database, then you're almost certainly within 6 degrees.

Day 2 Wrap-Up

On Day 2, we broadened our ability to interact with Neo4j by taking a look at the REST interface. You saw how, using the Cypher plugin, you can execute Cypher code on the server and have the REST interface return results. We played around with a larger dataset and finally finished up with a handful of algorithms for diving into that data.

Day 2 Homework

Find

1. Bookmark the documentation for the Neo4j REST API.

2. Bookmark the API for the JUNG project and the algorithms it implements.

3. Find a binding or REST interface for your favorite programming language.

Do

1. Turn the path-finding portion of the Kevin Bacon algorithm into its own step. Then implement a general-purpose Groovy function (for example, def actor_path(g, name1, name2) {...}) that accepts the graph and two names and compares the distance.

2. Choose and run one of the many JUNG algorithms on a node (or the dataset, if the API demands it).

3. Install your driver of choice, and use it to manage your company graph with the people and the roles they play, with edges describing their interactions (reports to, works with). If your company is huge, just try your close teams; if you're with a small organization, try including some customers. Find the most well-connected person in the organization by closest distance to all other nodes.

Day 3: Distributed High Availability

Let's wrap up our Neo4j investigation by learning how to make Neo4j more suitable for mission-critical, production uses. We'll see how Neo4j keeps data stable via ACID-compliant transactions. Then we'll install and configure a Neo4j high availability (HA) cluster to improve availability when serving high-read traffic. Then we're going to look into backup strategies to ensure that our data remains safe.

Transactions and Only Transactions with Cypher

Neo4j is an Atomic, Consistent, Isolated, Durable (ACID) transaction database, similar to PostgreSQL. This makes it a good option for important data that you may have otherwise picked a relational database for. Just like transactions you've seen before, Neo4j transactions are all-or-nothing operations. When a transaction starts, every following operation will succeed or fail as an atomic unit—failure of one means failure of all. Much like specifying BEGIN and COMMIT delimiters as in Postgres, Cypher enables you to do the same thing in the Cypher shell using :begin and :commit (the debts to the SQL world should be quite clear here!).

If you're using Cypher from a non-shell client, *all* queries are automatically treated as transactions and thus completely succeed or completely fail. Explicit transaction logic is necessary only in the shell.

High Availability

High availability mode is Neo4j's answer to the question, "Can a graph database scale?" Yes, but with some caveats. A write to one slave is not immediately synchronized with all other slaves, so there is a danger of losing consistency (in the CAP sense) for a brief moment (making it eventually consistent). HA will lose pure ACID-compliant transactions. It's for this reason that Neo4j HA is touted as a solution largely for increasing capacity for reads.

Just like Mongo, the servers in the cluster will elect a master that holds primary responsibility for managing data distribution in the cluster. Unlike in Mongo, however, slaves in Neo4j accept writes. Slave writes will synchronize with the master node, which will then propagate those changes to the other slaves.

HA Cluster

To use Neo4j HA, we must first set up a cluster. Previously, Neo4j clusters relied on ZooKeeper as an external coordination mechanism, which worked well but required a lot of additional administration, as ZooKeeper would have to be run separately. That has changed in more recent versions. Now, Neo4j clusters are self-managing and self-coordinating. Clusters can choose their own master/slave setup and re-coordinate when servers go offline.

You can see an illustration of this in the following figure, which shows a 4-node Neo4j cluster.

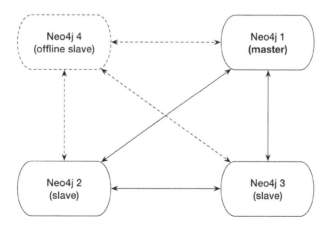

Nodes 1, 2, and 3 are currently online and replicating to one another properly, while node 4 is offline. When node 4 comes back online, it will re-enter as a slave node. If node 1, the current master node, went offline, the other nodes would automatically elect a leader (without the help of an external coordinating service). This is a fairly standard HA setup in the industry today, and the engineers behind Neo4j have done administrators a great service by enabling a ZooKeeper-free HA setup.

Building and Starting the Cluster

To build a cluster, we're going to run three instances of Neo4j Enterprise version 3.1.4. You can download a copy from the website for your operating system (be sure you select the correct edition)[5] and then unzip it and create two more copies of the directory. Let's name them neo4j-1.local, neo4j-2.local, and neo4j-3.local.

```
$ tar fx neo4j-enterprise-3.1.4-unix.tar.gz
$ mv neo4j-enterprise-3.1.4 neo4j-1.local
$ cp -R neo4j-1.local neo4j-2.local
$ cp -R neo4j-1.local neo4j-3.local
```

Now we have three identical copies of our database. Normally, you would unpack one copy per server and configure the cluster to be aware of the other servers. In order to build a local cluster, we need to make a few small configuration changes and start the nodes one by one. Each node contains a conf/neo4j.conf configuration file. At the top of that file in the folder for node 1, neo4j-1.local, add this:

```
dbms.mode=HA
dbms.memory.pagecache.size=200m
dbms.backup.address=127.0.0.1:6366
dbms.backup.enabled=true
ha.server_id=1
ha.initial_hosts=127.0.0.1:5001,127.0.0.1:5002,127.0.0.1:5003
ha.host.coordination=127.0.0.1:5001
ha.host.data=127.0.0.1:6363
dbms.connector.http.enabled=true
dbms.connector.http.listen_address=:7474
dbms.connector.bolt.enabled=true
dbms.connector.bolt.tls_level=OPTIONAL
dbms.connector.bolt.listen_address=:7687
dbms.security.auth_enabled=false
```

Copy and paste the same thing into the other two nodes' config files, except increase the following values by 1 *for each node* (producing three separate values for each—for example, 7474, 7475, and 7476 for dbms.connector.http.listen_address):

- ha.server_id
- ha.host.coordination
- ha.host.data
- dbms.connector.http.listen_address
- dbms.connector.bolt.listen_address

---

5. http://neo4j.org/download/

So, ha.server_id should have values of 1, 2, and 3 on the different nodes, respectively, and so on for the other configs. This is to ensure that the nodes aren't attempting to open up the same ports for the same operations. Now we can start each node one by one (the order doesn't matter):

```
$ neo4j-1.local/bin/neo4j start
$ neo4j-2.local/bin/neo4j start
$ neo4j-3.local/bin/neo4j start
```

You can watch the server output of any of the three running nodes by tailing the log file.

```
$ tail -f neo4j-3.local/logs/neo4j.log
```

If the cluster has been set up successfully, you should see something like this:

```
2017-05-08 03:38:06.901+0000 INFO  Started.
2017-05-08 03:38:07.192+0000 INFO  Mounted REST API at: /db/manage
2017-05-08 03:38:07.902+0000 INFO  Remote interface available at https://...
```

You should also be able to use three different Neo4j browser consoles at http://localhost:7474, as before, but also on ports 7475 and 7476. Don't use the browser console for now, though. We're going to experiment with the cluster via the CLI instead.

Verifying Cluster Status

We now have three different nodes running alongside one another in a cluster, ready to do our bidding. So let's jump straight in and write some data to make sure that things are being properly replicated across the cluster.

Jump into the Cypher shell (as we did on Day 2) for the first node:

```
$ neo4j-1.local/bin/cypher-shell
Connected to Neo4j 3.1.4 at bolt://localhost:7687 as user neo4j.
Type :help for a list of available commands or :exit to exit the shell.
Note that Cypher queries must end with a semicolon.
neo4j>
```

Now let's write a new data node to our cluster and exit the Cypher shell for node 1...

```
neo4j> CREATE (p:Person {name: "Weird Al Yankovic"});
neo4j> :exit
```

...and then open up the shell for node 2...

```
$ neo4j-2.local/bin/cypher-shell -u neo4j -p pass
```

...and finally see which data nodes are stored in the cluster:

```
neo4j> MATCH (n) RETURN n;
(:Person {name: "Weird Al Yankovic"})
```

And there you have it: Our data has been successfully replicated across nodes. You can try the same thing on node 3 if you'd like.

Master Election

In HA Neo4j clusters, master election happens automatically. If the master server goes offline, other servers will notice and elect a leader from among themselves. Starting the previous master server again will add it back to the cluster, but now the old master will remain a slave (until another server goes down).

High availability allows very read-heavy systems to deal with replicating a graph across multiple servers and thus sharing the load. Although the cluster as a whole is only eventually consistent, there are tricks you can apply to reduce the chance of reading stale data in your own applications, such as assigning a session to one server. With the right tools, planning, and a good setup, you can build a graph database large enough to handle billions of nodes and edges and nearly any number of requests you may need. Just add regular backups, and you have the recipe for a solid production system.

Backups

Backups are a necessary aspect of any professional database use. Although backups are effectively built in when using replication in a highly available cluster, periodic backups—nightly, weekly, hourly, and so on—that are stored off-site are always a good idea for disaster recovery. It's hard to plan for a server room fire or an earthquake shaking a building to rubble.

Neo4j Enterprise offers a tool called neo4j-admin that performs a wide variety of actions, including backups.

The most powerful method when running an HA server is to craft a full backup command to copy the database file from the cluster to a date-stamped file on a mounted drive. Pointing the copy to every server in the cluster will ensure you get the most recent data available. The backup directory created is a fully usable copy. If you need to recover, just replace each installation's data directory with the backup directory, and you're ready to go.

You must start with a full backup. Let's back up our HA cluster to a directory that ends with today's date (using the *nix date command). The neo4j-admin command can be run from any server and you can choose any server in the cluster when using the --from flag. Here's an example command:

```
$ neo4j-1.local/bin/neo4j-admin backup \
  --from 127.0.0.1:6366 \
  --name neo4j-`date +%Y.%m.%d`.db \
  --backup-dir /mnt/backups
```

Once you have done a full backup, you can choose to do an incremental backup by specifying an existing .db database directory as the target directory. But keep in mind that incremental backups only work on a fully backed-up directory, so ensure the previous command is run on the same day or the directory names won't match up.

Day 3 Wrap-Up

Today we spent some time keeping Neo4j data stable via ACID-compliant transactions, high availability, and backup tools.

It's important to note that all of the tools we used today require the Neo4j Enterprise edition, and so use a dual license—GPL/AGPL. If you want to keep your server closed source, you should look into switching to the Community edition or getting an OEM from Neo Technology (the company behind Neo4j). Contact the Neo4j team for more information.

Day 3 Homework

Find

1. Find the Neo4j licensing guide.

2. Answer the question, "What is the maximum number of nodes supported?" (Hint: It's in Questions & Answers in the website docs.)

Do

1. Replicate Neo4j across three physical servers.

2. Set up a load balancer using a web server such as Apache or Nginx, and connect to the cluster using the REST interface. Execute a Cypher script command.

3. Experiment further with the neo4j-admin tool. Acquire a solid understanding of *three* subcommands beyond backup.

Wrap-Up

Neo4j is a top open source implementation of the (relatively rare) class of graph databases. Graph databases focus on the relationships between data, rather than the commonalities among values. Modeling graph data is simple.

You just create nodes and relationships between them and optionally hang key-value pairs from them. Querying is as easy as declaring how to walk the graph from a starting node.

Neo4j's Strengths

Neo4j is one of the finest examples of open source graph databases. Graph databases are perfect for unstructured data, in many ways even more so than document databases. Not only is Neo4j typeless and schemaless, but it puts no constraints on how data is related. It is, in the best sense, a free-for-all. Currently, Neo4j can support 34.4 billion nodes and 34.4 billion relationships, which is more than enough for most use cases. (Neo4j could hold more than 15 nodes for each of Facebook's 2.2 billion users in a single graph.)

The Neo4j distributions provide several tools for fast lookups with Lucene, the Cypher querying language, and the REST interface. Beyond ease of use, Neo4j is fast. Unlike join operations in relational databases or map-reduce operations in other databases, graph traversals are constant time. Like data is only a node step away, rather than joining values in bulk and filtering the desired results, which is how most of the databases we've seen operate. It doesn't matter how large the graph becomes; moving from node A to node B is always one step if they share a relationship. Finally, the Enterprise edition provides for highly available and high read-traffic sites by way of Neo4j HA.

Neo4j's Weaknesses

Neo4j does have a few shortcomings. We found its choice of nomenclature (*node* rather than *vertex* and *relationship* rather than *edge*) to add complexity when communicating. Although HA is excellent at replication, it can only replicate a full graph to other servers. It cannot currently shard subgraphs, which still places a limit on graph size (though, to be fair, that limit measures in the tens of billions). Finally, if you are looking for a business-friendly open source license (like MIT), Neo4j may not be for you. Although the Community edition (everything we used in the first two days) is GPL, you'll probably need to purchase a license if you want to run a production environment using the Enterprise tools (which includes HA and backups).

Neo4j on CAP

The term "high availability cluster" should be enough to give away Neo4j's strategy. Neo4j HA is available and partition tolerant (AP). Each slave will return only what it currently has, which may be out of sync with the master node temporarily. Although you can reduce the update latency by increasing a slave's pull interval, it's still technically eventually consistent. This is why Neo4j HA is recommended for read-mostly requirements.

Parting Thoughts

Neo4j's simplicity can be off-putting if you're not used to modeling graph data. It provides a powerful open-source API with years of production use and yet it hasn't gotten the same traction as other databases in this book. We chalk this up to lack of knowledge because graph databases mesh so naturally with how humans tend to conceptualize data. We imagine our families as trees, or our friends as graphs; most of us don't imagine personal relationships as self-referential datatypes. For certain classes of problems, such as social networks, Neo4j is an obvious choice. But you should give it some serious consideration for non-obvious problems as well—it just may surprise you how powerful and easy it is.

## CHAPTER 7

DynamoDB

Earth movers are epic pieces of machinery, able to shuffle around massive bits of dirt and other materials with great ease. DynamoDB is a bit like the rented earth mover of NoSQL databases. You don't have to build it yourself or fix it when it's broken; you just have to drive it and pay for your usage. But it's complex to handle so you'll need to make very intelligent decisions about how to use it lest you end up incurring unexpected costs or jamming the engine.

DynamoDB is a cloud-based database available through Amazon Web Services (AWS), the cloud computing division of e-commerce giant Amazon (the same Amazon from which you may have purchased this book). You may know AWS as the creator of a dizzying, ever-expanding array of widely used cloud services, from the Simple Storage Service (S3) to the Elastic Compute Cloud (EC2) and far beyond (there could be over 100 services by the time you read this).

Despite the emergence of serious competitors, such as Microsoft Azure and Google Cloud Platform, AWS remains the leader of the Infrastructure-as-a-Service (IaaS) paradigm that has brought cloud computing to the masses, and DynamoDB is AWS's most significant contribution—thus far—to the world of NoSQL. The cloud has opened vast new horizons for everyone from lone-wolf developers to Fortune 500 companies, and any book on the NoSQL paradigm would be incomplete without this pioneering cloud database.

DynamoDB: The "Big Easy" of NoSQL

Six out of the seven databases that we cover in this book are easy enough to run on your laptop. But running systems such as HBase, CouchDB, and others in production—and using them for applications handling massive workloads—is a much different matter. Even databases that are a famously easy to operate at smaller scale, such as Redis, present major challenges in production environments, usually requiring skilled (and expensive!) admins and operations specialists on hand.

DynamoDB is a different story—and an outlier in this book. You don't have to install it, start it, or maintain it. You can sign up for an AWS account, create a DynamoDB table, and just go. As you'll see, DynamoDB does require *some* operations-style thinking and preparation, but you'll never need to provide it an XML configuration à la HBase or set up a complex cluster à la Mongo. DynamoDB is a database that runs itself and yet is capable of fulfilling some of your most ambitious "webscale" dreams, offering consistently fast performance no matter how much data you're storing.

So just how "webscale" are we talking here? Some facts:

- You can store as many items as you want in any DynamoDB table (more on tables and items later).

- Each item (the equivalent of a row in an SQL database) can hold as many attributes as you want, although there is a hard size limit of 400 KB per item (that limit will likely grow in the future).

- If you get data modeling right, which will occupy a decent chunk of this chapter, you should experience very little performance degradation even when your tables store petabytes of data.

- Over 100,000 AWS customers currently use DynamoDB.

- DynamoDB handles well over a trillion total requests a day (across all AWS customers).

But DynamoDB isn't interesting just because it's big and cloud-based and managed by experts you don't have to hire and fire. It's also a system very much worth learning in its own right, providing a familiar yet unique data model and an array of features you won't find in any of the other databases in this book. While some folks may be reticent to trust a cloud database that's managed by someone else, a variety of forward-thinking tech companies, including Airbnb, Adobe, Siemens, and Comcast, have taken the plunge and use DynamoDB as one of the core databases driving their platforms.

DynamoDB and the (Almost) Ops-Free Lifestyle

If you're running a database yourself or as part of a team, you can expect many of the following to keep you awake at night: ensuring speedy, predictable performance; handling unforeseeable hardware outages and network failures; scaling out disk capacity to meet unexpected spikes in demand; and enabling application developers to quickly get up and running using your database.

On top of that, DBAs with a background in NoSQL aren't exactly a dime a dozen, so hiring, training, and scaling out a team of DBAs for Mongo, HBase, or another NoSQL database is nothing to sneeze at. DynamoDB doesn't completely rid your life of these kinds of issues, but if you use it right it can take an enormous bite out of them.

There are also a number of secondary reasons why you might want to consider DynamoDB:

- You can use it in any of AWS's many datacenters across the entire globe. As of July 2017, AWS offers DynamoDB in forty-two Availability Zones (AZs) in sixteen geographic regions, with plans to expand into at least eight more AZs in three additional regions.

- All data in DynamoDB is stored on high-performing Solid State Disks (SSDs) and automatically replicated across multiple availability zones within an AWS region (which guarantees redundancy even within a single region).

- You can expect genuine downtime out of DynamoDB only in the rare event that an entire AWS datacenter goes down.

Datacenter outages are the Achilles heel of the cloud, and a very real risk that you should keep in mind. We've all experienced Netflix, Instagram, and other widely used services going down for hours at a time due to outages in Amazon's massive us-east-1 datacenter in Northern Virginia. AWS and DynamoDB aren't perfect, but their track record is exceedingly good, if not downright pristine. Using a database like DynamoDB won't grant you a *completely* ops-free lifestyle, but it may just enable you to refocus a huge chunk of your attention and resources onto other things, and for that reason alone it's worth a look.

The Core Storage Concepts: Tables, Items, and More

DynamoDB's data model is a bit tricky to define using standard "NoSQL" categories. It strongly resembles the data model of a key-value store such as Redis in that it wasn't really built to provide the rich queryability of an RDBMS such as Postgres. Although DynamoDB *does* have some interesting querying features, which we'll learn about shortly, it really soars when you know what you're looking for in advance, which is a hallmark of key-value stores. If you're building an application that uses DynamoDB, you should always strive to architect it so that your data is associated with certain "natural" keys that allow for easy discoverability—for example, the ability to find user data on the basis of unique usernames.

Not to Be Confused with Dynamo

Technologically, DynamoDB originally drew heavily on concepts derived from a distributed, eventually consistent storage system called *Dynamo* created to address Amazon's own data storage problems (and massive ones at that). Amazon's theoretical research into the distributed database domain resulted in the so-called "Dynamo paper" (actually titled *Dynamo: Amazon's Highly Available Key-value Store*),[a] which exerted a seminal influence on widely used NoSQL databases such as Riak, Cassandra, and Voldemort.

It's unclear how faithful DynamoDB is to the concepts in the Dynamo paper, as Amazon keeps most under-the-hood implementation details under wraps, but the paper itself is a treasure trove of rich theoretical explorations of distributed database concepts. Throughout this book, we'll be careful to always use the term *DynamoDB* to distinguish the public-facing AWS service from the internal Dynamo and its associated paper.

a.   http://dl.acm.org/citation.cfm?id=1294281

There are aspects of DynamoDB's data model, however, that are reminiscent of RDBMSs such as Postgres. The first point of overlap is that all data in DynamoDB is stored in *tables* that you have to create and define in advance, though tables have some flexible elements and can be modified later. You can create, modify, and delete DynamoDB tables at will using an interface called the *control plane*. If you're used to interfaces like Postgres's psql, which we explored in Chapter 2, *PostgreSQL*, on page 9, then the control plane should be familiar to you.

The second point of overlap is that you store *items* inside of tables. Items roughly correspond to *rows* in RDBMSs; they consist of one or more *attributes*, which roughly correspond to RDBMS columns. Earlier in the book, you learned about databases such as Mongo and Couch that have no concept whatsoever of predefined tables. DynamoDB requires you to define only *some* aspects of tables, most importantly the structure of keys and local secondary indexes, while retaining a schemaless flavor.

The last point of overlap with RDBMSs is that DynamoDB enables you to query data based on *secondary indexes* rather than solely on the basis of a primary key (think back to secondary indexes in Postgres). This means that you can perform queries in DynamoDB that are essentially equivalent to SQL queries like these:

```
/* Remember: you can't actually use SQL syntax with DynamoDB;
   these examples are just for show */
SELECT * FROM chevys WHERE make = "nova";
SELECT * FROM pro_sports_teams WHERE city = "cleveland";
SELECT * FROM presidents WHERE first_name = "Jethro"; /* OOPS! None found! */
```

You can even perform *range queries*:

```
SELECT * FROM pearl_jam_albums WHERE
  title <= "Ten";
SELECT * FROM john_cusack_films WHERE
  title BETWEEN "Better Off Dead" AND "High Fidelity";
SELECT * FROM oscar_wilde_quotes WHERE
  quote LIKE 'I have nothing to declare%';
```

DynamoDB's Consistency Model

Now that we have a basic outline of DynamoDB's "key-value plus" data model, a question naturally emerges: How does DynamoDB fit in with the so-called CAP theorem that we discussed in the last chapter? Are we dealing with an eventually consistent database that may turn up stale data from time to time (such as CouchDB and others in the NoSQL landscape)? Or are we dealing with a strongly consistent, ACID-compliant, transactional database that only ever returns the most up-to-date value that we're seeking?

The answer: Yes, please! Everybody gets a car! DynamoDB actually supports *both* consistency models. Even better, you can specify which consistency model you want on a *per-read basis*.

So when you query DynamoDB, your application can say either...

- I want the most up-to-date value, even if it costs me some extra latency or, heaven forbid, the value isn't currently available at all, *or*

- I've got a tight schedule, so give me what you've got right now, even if it's a bit stale.

Always bear in mind, however, that "stale" in the universe of DynamoDB doesn't mean hours; it probably means milliseconds, and the trade-off may be acceptable in plenty of cases (make sure to run it by your CTO, though). The flexibility, however, is nice, and the ability to query the *same data* using both models can really come in handy.

The downside of strongly consistent reads, as in other systems, is that they may not be available in case of network, hardware, or other outages. Death, taxes, and the CAP theorem: there's no escaping them. The only real "solution" is to use strong consistency only when truly necessary and to design your application to be prepared to deal with an unresponsive database (rare as it may be with DynamoDB). Consistent reads also "cost" twice as much in terms of read capacity than non-consistent reads.

Another important thing to note about consistency is that DynamoDB *supports only item-level consistency*, which is analogous to row-level consistency in RDBMSs. There are *no* atomic operations across items, which means no consistency for batch operations. And when you run queries against indexes or whole tables, do not *ever* expect that the result set will be 100 percent up-to-date. Item-level consistency is a good thing to have, but if consistency across items is a necessity for your use case, you should explore other databases.

As you can see, these kinds of querying capabilities take DynamoDB beyond what you'd find in a more straightforward key-value store (like the one you'll see in the next chapter, on Redis). So we'll call DynamoDB's data model *key-value plus* for short to account for these borrowings from the relational paradigm.

In spite of these SQL-flavored capabilities, though, there are firm limits to the DynamoDB/RDBMS parallels. Most importantly, if you need querying capabilities that go beyond the simple ones in the previous example, you'll have to implement them on the application side, or just use a different database (or use other cloud services in conjunction with DynamoDB, as we'll do on Day 3). Furthermore, DynamoDB has no concept of things like joins between tables; the table is the highest level at which data can be grouped and manipulated, and any join-style capabilities that you need will have to be implemented on the application side, which has its own downsides.

So that provides a little bit of background, historical and technological, for DynamoDB. It's time to dig much deeper using real interactions with the database.

Day 1: Let's Go Shopping!

Fun fact: Dynamo—the database that inspired the later DynamoDB—was originally built with the very specific purpose of serving as the storage system for Amazon's famous shopping cart. When you're building a shopping cart application, the absolute, unbreakable categorical imperative guiding your database should be this: *do not lose data under any circumstances*. Losing shopping cart data means losing money directly. If a user puts a $2,500 mattress in their Amazon shopping cart and the database suddenly forgets that, then that's money potentially lost, especially if the data is lost just before checkout.

Multiply a mistake like that times thousands or even millions and you get a clear sense of why Amazon needed to build a fault-tolerant, highly available database that never loses data. The good news is that you get to reap the benefits of Amazon's efforts and use DynamoDB to your own ends in your own applications.

As a first practical taste of DynamoDB, we'll set up a DynamoDB table that could act as the database for a simple shopping cart application. This table will be able to store shopping cart items (it looks like Amazon's use of the "item" terminology was no accident). We'll perform basic CRUD operations against this table via the command line.

But first, a stern warning: *DynamoDB is not free!* It is a paid service. AWS offers a free tier for virtually all of its services so that you can kick the tires without immediately incurring costs, but make sure to check the pricing guide[1] before you start going through the examples in this book. We won't make super intensive use of AWS services, so it should cost you at most a few dollars, but due diligence may just save you from an unpleasant end-of-the-month surprise.

Before you can get started with this section, you'll need to create an AWS account for yourself using the AWS console.[2] That part is pretty self-explanatory. Don't worry about familiarizing yourself with the AWS console for now, as most of the examples in this chapter will use the command line. Once you've signed up with AWS and can access your user console (which shows you all of AWS's currently available services on the landing page), download the official AWS CLI tool using pip, the Python package manager:

```
$ sudo pip install aws
```

If you run aws --version and get a version string like aws-cli/1.11.51 Python/2.7.10 Darwin/16.1.0 botocore/1.5.14, you should be ready to go. All of the aws tool's commands are of the form aws [service] [command], where service can be dynamodb, s3, ec2, and so on. To see the commands and options available for DynamoDB specifically, run aws dynamodb help.

Once the CLI tool is installed, you'll need to configure it by running the following:

```
$ aws configure
```

Running DynamoDB Locally

If you ever decide to develop a full-fledged application of your own using DynamoDB, you might want to check out DynamoDB Local,[a] which is a version of DynamoDB that you can run on your own machine that's fully API compatible with hosted DynamoDB. It's available as a Java JAR and works on Windows, Mac OS, and Linux.

We won't use DynamoDB Local for the exercises here because we'll need to use the hosted version in conjunction with other AWS services, but it's a very nice thing to have in your development toolbelt.

a.   https://aws.amazon.com/blogs/aws/dynamodb-local-for-desktop-development

---

1.   https://aws.amazon.com/pricing
2.   https://console.aws.amazon.com

That will prompt you to input the AWS access key ID and secret access key for your account and enable you to choose a default AWS region when using the tool (us-east-1 is the default) and output format for CLI commands (json is the default).

The DynamoDB *control plane* is the set of commands used to manage tables. Our first action using the control plane will be to see which tables are associated with our account:

```
$ aws dynamodb list-tables
{
  "TableNames": []
}
```

As expected, there are no tables associated with our account, so let's make a very simple shopping cart table in which each item has just one attribute: an item name stored as a string.

```
$ aws dynamodb create-table \
  --table-name ShoppingCart \
  --attribute-definitions AttributeName=ItemName,AttributeType=S \
  --key-schema AttributeName=ItemName,KeyType=HASH \
  --provisioned-throughput ReadCapacityUnits=1,WriteCapacityUnits=1
```

DynamoDB's *Almost* Schemaless Data Model

In the create-table operation, it *seems* like the ShoppingCart table is being created with a strict schema according to which items in the table can have only an ItemName attribute. But DynamoDB doesn't work that way. Whenever you create a table, you only have to define attributes *that function as keys* (sometimes referred to as *key attributes*).

So we could store items in our shopping cart table that have any number of other properties (brand name, year manufactured, ISBN, whatever) if we wanted to, without having to specify those attributes when we create the table. The only restriction on our ShoppingCart table is that each item must have an ItemName.

But there's a catch here: although schema restraints apply only to key attributes, you can't query for attributes that aren't specified as keys or indexes when you create the table (more on indexes later). So if you started storing items with a brand name attribute in the ShoppingCart table, you wouldn't be able to discover items by brand name. If you wanted to do that, you'd have to create a new table and add the brand name as a key or index. And so even though schema design doesn't force you into a straitjacket, you should make that decision very carefully.

This is in contrast to a database like Mongo, which is schemaless but allows you to query for whatever fields you want at any time.

The output of that command should be a JSON object describing our newly created table:

```
{
    "TableDescription": {
        "TableArn": "arn:aws:dynamodb:...:table/ShoppingCart",
        "AttributeDefinitions": [
            {
                "AttributeName": "ItemName",
                "AttributeType": "S"
            }
        ],
        "ProvisionedThroughput": {
            "NumberOfDecreasesToday": 0,
            "WriteCapacityUnits": 1,
            "ReadCapacityUnits": 1
        },
        "TableSizeBytes": 0,
          "TableName": "ShoppingCart",
        "TableStatus": "CREATING",
        "KeySchema": [
            {
                "KeyType": "HASH",
                "AttributeName": "ItemName"
            }
        ],
        "ItemCount": 0,
        "CreationDateTime": 1475032237.808
    }
}
```

We could get that same output using the describe-table command at any time (except that the TableStatus parameter will change to ACTIVE very quickly after creation):

```
$ aws dynamodb describe-table \
  --table-name ShoppingCart
```

So now we've reserved a little nook and cranny in an AWS datacenter to hold our shopping cart data. But that create-table command is probably still a bit cryptic because there are some core concepts we haven't gone over yet. Let's start with supported data types.

DynamoDB's Data Types

DynamoDB's type system is, in essence, a stripped-down version of the type system that you'd find in a relational database. DynamoDB offers simple types such as Booleans, strings, and binary strings, but none of the more purpose-specific types that you'd find in, say, Postgres (such as currency values or geometric types). DynamoDB offers these five *scalar types*, which can be thought of as its atomic types:

Type	Symbol	Description	JSON Example
String	S	A typical string like you'd find in most programming languages.	"S": "this is a string"
Number	N	Any integer or float. Sent as a string for the sake of compatibility between client libraries.	"N": "98", "N":"3.141592"
Binary	B	Base64-encoded binary data of any length (within item size limits).	"B": "4SrNYKrcv4wjJczEf6u+ TgaT2YaWGgU76YPhF"
Boolean	BOOL	true or false.	"BOOL": false
Null	NULL	A null value. Useful for missing values.	"NULL": true

Warning! No Empty Strings

String values cannot be empty in DynamoDB. You must provide some kind of place-holder when using strings, perhaps something like "nil" or "empty". This is frankly one of the oddest things about DynamoDB and something to always bear in mind when building applications using it.

In addition to the scalar types, DynamoDB also supports a handful of *set types* and *document types* (list and map):

Type	Symbol	Description	JSON Example
String set	SS	A set of strings.	"SS": ["Larry", "Moe"]
Number set	NS	A set of numbers.	"NS": ["42", "137"]
Binary set	BS	A set of binary strings.	"BS": ["TGFycnkK", "TW9lCg=="]
List	L	A list that can consist of data of any scalar type, like a JSON array. You can mix scalar types as well.	"L": [{"S": "totchos"}, {"N": "741"}]
Map	M	A key-value structure with strings as keys and values of any type, including sets, lists, and maps.	"M": {"FavoriteBook": {"S": "Old Yeller"}}

Set types act just like sets in most programming languages. All items in a set must be unique, which means that attempting to add the string "totchos" to a string set that already included it would result in no change to the set.

JSON in DynamoDB

And last but certainly not least, DynamoDB also allows you to store *any valid JSON* as an item attribute. So if your application's data model uses data types that are JSON serializable/deserializable, then you can store those types directly rather than wrangling them into the supported types you just saw. Keep two things in mind, though: Individual items can't be larger than 400 KB, so don't go too crazy using DynamoDB as a store for large JSON objects or BLOBs; and you can't query inside of JSON objects (your application will need to supply that logic).

DynamoDB's set of supported data types is fairly limited compared to what you would find in an RDBMS such as Postgres but quite rich in comparison with something like HBase, which only holds binary data and makes the application responsible for all serialization and deserialization.

Here's an example put operation that uses JSON:

```
$ aws dynamodb put-item --table-name Books \
  --item '{
    "Title": {"S": "Moby Dick"},
    "PublishYear": {"N": "2012"},
    "ISBN": {"N": "98765"},
    "PublisherInfo": {
      "Name": "Something"
    }
  }'
```

Basic Read/Write Operations

Now that you have a better sense of what actually goes on in tables and inside of items, you can begin actually working with data. Let's add a few items to our shopping cart using the put-item command:

```
$ aws dynamodb put-item --table-name ShoppingCart \
  --item '{"ItemName": {"S": "Tickle Me Elmo"}}'
$ aws dynamodb put-item --table-name ShoppingCart \
  --item '{"ItemName": {"S": "1975 Buick LeSabre"}}'
$ aws dynamodb put-item --table-name ShoppingCart \
  --item '{"ItemName": {"S": "Ken Burns: the Complete Box Set"}}'
```

As you can see, when we need to add data using the command line we need to send it across the wire as JSON. We now have three items in our shopping cart. We can see a full listing using the scan command (which is the equivalent of an SQL SELECT * FROM ShoppingCart statement):

```
$ aws dynamodb scan \
  --table-name ShoppingCart
{
  "Count": 3,
  "Items": [
    {
      "ItemName": {
        "S": "1975 Buick LeSabre"
      }
    },
    {
      "ItemName": {
        "S": "Ken Burns: the Complete Box Set"
      }
    },
    {
      "ItemName": {
        "S": "Tickle Me Elmo"
      }
    }
  ],
  "ScannedCount": 3,
  "ConsumedCapacity": null
}
```

Scan operations involve all of the items in a table. It's perfectly fine to use them when you're not storing much data, but they tend to be very expensive options, so in a production table you should use them only if your use case absolutely requires processing every item in a table (and if you do require this, you may need to rethink your application logic!).

So how do you fetch, update, or delete specific items? This is where *keys* come in. In DynamoDB tables, you need to specify in advance which fields in the table are going to act as keys. In our case, our table has only one field, so the ItemName attribute will need to act as our key. But DynamoDB doesn't infer this automatically. This line in our create-table command specified the key: --key-schema AttributeName=ItemName,KeyType=HASH.

What happened here is that we told DynamoDB that we wanted the ItemName attribute to act as a key of type HASH. This means that we're using ItemName the way that we'd use keys in a standard key-value store like Redis: we simply provide DynamoDB with the "address" of the item and the database knows where to find it. In the next section, you'll see why keys in DynamoDB can also be much more complex—and powerful—than this.

For now, we can fetch specific items from our shopping cart, by key, using the --key flag:

```
$ aws dynamodb get-item --table-name ShoppingCart \
  --key '{"ItemName": {"S": "Tickle Me Elmo"}}'
{
    "Item": {
        "ItemName": {
            "S": "Tickle Me Elmo"
        }
    }
}
```

As discussed in the intro to this chapter, DynamoDB enables you to specify whether or not you want to perform a consistent read on every request using the --consistent-read flag when you make a get-item request. This GET request would guarantee item-level consistency:

```
$ aws dynamodb get-item --table-name ShoppingCart \
  --key '{"ItemName": {"S": "Tickle Me Elmo"}}' \
  --consistent-read
```

But let's be honest: Tickle Me Elmo isn't exactly all the rage these days so let's eliminate that from our cart (though we may regret it if Tickle Me Elmos experience a spike in resale value). We can do that on the basis of the hash key as well:

```
$ aws dynamodb delete-item --table-name ShoppingCart \
  --key '{"ItemName": {"S": "Tickle Me Elmo"}}'
```

If we run the same scan operation as before, the Count field in the returned JSON will indicate that we now only have two items in our shopping cart.

Two Key Types, Many Possibilities

DynamoDB is, at root, a key-value store. But it's a special key-value store in that it provides two types of key that you can choose on a table-by-table basis. You can use either a *hash key* (aka partition key) by itself *or* you can use a *composite key* that combines a hash key and a *range key* (aka sort key), as shown in the figure on page 224.

A hash key can be used to find items the same way you perform lookups in key-value databases such as HBase and Redis. You provide DynamoDB with a key and it checks the table to see if there's an item associated with the key. Imagine fetching information about NFL teams that have won the Super Bowl using the year as the hash key. Or imagine retrieving information about an

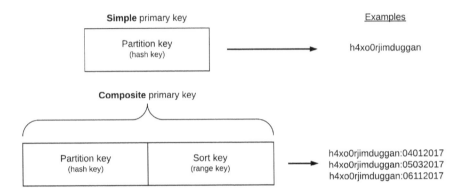

employee from a human resources database using the employee's Social Security Number as the hash key.

A combination partition and sort key, however, enables you to find items on the basis of the hash key if you know it in advance *or* to find multiple items via a *range query*.

Imagine a table storing information about books in which each book item has two properties: a title (string) and the year published (number). In this case, you could use the title as a hash key and the year published as a range key, which would enable you to fetch book data if you already know the title *or* if you only know a range of years that you're interested in.

Here's an example aws command that creates a table with that key combination:

```
$ aws dynamodb create-table \
  --table-name Books \
  --attribute-definitions AttributeName=Title,AttributeType=S \
    AttributeName=PublishYear,AttributeType=N \
  --key-schema AttributeName=Title,KeyType=HASH \
    AttributeName=PublishYear,KeyType=RANGE \
  --provisioned-throughput ReadCapacityUnits=1,WriteCapacityUnits=1
```

A book like *Moby Dick* has been published many times since its initial run. The structure of our Book table would enable us to store many items with a title of Moby Dick and then fetch specific items on the basis of which year the edition was published. Let's add some items to the table:

```
$ aws dynamodb put-item --table-name Books \
  --item '{
    "Title": {"S": "Moby Dick"},
    "PublishYear": {"N": "1851"},
    "ISBN": {"N": "12345"}
  }'
```

```
$ aws dynamodb put-item --table-name Books \
  --item '{
    "Title": {"S": "Moby Dick"},
    "PublishYear": {"N": "1971"},
    "ISBN": {"N": "23456"},
    "Note": {"S": "Out of print"}
  }'
$ aws dynamodb put-item --table-name Books \
  --item '{
    "Title": {"S": "Moby Dick"},
    "PublishYear": {"N": "2008"},
    "ISBN": {"N": "34567"}
  }'
```

You may have noticed that we supplied an ISBN attribute for each item without specifying that in the table definition. That's okay because remember that we only need to specify key attributes when creating tables. This gives DynamoDB its relative schemalessness, which you can also see at work in the second item we created, which has a Note attribute while the others do not.

To see which books were published after the year 1980, for example, we could use a range query:

```
$ aws dynamodb query --table-name Books \
  --expression-attribute-values '{
    ":title": {"S": "Moby Dick"},
    ":year": {"N": "1980"}
  }' \
  --key-condition-expression 'Title = :title AND PublishYear > :year'
{
  "Count": 1,
  "Items": [
      {
          "PublishYear": {
              "N": "2008"
          },
          "ISBN": {
              "N": "34567"
          },
          "Title": {
              "S": "Moby Dick"
          }
      }
  ],
  "ScannedCount": 1,
  "ConsumedCapacity": null
}
```

With the query command, the --expression-attribute-values flag enables us to provide values for variables that we want to use as JSON. The --key-condition-expression flag enables us to provide an actual query string strongly reminiscent of SQL, in this case Title = :title AND PublishYear > :year (which becomes Title = "Moby Dick" AND PublishYear > 1900 via interpolation).

If you've used a SQL driver for a specific programming language, then you've probably constructed parameterized queries like this. As output, we got one of three books currently in the Books table, as expected.

Whenever you provide key condition expressions, you must match directly on the hash key (in this case Title = :title) and then you can optionally provide a query for the range key using one of these operators: =, >, <, >=, <=, BETWEEN, or begins_with. A BETWEEN a AND b expression is the direct equivalent of >= a AND <= b and begins_with enables you to create an expression like begins_with(Title, :str) where :str could be a string.

But what if we wanted our result set to include only, say, ISBN data? After all, we know that all the books are titled Moby Dick, so we may not need that as part of our result set. We can tailor that result set using *attribute projection*. On the command line, you can perform attribute projection using the --projection-expression flag, which enables you to specify a list of attributes that you want returned for each item. This query would return only the ISBN for each edition of *Moby Dick* published after 1900:

```
$ aws dynamodb query --table-name Books \
  --expression-attribute-values \
    '{":title": {"S": "Moby Dick"},":year": {"N": "1900"}}' \
  --key-condition-expression \
    'Title = :title AND PublishYear > :year' \
  --projection-expression 'ISBN'
{
    "Count": 2,
    "Items": [
        {
            "ISBN": {
                "N": "23456"
            }
        },
        {
            "ISBN": {
                "N": "34567"
            }
        }
    ],
    "ScannedCount": 2,
    "ConsumedCapacity": null
}
```

If the attribute isn't defined for a specific item, then an empty object will be returned. Remember that only one of our book items has a Note attribute. Here's the result set when projecting for that attribute:

```
$ aws dynamodb query --table-name Books \
  --expression-attribute-values \
    '{":title": {"S": "Moby Dick"},":year": {"N": "1900"}}' \
  --key-condition-expression \
    'Title = :title AND PublishYear > :year' \
  --projection-expression 'Note'
{
    "Count": 2,
    "Items": [
        {
            "Note": {
                "S": "Out of print"
            }
        },
        {}
    ],
    "ScannedCount": 2,
    "ConsumedCapacity": null
}
```

Note the empty object, {}, returned for one of the Items.

As you can see in this section, choosing the right key setup for any DynamoDB table is extremely important because that will determine how your application is able to discover the items it's looking for. A good rule of thumb is this: If your application is built to know *in advance* where an item lives, then use just a hash key. An example here would be a user info database where you find items based on usernames already known to the application.

Spreading the Data Around: Partitioning in DynamoDB

Behind the scenes, DynamoDB's system for distributing item data across servers—*partitions* in DynamoDB parlance—is likely very complex. But from your perspective as a user it's really fairly simple. You can see a basic visual illustration of data partitioning in the figure on page 228.

When you start writing data to a DynamoDB table, it begins filling in a first partition (partition 1 in the diagram). Eventually, that partition will fill up and data will start being distributed to partition 2, then at some point to partition 3, and so on out to N partitions. That N can be pretty much as large as you want; AWS provides no guidelines for limits to the number of partitions. The logic will simply repeat itself until you stop feeding data to the table.

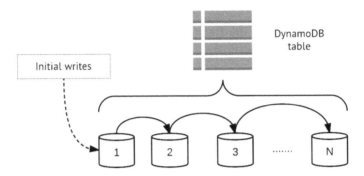

How DynamoDB makes decisions about when to redistribute data between partitions isn't something that Amazon makes transparent to the user. It *just works*. The only thing you have to worry about is ensuring as even a distribution of partition keys as possible, as laid out in the next section.

So just how *big* are these partitions? That's determined by how much provisioned throughput you specify for the table. Think back to the read- and write-capacity units you specified in the create-table operation for the ShoppingCart table. There, one read capacity unit and one write capacity unit were specified. That provided the initial space allocation for the table. DynamoDB will add new partitions either when that first partition fills up *or* when you change your provisioned throughput settings in a way that's incompatible with the current settings.

Location, Location, Location

As in any key-value store with limited querying capabilities, *where* you store things is an essential concern in DynamoDB and one that you should plan for from the get-go because it will have a huge impact on performance—and always remember that speedy, reliable performance is essentially the *whole point* of using DynamoDB.

As laid out in the previous section, DynamoDB uses a partition-based scheme for managing data within tables. You create a table and begin writing to it; over time, data is spread around across N partitions in an optimized way. But even though partitioning is automated, there are still some guidelines that you should follow when using tables.

The tricky part of partitioning is it's possible to create an uneven distribution of items across partitions. For a basic illustration, see the figure on page 229.

DynamoDB *always* performs best—in terms of read and write speed—when access to partition keys is balanced. In this illustration, the size of each

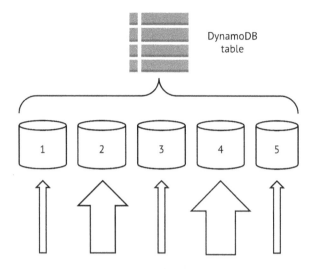

upward-facing arrow shows how intensively each partition is accessed. Partitions 2 and 4 here take significantly more traffic than partitions 1, 3, and 5, making partitions 2 and 4 so-called "hotspots." The presence of hotspots is likely to detract from performance for *all* partitions and should be avoided whenever possible.

In general, you can crystallize best practices for DynamoDB performance into just a few basic maxims.

First, if you're using a hash key as your partition key, you should always strive for a data model in which the application *knows the key in advance* because this will enable you to target the item directly rather than relying on range and other queries. You should make the hash key something meaningful —for example, the username of each user in a CRM table, the device ID for each sensor in an "Internet of Things" table (more on that in Day 2), or a UUID-based transaction identifier in an inventory table. When working with key-value stores, this is simply the nature of the beast, and DynamoDB is no different here.

Second, because the partition key determines where data is stored, you should use partition keys that don't cluster around just a few values. If you had a partition key with only a few possible values, for example good, bad, and ugly, you would produce hotspots around those values.

Third, in cases where you need to use a composite key—a hash key plus a range key—you should opt for *fewer partition keys and more range keys*. This is best illustrated with an example. Let's say that you're a video game company that makes the game Bonestorm. Bonestorm has over a million players and you want to store daily total stats for each player on each day that they play the game. You could use username/date composite keys that look like this:

```
h4x0rjimduggan:04012017
h4x0rjimduggan:05032017
pitythefool:11092016
pitythefool:07082016
```

A less-optimal strategy here would be to make the date the hash key and usernames the sort key. Because there are far more users than there are dates—by a favor of thousands—the number of items with the same hash key would be much higher.

As is always the case with key-value stores, even a "key-value plus" store like DynamoDB, your application needs to be smart about how it stores data and how keys are structured. One of the great things about RDBMSs that we've discovered after years of experimenting with NoSQL databases is just how flexible they can be. DynamoDB is more flexible than other key-value stores —composite keys provide for that—but careful planning, before you write even your first items, is nonetheless essential.

Tables Within Tables: Indexes in DynamoDB

The last core component of DynamoDB that we'll explore on Day 1 is *indexing*. Indexes are essentially mini tables that enable you to look up data more efficiently. Indexes in DynamoDB work much like they do in relational systems, storing lists of keys for objects based on some set of criteria.

Indexes usually offer a crucial performance boost because they prevent you from needing to run some of your more expensive queries. Instead of scanning an entire table and then selecting a subset of the results, which is almost never a good idea, you can *query or scan the index instead*. The price you pay for indexes is that they take up additional disk space. Whether or not that price is worth the performance boost depends on your use case and is difficult to decide in advance without knowing a lot of particulars. In DynamoDB, indexes come in two flavors: local and global.

Local Secondary Indexes

Local secondary indexes (LSIs) let you query or scan attributes *outside of your primary hash and sort key*. The "local" in "local secondary index" means *among items sharing a partition key*. You can see an example of this in the following figure. Here, a local secondary index is created for the High Score attribute.

The LSI on the High Score attribute here means that we can perform scans or queries related to high scores *for a specific user.*

Partition key

Username (hash key)	Date (range key)	High score	Avatar
h4x0rjimduggan	04012017	751	Lion
h4x0rjimduggan	05032017	852	Skull
beboprocksteady75	04262017	451	Raptor
beboprocksteady75	05032017	562	Lion
beboprocksteady75	06122017	567	Narwhal

Local secondary index — High score

No index — Avatar

Here's an example range query for the HighScore attribute that shows all of the dates on which the player h4x0rjimduggan scored over 800 points:

```
$ aws dynamodb query --table-name BonestormData \
  --expression-attribute-values \
    '{":user": {"S": "h4x0rjimduggan"},":score": {"N": "800"}}' \
  --key-condition-expression \
    'Username = :user AND HighScore > :score' \
  --projection-expression 'Date'
```

Always bear in mind that *LSIs can't be modified after a table has been created,* so be extra careful to plan for them in advance (or, even better, thoroughly test different indexing models in development).

Global Secondary Indexes

Global secondary indexes (GSIs) are indexes that aren't restricted to items with the same partition key. The "global" here essentially means "any attribute in the table." See the figure on page 232 for an example. You can find *any* items in the table using the Avatar attribute.

Here's an example query that finds all items for which the Avatar field equals Lion and returns the Username and Date for each of those items:

```
$ aws dynamodb query --table-name BonestormData \
  --expression-attribute-values \
    '{":avatar": {"S": "Lion"}}' \
  --key-condition-expression \
    'Avatar = :avatar' \
  --projection-expression 'Username, Date'
```

Username (hash key)	Date (range key)	High score	Avatar
h4x0rjimduggan	04012017	751	Lion
h4x0rjimduggan	05032017	852	Skull
beboprocksteady75	04262017	451	Raptor
beboprocksteady75	05032017	562	Lion
beboprocksteady75	06122017	567	Narwhal

An important thing to note is that GSIs can be modified *after* a table has been created, whereas LSIs cannot. This makes it somewhat less crucial to get your GSIs right from the get-go, but it's still never a bad idea to make a thorough indexing plan in advance.

Day 1 Wrap-Up

Here on Day 1 we did a *lot* of conceptual exploration, from supported data types to indexing to the core philosophy of DynamoDB, but we didn't really *do* anything all that exciting with DynamoDB. That will change on Day 2, when we'll embark on one of the most ambitious practical projects in this book, building a streaming data pipeline that ties together multiple AWS services to create a streaming data pipeline that uses DynamoDB as a persistent data store.

Day 1 Homework

Find

1. DynamoDB does have a specific formula that's used to calculate the number of partitions for a table. Do some Googling and find that formula.

2. Browse the documentation for the DynamoDB streams feature.[3]

3. We mentioned limits for things like item size (400 KB per item). Read the Limits in DynamoDB documentation[4] to see which other limitations apply when using DynamoDB so that you don't unknowingly overstep any bounds.

---

3. http://docs.aws.amazon.com/amazondynamodb/latest/developerguide/Streams.html
4. http://docs.aws.amazon.com/amazondynamodb/latest/developerguide/Limits.html

Do

1. Using the formula you found for calculating the number of partitions used for a table, calculate how many partitions would be used for a table holding 100 GB of data and assigned 2000 RCUs and 3000 WCUs.

2. If you were storing tweets in DynamoDB, how would you do so using DynamoDB's supported data types?

3. In addition to PutItem operations, DynamoDB also offers *update item* operations that enable you to modify an item if a *conditional expression* is satisfied. Take a look at the documentation for conditional expressions[5] and perform a conditional update operation on an item in the ShoppingCart table.

Day 2: Building a Streaming Data Pipeline

On Day 1, we made some solid progress on understanding the core concepts of DynamoDB, from how DynamoDB partitions data to the data types that it supports to secondary indexes. We worked through some simple table management commands and some basic CRUD operations on that table to see the concepts in action.

We were exposed to some features that set DynamoDB apart from other, more strict key-value stores, but those features are mostly garnishes. The main dish is DynamoDB's unique blend of extreme scalability, predictably solid performance as you scale out, and freedom from operational burdens.

On Day 2, we'll build something that can take full advantage of those features in a way that we couldn't in our Day 1 CRUD exercises. We'll build a streaming data pipeline that pumps sensor data into DynamoDB (we'll use a Ruby script to act as mock sensors). Those mock sensors will populate our table with three pieces of data per "reading":

*   An identifier for the sensor—for example, sensor-1 or temp-a1b2c3
*   A timestamp for the reading in Unix time (this will allow for easier sorting)
*   The current temperature picked up by the sensor—for example, 81.4 or 73.2

But instead of writing to DynamoDB directly, we'll use a streaming data service called Kinesis that's built for handling massive write throughput; messages passing through Kinesis will be written to DynamoDB using functions deployed to AWS's Lambda service.

It may seem a bit odd to focus on connecting AWS services in a chapter devoted to DynamoDB. But it's important to note that cloud databases are

---

5. http://docs.aws.amazon.com/amazondynamodb/latest/developerguide/Expressions.ConditionExpressions.html

rarely used as standalone tools. Cloud providers typically offer lots and lots of services that can run in the same datacenter as your database, built to supplement one another. To use multiple services together is to go with the grain of cloud computing.

A Data Model for Sensor Data

The data pipeline that we build later today will be capable of handling *lots* of streaming data, to the tune of many megabytes per second. But before we open up that pipeline, we need to make some big choices about our data model. For reasons we went over on Day 1, getting data modeling right is *everything* in DynamoDB and any missteps can get you into trouble, especially in a big production system.

Getting Our Keys Right

Keys are extremely important in DynamoDB because they not only act as "addresses" for items, as in systems like Redis, in DynamoDB they also determine *how* your data is distributed between partitions, which in turn affects the write/read performance of the table.

We'll call our DynamoDB table SensorData, and it will consist of the following columns:

- The hash key will be a ReadingId attribute that will be randomly generated. This will ensure that our partition keys are evenly distributed across partitions. There will be no range key, as each item will have a different partition key; range keys can only sort across items with the same partition key, and in this case a range key for a single partition key would be nonsensical.

- The ID of the device emitting the data (sensor1, factory-sensor-1337, and so on).

- A timestamp number expressing the current Unix time.

- The temperature for the reading.

When creating DynamoDB tables via the command line, you can either use flags (as for the previous ShoppingCart table) or you can use a JSON specification. The spec for our SensorData table will be complex enough that using CLI flags will be too unwieldy. So we'll do it this way instead:

```
$ aws dynamodb create-table \
  --cli-input-json file://sensor-data-table.json
```

And here's the JSON spec itself:

dynamodb/sensor-data-table.json

```json
{
  "TableName": "SensorData",
  "KeySchema": [
    {
      "AttributeName": "SensorId",
      "KeyType": "HASH"
    },
    {
      "AttributeName": "CurrentTime",
      "KeyType": "RANGE"
    }
  ],
  "AttributeDefinitions": [
    {
      "AttributeName": "SensorId",
      "AttributeType": "S"
    },
    {
      "AttributeName": "CurrentTime",
      "AttributeType": "N"
    },
    {
      "AttributeName": "Temperature",
      "AttributeType": "N"
    }
  ],
  "LocalSecondaryIndexes": [
    {
      "IndexName": "TemperatureIndex",
      "KeySchema": [
        {
          "AttributeName": "SensorId",
          "KeyType": "HASH"
        },
        {
          "AttributeName": "Temperature",
          "KeyType": "RANGE"
        }
      ],
      "Projection": {
        "ProjectionType": "ALL"
      }
    }
  ],
  "ProvisionedThroughput": {
    "ReadCapacityUnits": 2,
    "WriteCapacityUnits": 2
  }
}
```

Keep in mind that this data model is highly specific to our use case. Many use cases may involve more complex column structures, more secondary indexes, more attributes, and so on. The important thing is making sure that you go through a similar decision-making process whenever you use DynamoDB; missteps here will cost you, and we do mean actual money.

Navigating Trade-offs in Performance Tuning

As we've stressed before, you simply shouldn't use DynamoDB if you're after anything but extremely good performance at massive scale. But as with any complex system, performance and scalability in DynamoDB are *not* guaranteed. There's a wide variety of missteps that will ensure that you have a deeply sub-optimal experience, spend too much money, or both.

On Day 1, we talked about performance optimization from the standpoint of data modeling and how the distribution of primary keys is very important. In this section, the focus will be more operational. DynamoDB provides a small handful of knobs you can adjust that can have a big impact on performance. These knobs are the closest thing you get to "ops" in DynamoDB, but they aren't terribly complex. You just need to keep a few basic principles in view.

Throughput is the central concept here. When we created the ShoppingCart table on Day 1, we used this command but didn't provide much explanation of the --provisioned-throughput flag:

```
$ aws dynamodb create-table --table-name ShoppingCart \
  --attribute-definitions AttributeName=ItemName,AttributeType=S \
  --key-schema AttributeName=ItemName,KeyType=HASH \
  --provisioned-throughput ReadCapacityUnits=1,WriteCapacityUnits=1
```

Read capacity and write capacity units are handled differently in DynamoDB. Write capacity units (WCUs) are measured in units of 1 KB per second while read capacity units (RCUs) are measured in units of 4 KB per second. You can set both read and write throughput on a per-table basis. For workloads that are more write heavy, you could provision just one RCU and many WCUs, or vice versa for read-heavy workloads.

We won't delve too far into DynamoDB throughput tuning here. Just keep a few things in mind:

- Strive to match the RCUs and WCUs in a table to balance between read and write intensity. Perform regular checks—Amazon offers numerous services to help with this, such as CloudWatch—to ensure that you haven't over- or under-provisioned throughput on either the read or the write side. Perhaps even set up an automated system to re-provision when necessary.

- Considerations about read and write throughput *include secondary indexes*, both local and global. Throughput should be provisioned based on the size of index entries, *not* the size of the actual table items.

- Strongly consistent reads are about twice as expensive as eventually consistent reads.

If you're ever concerned about costs, the DynamoDB console on the AWS website provides an interface that you can use to get cost estimates, as shown in the figure that follows.

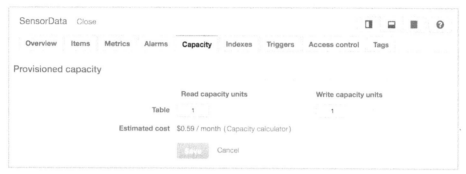

Throughput settings for a table are *not* fixed for all time and can be updated at will. For our purposes here, 1 unit of RCU and WCU will suffice for our table. But we couldn't let you proceed beyond this section without mentioning this second, essential element of DynamoDB performance.

Now that we have a `SensorData` table ready to accept writes, we can get back to building our streaming sensor data pipeline.

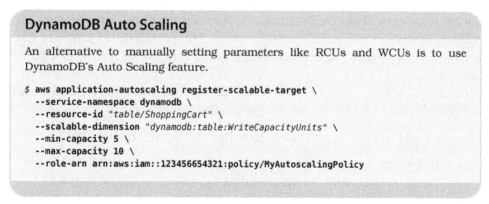

DynamoDB Auto Scaling

An alternative to manually setting parameters like RCUs and WCUs is to use DynamoDB's Auto Scaling feature.

```
$ aws application-autoscaling register-scalable-target \
  --service-namespace dynamodb \
  --resource-id "table/ShoppingCart" \
  --scalable-dimension "dynamodb:table:WriteCapacityUnits" \
  --min-capacity 5 \
  --max-capacity 10 \
  --role-arn arn:aws:iam::123456654321:policy/MyAutoscalingPolicy
```

It's a Streaming World

Data *streams* are best understood in contrast to data *batches*. When you process a batch—maybe a huge CSV file or a massive Postgres table—you take a well-defined mass of data and apply some kind of logic to it, for example selecting all values that satisfy a WHERE clause in an SQL query or parsing all the values in a column in an Excel spreadsheet.

When you process a stream of data, however, you don't know in advance how many items will pass through the stream for processing. Instead, you design some kind of processing logic, open up a pipe, and handle things as they come through. Although there's still plenty of room for batch processing in today's data landscape, streaming models have become more popular with the predominance of realtime inputs from devices such as smartphones and, in our case, sensors.

A Realtime, Streaming, Functional Data Pipeline

For today's practical exercise, we'll use a combination of three AWS services —DynamoDB, Lambda, and Kinesis—to build a data pipeline that's capable of accepting *lots* of incoming data, processing it, and finally storing it in DynamoDB.

Amazon's *Kinesis* is a service that enables you to manage data streams that you can pipe to any number of destinations, from S3 buckets to Redshift warehouses to, in our case, AWS Lambda functions (more on that in a minute). You can think of Kinesis as a managed, cloud-only version of Apache Kafka, and if you've worked with Kafka then some of the core primitives driving Kinesis may be familiar to you already: topics, producers, consumers, records, and so on. Not a perfect analogy, but it should suffice for our exercise.

Lambda is a Functions-as-a-Service (FaaS) platform that enables you to manage functions that run in Amazon datacenters without *any* concern for running servers or managing infrastructure. The popularity of Lambda has spawned the so-called "serverless" paradigm of computing, which is a bit of misnomer in that Lambda functions do, of course, run on servers, but the fact that you simply write functions that process inputs however you'd like and upload them to AWS makes it at least *feel* serverless.

What we build today will ultimately look like the figure on page 239.

Data will flow through a Kinesis stream to a Lambda function that then processes the data. The Lambda processing step writes the incoming data to a DynamoDB table. Once we've built this, we'll feed some example data into Kinesis using the aws CLI tool to test things and then start pumping sensor data in.

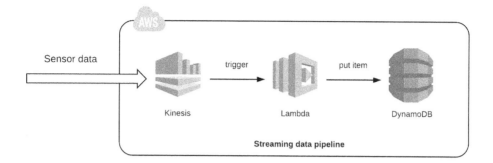

Before you start going through the CLI examples here, do two things. First, cd into the code/dynamodb folder for the DynamoDB chapter. Then, create a Kinesis stream using the aws tool:

```
$ export STREAM_NAME=temperature-sensor-data
$ aws kinesis create-stream \
  --stream-name ${STREAM_NAME} \
  --shard-count 1
```

When creating this stream, we gave it a name and specified a *shard count*. The shard count essentially determines how much parallel processing power you want your stream to have. More shards means more power but also more cost, so we'll use just one shard for our example here as it's all we'll really need. Now let's have a look at how AWS sees our stream:

```
$ aws kinesis describe-stream \
  --stream-name ${STREAM_NAME}
{
    "StreamDescription": {
        "RetentionPeriodHours": 24,
        "StreamName": "iot-temperature-data",
        "Shards": [],
        "StreamARN": "arn:aws:kinesis:...:stream/iot-temperature-data",
        "EnhancedMonitoring": [
            {
                "ShardLevelMetrics": []
            }
        ],
        "StreamStatus": "CREATING"
    }
}
```

At first, the status of the stream will be CREATING, but within a few seconds the status should change to ACTIVE. Once that happens, you can write some data to the stream. Each record that you write to Kinesis needs to contain two things: a partition key and a binary large object (BLOB) of data. The partition key determines which shard the record is written to (as with DynamoDB's partitioning system). Set the STREAM_ARN environment variable to the StreamARN shown in the output, which should begin with arn:aws:kinesis.

Here's an example write to the temperature-sensor-data stream that we just created:

```
$ aws kinesis put-record \
  --stream-name ${STREAM_NAME} \
  --partition-key sensor-data \
  --data "Baby's first Kinesis record"
{
    "ShardId": "shardId-000000000000",
    "SequenceNumber": "4957192301...3577493926"
}
```

Don't worry too much about partitions, shards, and the returned JSON here, as we won't delve too deeply into Kinesis in this book. The important thing to know for now is that our stream is ready to accept incoming records and pass them along to the Lambda function that we'll create later.

Now one essential piece of our pipeline is in place, but there are more puzzle pieces we need to connect. Kinesis is a powerful system but it's really just a fancy pipe. It doesn't actually *process* or write data, so we can't use it to actually store items in DynamoDB. We'll need to create a processing layer that ingests records from Kinesis and actually does something with them.

Up until very recently, the default way to create this kind of processing layer in AWS would be to write an application that can handle incoming streams of data and run that application on Elastic Compute Cloud (EC2) servers. That's a perfectly reasonable approach, but it requires you to fire up and manage servers. We can avoid that by using Lambda, which requires us to simply write some code, run some basic CLI commands, and let AWS do the work.

First, we need to write our function. Lambda supports several languages for Lambda functions, but let's use JavaScript because its callback-based logic is a natural fit for Lambda (and perhaps even an inspiration for Lambda!). Here is the code for our handler:

```javascript
dynamodb/ProcessKinesisRecords.js
var AWS = require('aws-sdk');
var DynamoDB = new AWS.DynamoDB({
  apiVersion: '2012-08-10',
  region: 'us-east-1',
});
```

```javascript
exports.kinesisHandler = function(event, context, callback) {
  // We only need to handle one record at a time
  var kinesisRecord = event.Records[0];

  // The data payload is base 64 encoded and needs to be decoded to a string
  var data    =
    Buffer.from(kinesisRecord.kinesis.data, 'base64').toString('ascii');
  // Create a JSON object out of that string
  var obj     = JSON.parse(data);
  var sensorId    = obj.sensor_id,
      currentTime = obj.current_time,
      temperature = obj.temperature;

  // Define the item to write to DynamoDB
  var item = {
    TableName: "SensorData",
    Item: {
      SensorId: {
        S: sensorId
      },
      CurrentTime: {
        // Remember that all numbers need to be input as strings
        N: currentTime.toString()
      },
      Temperature: {
        N: temperature.toString()
      }
    }
  };

  // Perform a put operation, logging both successes and failures
  DynamoDB.putItem(item, function(err, data) {
    if (err) {
      console.log(err, err.stack);
      callback(err.stack);
    } else {
      console.log(data);
      callback(null, data);
    }
  });
}
```

When writing any Lambda handler function, you are given three JavaScript objects to work with when your function is triggered:

- The event object contains the data that has been passed to the function, in our case the JSON object written to Kinesis.

- The context object holds information about the environment in which the function is running.

- The `callback` object signals that the operation is finished. If called with a single argument, that means that the function returns an error; if called with `null` and a string, then the function is deemed successful and the string represents the success message.

The event object that our function receives from Kinesis is a JSON object with a `Records` field that will hold the data for each record. In our pipeline, Kinesis will only deliver a single record at a time. For each record that arrives, we'll put an item to our `SensorData` table.

Before we can stitch Kinesis and Lambda together, however, we need to create an AWS *security role* that enables us to do that. Role management in AWS is handled by a service called Identity and Access Management, or IAM. If you've managed users, roles, and groups in database systems such as Postgres, the concepts here are quite similar. The following set of commands will:

- Create the role using a JSON document that you can peruse in the `lambda-kinesis-role.json` file.

- Attach a *policy* to that role that will enable Kinesis to pass data to Lambda.

- Store the ARN for this role in an environment variable.

```
$ export IAM_ROLE_NAME=kinesis-lambda-dynamodb
$ aws iam create-role \
  --role-name ${IAM_ROLE_NAME} \
  --assume-role-policy-document file://lambda-kinesis-role.json
$ aws iam attach-role-policy \
  --role-name ${IAM_ROLE_NAME} \
  --policy-arn \
    arn:aws:iam::aws:policy/service-role/AWSLambdaKinesisExecutionRole
$ aws iam attach-role-policy \
  --role-name ${IAM_ROLE_NAME} \
  --policy-arn \
    arn:aws:iam::aws:policy/AmazonDynamoDBFullAccess
```

Now you need to get the ARN for that role. Run this command and set the `ROLE_ARN` environment variable to the proper Arn, which should begin with `arn:aws:iam`:

```
$ aws iam get-role --role-name ${IAM_ROLE_NAME}
```

In order to upload our function to Lambda, we need to create a Zip file out of it and then upload the zipped payload using the `create-function` command:

```
$ zip ProcessKinesisRecords.zip ProcessKinesisRecords.js
$ aws lambda create-function \
  --region us-east-1 \
  --function-name ProcessKinesisRecords \
```

```
  --zip-file fileb://ProcessKinesisRecords.zip \
  --role ${ROLE_ARN} \
  --handler ProcessKinesisRecords.kinesisHandler \
  --runtime nodejs6.10
{
    "CodeSha256": "LdmN2sMF5kwdZiRbIYAtdhs4J8pX39Qa6EhvGdGAcOQ=",
    "FunctionName": "kinesis-dynamodb-processor",
    "CodeSize": 530,
    "MemorySize": 128,
    "FunctionArn": "arn:aws:lambda:...",
    "Version": "$LATEST",
    "Role": "arn:aws:iam:...",
    "Timeout": 3,
    "LastModified": "2017-04-13T04:07:36.833+0000",
    "Handler": "kinesisHandler",
    "Runtime": "nodejs4.3",
    "Description": ""
}
```

If you have any modifications that you want to make to the function on your own, you can update it at any time by creating a new Zip file and using the update-function-code command:

```
$ zip ProcessKinesisRecords.zip ProcessKinesisRecords.js
$ aws lambda update-function-code \
  --function-name ProcessKinesisRecords \
  --zip-file fileb://ProcessKinesisRecords.zip
```

We can run a test invocation of the new function using a mock input from a text file and storing the output in another text file (that you can peruse on your own):

```
$ aws lambda invoke \
  --invocation-type RequestResponse \
  --function-name ProcessKinesisRecords \
  --payload file://test-lambda-input.txt \
  lambda-output.txt
{
    "StatusCode": 200
}
```

Success! We've triggered a Lambda function using a mock data input payload mimicking a Kinesis stream. Lambda then handled the data, turned it into a DynamoDB item, and made a successful write. What's missing now is that Kinesis isn't yet able to trigger and pass data to our Lambda function. For that, we need to create a *source mapping* that tells AWS that we want our iot-temperature-data to trigger our ProcessKinesisRecords Lambda function whenever a record passes into the stream. This command will create that mapping:

```
$ aws lambda create-event-source-mapping \
  --function-name ProcessKinesisRecords \
  --event-source-arn ${KINESIS_STREAM_ARN} \
  --starting-position LATEST
{
    "UUID": "0f56a8c7-de6d-4a77-b536-9ec87be5a065",
    "StateTransitionReason": "User action",
    "LastModified": 1492057092.585,
    "BatchSize": 100,
    "EventSourceArn": "arn:aws:kinesis:...",
    "FunctionArn": "arn:aws:lambda:...",
    "State": "Creating",
    "LastProcessingResult": "No records processed"
}
```

You can see a description of the event source mapping:

```
$ aws lambda list-event-source-mappings
{
    "EventSourceMappings": [
        {
            "UUID": "0f56a8c7-de6d-4a77-b536-9ec87be5a065",
            "StateTransitionReason": "User action",
            "LastModified": 1492057140.0,
            "BatchSize": 100,
            "State": "Enabled",
            "FunctionArn": "arn:aws:lambda:...",
            "EventSourceArn": "arn:aws:kinesis:...",
            "LastProcessingResult": "No records processed"
        }
    ]
}
```

If the value of State isn't yet Enabled, wait a few seconds and that should change.

At this point, the pipeline is in place. Records that are written to the temperature-sensor-stream stream in Kinesis will be processed by a Lambda function, which will write the results to the SensorData table in DynamoDB. Just to be sure, let's put a record to the stream and see what happens:

```
$ export DATA=$(
  echo '{
    "sensor_id":"sensor-1",
    "temperature":99.9,"current_time":123456789
  }' | base64)
$ aws kinesis put-record \
  --stream-name ${STREAM_NAME} \
  --partition-key sensor-data \
  --data ${DATA}
```

That should return a JSON object with a ShardId and SequenceNumber as before. But let's see if that mock temperature sensor reading ended up in DynamoDB:

```
$ aws dynamodb scan --table-name SensorData
{
    "Count": 1,
    "Items": [
        {
            "CurrentTime": {
                "N": "123456789"
            },
            "Temperature": {
                "N": "99.9"
            },
            "SensorId": {
                "S": "sensor-1"
            }
        }
    ]
}
```

Success again! Our pipeline is now all set up and ready to handle sensor data inputs. On Day 3, we'll begin pumping data into Kinesis and letting Lambda do its magic.

Day 2 Homework

Find

1. Read some documentation for the DynamoDB Streams feature (not to be confused with Kinesis).[6] Think of a compelling use case for this feature.

2. Find one or more DynamoDB client libraries for your favorite programming language. Explore how to perform CRUD operations using that library.

3. DynamoDB supports object expiry using time to live (TTL). Find some documentation on TTL in DynamoDB and think of some use cases for it.

Do

1. One way to improve the performance of Kinesis is to write records to different partitions. Find some documentation on partitioning in Kinesis and think of a stream partitioning scheme that would work with our sensor data model (rather than writing all records to the sensor-data partition).

---

6. http://docs.aws.amazon.com/amazondynamodb/latest/developerguide/Streams.html

2. Modify various elements of our data pipeline—the SensorData table definition, the Lambda function, and so on—to enable sensors to write humidity-related data to the pipeline (as a percentage). Make sure that *all* of these components line up properly!

Day 3: Building an "Internet of Things" System Around DynamoDB

On Day 2, we delved into DynamoDB's streaming feature and turned our DynamoDB database from a fairly standard cloud storage mechanism into a much more dynamic processing system consisting of a Kinesis-Lambda-DynamoDB system. What we *didn't* do on Day 2 was provide any data inputs beyond some CLI test runs. On Day 3, we'll provide some "Internet of Things"-style data from mock sensors.

The term "Internet of Things" (aka IoT) is kind of like "Big Data" or "the Cloud." Its use is controversial because there's a lot of buzz surrounding it, and what it points to isn't so much something that already exists as much as it is a set of emerging technological possibilities. The "things" in the expression can refer to everything from moisture sensors in your refrigerator to a heart-rate monitor you wear on your wrist—essentially anything that isn't a "normal" computer (laptop, smartphone, cloud server) and is capable of producing data and transmitting it to some part of the Internet.

The interesting thing about the IoT from the perspective of this book is that things like sensors can produce *tons* of data, especially when aggregating across many data-producing devices. Imagine a 50-acre vineyard with moisture and temperature sensors hooked up every few feet along the rows of vines, or a high-tech manufacturing facility where each machine in an assembly line is feeding all kinds of data to some centralized source. In both cases, these devices might be sending data every few hours or they might be sending it more than once a second. IoT data usually comes in small chunks (maybe just a few sensor readings at a time), but those small chunks can really add up.

DynamoDB is a good choice for an IoT database because it's built to handle not just huge data sets but data sets whose size can't be determined in advanced. The downside of DynamoDB, as we discussed before, is that it isn't built for complex queries of the type you'd be able to run on a relational database. For our needs here, though, DynamoDB's "key-value plus" querying system will do just fine. Our tables will be fairly simple, and range queries will enable us to use DynamoDB as a powerful timeseries database. Any processing logic we need to apply beyond this can happen on the application side if we need it to.

Mock Data Inputs

In a real sensor data setup, you would likely use a protocol like Message Queue Telemetry Transport (MQTT)[7] as a device messaging protocol to feed data into a streaming data pipeline like ours, perhaps in conjunction with a broker interface like Amazon's IoT service.[8]

Here, we'll do something a bit simpler that doesn't require having actual sensor devices on hand. We'll use a Ruby script that auto-generates temperature data and writes that data to our data pipeline as JSON.

```ruby
dynamodb/upload-sensor-data.rb
require 'aws-sdk'
require 'random-walk'
require 'time'

STREAM_NAME = 'temperature-sensor-data'

# Make sure that both a sensor ID and number of iterations are entered
if ARGV.length != 2
  abort("Must specify a sensor ID as the first arg and N as the second")
end

@sensor_id = ARGV[0]
@iterator_limit = ARGV[1].to_i

# The Kinesis client object. Supply a different region if necessary
@kinesis_client = Aws::Kinesis::Client.new(region: 'us-east-1')

# An array used to generate random walk values
@temp_walk_array = RandomWalk.generate(6000..10000, @iterator_limit, 1)

# The iterator starts at 0
@iterator = 0

def write_temp_reading_to_kinesis
  # Generate a random current temperature from the walk array
  current_temp = @temp_walk_array[@iterator] / 100.0

  # The JSON payload for the reading
  data = {
    :sensor_id    => @sensor_id,
    :current_time => Time.now.to_i,
    :temperature  => current_temp,
  }

  # The record to write to Kinesis
  kinesis_record = {
    :stream_name  => STREAM_NAME,
    :data         => data.to_json,
```

---

7. http://mqtt.org
8. https://aws.amazon.com/iot

```
    # We'll use just a single partition key here
    :partition_key => 'sensor-data',
  }

  # Write the record to Kinesis
  @kinesis_client.put_record(kinesis_record)

  puts "Sensor #{@sensor_id} sent a temperature reading of #{current_temp}"

  @iterator += 1

  # Exit if script has iterated N times
  if @iterator == @iterator_limit
    puts "The sensor has gone offline"
    exit(0)
  end
  end
end

while true
  write_temp_reading_to_kinesis
  # Pause 2 seconds before supplying another reading
  sleep 2
end
```

In order to run the script, you'll need to install the random-walk and aws-sdk gems:

```
$ gem install random-walk aws-sdk
```

This script requires you to specify a sensor identifier, such as sensor-1 or whatever you'd like, as well as the number of times that you'd like the script to write data to the pipeline. To make the temp-sensor-1 sensor write 1,000 times to the pipeline:

```
$ ruby upload-sensor-data.rb temp-sensor-1 1000
```

A randomized temperature reading will be written to the pipeline every 2 seconds until it's gone through the supplied number of iterations. The temperature readings will be between 60 and 100 degrees and based on a *random walk* pattern, which means that the readings will follow a lightly meandering path rather than being truly random. A four-step random walk pattern would produce a series like 47.2, 47.3, 47.7, 47.6 as opposed to something like 47.2, 68.9, 50.3, 32.1. The script will also supply a Unix timestamp to each reading (which we can later use to run range queries).

Open up multiple shell sessions and run the script for multiple device IDs. Or use this command, which will write 1,000 sensor readings each for 10 sensors labeled sensor-1, sensor-2, and so on.

```
$ for n in {1..10}; do
    ruby upload-sensor-data.rb sensor-${n} 1000 &
  done
```

Let that run for as long as you'd like. You can shut down all the running mock sensors at any time:

```
$ pgrep -f upload-sensor-data | xargs kill -9
```

Scan the SensorData table a few times to see the number of items steadily increasing:

```
$ aws dynamodb scan --table-name SensorData
```

As the table fills up, scan operations will become increasingly slow. Now would be a good time to explore local secondary index queries. Remember that when we created the SensorData table we created a local secondary index for the Temperature attribute. Get two timestamp values for two temperature readings —the first and the 201st—like this:

```
$ T1=$(aws dynamodb scan --table-name SensorData \
  --query Items[0].CurrentTime.N | tr -d '"')
$ T2=$(aws dynamodb scan --table-name SensorData \
  --query Items[200].CurrentTime.N | tr -d '"')
```

Then run this query, substituting the values for T1 and T2 (make sure to use the larger of the two values for t2).

```
$ aws dynamodb query --table-name SensorData \
  --expression-attribute-values '{
    ":t1": {"N": "..."},
    ":t2": {"N": "..."},
    ":sensorId": {"S": "sensor-1"}
  }' \
  --key-condition-expression \
    'SensorId = :sensorId AND CurrentTime BETWEEN :t1 AND :t2' \
  --projection-expression 'Temperature'
```

That should return all the Temperature values for the sensor-1 sensor between the two timestamps (feel free to substitute a different name if you used a different naming scheme).

Now see how many items are currently in the table:

```
$ aws dynamodb scan --table-name SensorData \
  --query Count
```

At this point, you may be up to several hundreds of items. Let the count get above 1,000 or so and then stop the sensors using the kill -9 command we used before. At that point, there will be plenty of data in the SensorData table to move on to the next exercise.

An SQL Querying Interface

Our mock sensors have now streamed over 1,000 entries into our DynamoDB table. We've seen one way of accessing that data, which is fetching sensor readings based on a time range. This is a cool capability, but if we wanted to gather more meaningful metrics for our sensor data, we'd need a more powerful interface. What if you had, say, data analysts or climate scientists on your team that needed to perform much more complex queries or mathematical calculations using that sensor data?

One way that you can do this on AWS is to use plain old SQL. Now, don't get too excited just yet, because you can't perform SQL queries over DynamoDB tables *directly*—at least not yet—but what you *can* do instead is transfer data stored in DynamoDB tables into an S3 (Simple Storage Service) bucket using a service called Data Pipeline and then run SQL queries directly against that data using another AWS service called Athena.

Time for Another Pipeline

Amazon's Data Pipeline service enables you to create batch jobs that efficiently move data between Amazon services (including S3, the Redshift data warehousing service, and many more). You can write your own pipeline logic from scratch or you can use a template for ease of use. Fortunately for us, there's a predefined *Export DynamoDB table to S3* pipeline definition that will make this very simple. Ultimately, our streaming pipeline plus querying interface will look like the architecture in the figure that follows.

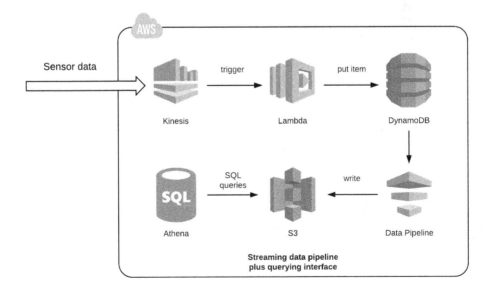

To begin, you'll need to create a new S3 bucket to store JSON data from the SensorData table in DynamoDB. You can call this bucket whatever you'd like, so long as it's globally unique (as in unique among *all* AWS users). Perhaps call it sensor-data, and add your local username and use the aws tool to create the bucket, like this:

```
$ export BUCKET_NAME=s3://sensor-data-$USER
$ aws s3 mb ${BUCKET_NAME}
```

To set up the pipeline, go to the Date Pipeline page in the AWS console[9] and select *Create new pipeline*, as you can see in the figure that follows.

When the pipeline creation page pops up, do the following:

- Give the pipeline any name you'd like.

- Under *Source*, select *Build using a template* and then the *Export DynamoDB table to S3* template.

- Under *Source DynamoDB table name* , specify the SensorData table, and under *Output s3 folder*, input the name of the S3 bucket that you created.

- Leave the *DynamoDB read throughput ratio* value as is and supply the AWS region (we've been using us-east-1 thus far in these examples but yours may differ).

- Under *Run* in the *Schedule* section, select *on pipeline activation*. Disable logging in the next section and select *Default* under *Security/Access*.

Now click *Activate*. That will bring you back to the data pipeline console. The pipeline job will go through several phases, beginning with WAITING. Behind the scenes, Data Pipeline is actually spinning up, using, and finally shutting down an Elastic MapReduce cluster to perform the data transfer (think back to Day 3 of the HBase chapter when we spun up our own EMR cluster to run HBase). The job should finish within a few minutes. Once it's done, every

---

9. https://console.aws.amazon.com/datapipeline

item in the SensorData table will be kept in a single file in S3, with each sensor reading as a JSON object on a separate line in the file.

Querying the Data Using Athena

Athena is an AWS service that enables you to query data files stored in S3 using plain SQL queries. We'll use Athena to get some aggregate metrics out of the data stored in our SensorData table. Go to the Athena console[10] and click on *Query Editor*. This is the interface that you can use to create tables and run queries. Run this query to create a sensor_data table (substituting the appropriate name for the S3 bucket that you created).

```
CREATE EXTERNAL TABLE sensor_data (
  sensorid      struct<s:string>,
  currenttime   struct<n:bigint>,
  temperature   struct<n:float>
)
ROW FORMAT SERDE 'org.openx.data.jsonserde.JsonSerDe'
with serdeproperties ('paths'='SensorId,CurrentTime,Temperature')
LOCATION 's3://YOUR-S3-BUCKET/';
```

A few things to note here. First, we're using data structures called *structs* as columns. That's because the JSON object for each item in our DynamoDB table looks like this:

```
{
  "SensorId": {
    "S": "..."
  },
  "CurrentTime": {
    "N": "..."
  },
  "Temperature": {
    "N": "..."
  }
}
```

Structs will enable us to easily handle this nested JSON data. Second, the ROW FORMAT information simply specifies that we're querying files storing JSON as well as which JSON fields we're interested in (SensorId and so on). Finally, the LOCATION points to our S3 bucket (don't forget the slash at the end).

The data from DynamoDB should all be in one file in a subfolder of the S3 bucket you created. The name of the subfolder is based on the current date and time. To see the name of that subfolder:

```
$ aws s3 ls ${BUCKET_NAME}/
```

---

10. https://console.aws.amazon.com/athena

Now, list the contents of that subfolder:

```
$ aws s3 ls ${BUCKET_NAME}/SUBFOLDER/
```

You'll see that there are three files: a data file with a name like 5d2bf1ba-829e-402f-a9a4-2849b974be01, a manifest file, and a _SUCCESS file. Delete the latter two files, as they only contain metadata from Data Pipeline and will interfere with our Athena queries:

```
$ aws s3 rm ${BUCKET_NAME}/SUBFOLDER/manifest
$ aws s3 rm ${BUCKET_NAME}/SUBFOLDER/_SUCCESS
```

Now come back to the Athena console because you're ready to run queries against the (now-sanitized) S3 folder. Let's start with fetching 10 rows at random (see the figure that follows):

```
SELECT * FROM sensor_data LIMIT 10;
```

	sensorid	timestamp	temperature
1	{s=sensor-2}	{n=1495247362}	{n=80.08000183105469}
2	{s=sensor-2}	{n=1495247364}	{n=80.06999969482422}
3	{s=sensor-2}	{n=1495247366}	{n=80.06999969482422}
4	{s=sensor-2}	{n=1495247369}	{n=80.08000183105469}
5	{s=sensor-2}	{n=1495247371}	{n=80.06999969482422}
6	{s=sensor-2}	{n=1495247373}	{n=80.08000183105469}
7	{s=sensor-2}	{n=1495247376}	{n=80.08000183105469}
8	{s=sensor-2}	{n=1495247378}	{n=80.06999969482422}
9	{s=sensor-2}	{n=1495247380}	{n=80.08000183105469}
10	{s=sensor-2}	{n=1495247383}	{n=80.08999633789062}

Here are some other queries that you can run:

```
/* List the sensors for which you have data */
SELECT DISTINCT sensorid.s AS SensorId FROM sensor_data;
/* Get the number of readings from a specific sensor */
SELECT COUNT(*) AS NumberOfReadings FROM sensor_data
  WHERE sensorid.s = 'some-sensor-id';
/* Find the average temperature measured by a specific sensor */
SELECT AVG(temperature.n) AS AverageTemp FROM sensor_data
  WHERE sensorid.s = 'some-sensor-id';
/* Find the average temperature across all sensors */
SELECT AVG(temperature.n) AS AverageTempAllSensors FROM sensor_data;
/* Find the average temperature from a specific sensor */
SELECT AVG(temperature.n) AS AverageTemp FROM sensor_data
  WHERE sensorid.s = 'some-sensor-id';
/* Find the maximum temperature across all sensors */
SELECT MAX(temperature.n) AS MaxTemp FROM sensor_data;
/* Find the standard deviation for temperature across all sensors */
SELECT STDDEV(temperature.n) AS StdDev FROM sensor_data;
```

Production Ready? Not Quite

The system that we've built here—the Kinesis/Lambda/DynamoDB pipeline plus Athena querying layer—has served us well in exploring these services, but you wouldn't want to use it as a production system. Why? Because it's built on the assumption that there's only one table.

In reality, data in DynamoDB is often spread across many tables, while querying that data involves knowing in which tables the right data lives (one *could* call this *tertiary indexing* but the authors are unaware of this usage in the wild!). For our sensor data use case, that may involve, for example, storing data from different days in different tables and automatically writing new sensor data to the correct table.

To make a setup like that work, you could auto-infer the table name from the current date in the Lambda function, like this:

```
var date = new Date().toJSON().slice(0,10).replace(/-/g, '-');
var tableName = `sensor-data-${date}`;
var item = {
  TableName: tableName,
  Item: {
    // item data
  }
}
```

The name of each table in this setup would be of the form sensor-data-YYYY-MM-DD. You could create DynamoDB tables for specific dates in advance, along with S3 buckets for holding JSON data and Athena external table definitions for those different buckets. This would, in turn, enable you to run queries *across* DynamoDB tables and thus to gather metrics across days. A query like this, for example, would find the average temperature for all sensors across two days' worth of readings:

```
SELECT (
  (SELECT SUM(temperature.n) FROM sensor_data_05_01_2017) +
    (SELECT SUM(temperature.n) FROM sensor_data_05_02_2017)
  ) / (
  (SELECT COUNT(temperature.n) FROM sensor_data_05_01_2017) +
    (SELECT COUNT(temperature.n) FROM sensor_data_05_02_2017)
);
```

What a ride! We just combined five AWS services—DynamoDB, Kinesis, Lambda, DataPipeline, and Athena, plus some helper services like IAM—into a cohesive platform for sensor data.

Day 3 Homework

Find

1. We added a global secondary index to our SensorData table, which increased our disk space usage. Read some documentation[11] to see how much space GSIs use.

2. The Athena service enables you to use a broad palette of SQL commands for running queries against S3 buckets—but not *all* the commands you may be used to. Do some Googling and find out which commands are and aren't supported.

Do

1. Exercise 1 in the homework for Day 2 called for modifying the data pipeline to handle humidity readings from our mock sensors. Modify the sensor data input script from Day 3 so that each sensor reading contains a humidity reading. Make sure to use a random walk logic to keep those readings relatively un-volatile. Then create a new external table in Athena that can run queries against that new data model.

2. In the last section of Day 3, we stated that the data pipeline we built isn't quite production ready because we have only one table and that a better system would store data from different days in different tables. Begin building that system to the best of your ability, given what you've learned so far.

Wrap-Up

This chapter has been quite a ride! We explored not just the very interesting and powerful DynamoDB but also a broad swathe of AWS offerings, and we built a pretty darned scalable data pipeline for use in a far-away datacenter. DynamoDB presents us not just with a relatively ops-free experience but always with a data model that sits in a nice middle point between the granularity of SQL and the minimalism of most NoSQL data models.

DynamoDB's Strengths

The strengths of DynamoDB have been on display throughout this chapter. It enables you to skip all the installation and setup steps and get started building immediately. And if you build something small, there are few intrinsic limits to

---

11. http://docs.aws.amazon.com/amazondynamodb/latest/developerguide/GSI.html

how big it can get (*if*, of course, you have the budget for it). DynamoDB can be tricky in places, especially when it comes to things like capacity provisioning, planning for indexes, and coming up with a data model that enables you to take advantage of DynamoDB's performance and scalability. But getting past the tricky parts unlocks a lot of possibilities.

Although DynamoDB requires you to give up some of the querying power of relational databases, its data and querying models provide some powerful constructs, such as indexes and range queries, that you won't find in a lot of NoSQL databases. And if you run into barriers, such as the inability to write SQL-style queries for tables, you may be able to use an external service to fill in the gaps, as we did on Day 3. Beyond all of this, DynamoDB's feature set continues to expand, as does the constellation of services surrounding DynamoDB in the AWS ecosystem.

DynamoDB's Weaknesses

The drawbacks presented by DynamoDB are directly reminiscent of other NoSQL databases. Despite some interesting querying and modeling constructs, you're probably better off using Postgres or another relational database unless you know for sure that you're dealing with a DynamoDB-shaped problem (or maybe an HBase-shaped problem, or Mongo, and so on). Even if you have a use case that truly calls for a big NoSQL database, you may have trouble getting your data model to mesh well with DynamoDB's partitioning system. And as always, there's the cost. Any database you use is going to cost money *somehow*, but DynamoDB and others don't always make financial sense. There may be times when it makes sense to run databases yourself, maybe on your own hardware and maybe in the cloud. Caveat emptor.

Parting Thoughts

Cloud databases aren't everyone's cup of tea. They require a lot of trust—trust in massive systems whose internals you can't see and trust in the future economic prospects of cloud providers themselves. These and other drawbacks are real, but there are some major upsides, as we hope to have shown in this chapter. We urge anybody with a strong interest in databases to give them a try. Even if you don't ever have a use case that requires a database like DynamoDB, we think that they're greatly empowering for developers and just downright fun. They turn your humble little laptop into a very powerful orchestration platform.

DynamoDB is a good place to start but we focused on it here mostly due to its influence and market share. There are *many* other options. If you want a DynamoDB-style experience with a SQL favor, have a look at Google's BigQuery or Amazon's Redshift. For globally distributed databases, try Google Cloud Spanner, CockroachDB, or FaunaDB. We reckon that the database landscape is starting to lean strongly in the direction of the cloud and the ops-free lifestyle. The next edition of this book may even feature several cloud databases.

## CHAPTER 8

Redis

Redis is like grease. It's most often used to lubricate moving parts and keep them working smoothly by reducing friction and speeding up their overall function. Whatever the machinery of your system, it could very well be improved with a bit poured over it. Sometimes the answer to your problem is simply a judicious use of more Redis.

First released in 2009, Redis (*REmote DIctionary Service*) is a simple-to-use key-value store with a sophisticated set of commands. And when it comes to speed, Redis is hard to beat. Reads are fast and writes are even faster, handling upwards of 100,000 SET operations per second by some benchmarks. Redis creator Salvatore Sanfilippo (aka antirez) refers to his project as a "data structure server" to capture its nuanced handling of complex datatypes and other features. Exploring this super-fast, more-than-just-a-key-value-store will round out our view of the modern database landscape.

Data Structure Server Store

It can be a bit difficult to classify exactly what Redis *is*. At a basic level, it's a key-value store, of course, but that simple label doesn't really do it justice. Redis supports advanced data structures, though not to the degree that a document-oriented database would. It supports set-based query operations but not with the granularity or type support you'd find in a relational database. And, of course, it's *fast*, trading durability for raw speed.

In addition to being an advanced data structure server, Redis can also be used as a blocking queue (or stack) and a publish-subscribe system. It features configurable expiry policies, durability levels, and replication options. All of this makes Redis more of a toolkit of useful data structure algorithms and processes than a member of any specific database genre.

Redis's expansive list of client libraries makes it a drop-in option for many programming languages. It's not simply easy to use; it's a joy. If an API is UX for programmers, then Redis should be in the Museum of Modern Art alongside the Mac Cube.

In Days 1 and 2, we'll explore Redis's features, conventions, and configuration. Starting with simple CRUD operations, like always, we'll quickly move on to more advanced operations involving more powerful data structures: lists, hashes, sets, and sorted sets. We'll create transactions and manipulate data expiry characteristics. We'll use Redis to create a simple message queue and explore its publish-subscribe functionality. Then we'll dive into Redis's configuration and replication options, learning how to strike an application-appropriate balance between data durability and speed.

Databases are often and increasingly used in concert with each other. Redis is introduced last in this book so that we can use it in just such a manner. In Day 3, we'll build our capstone system, a rich multidatabase music solution including Redis, CouchDB, Neo4J, and Postgres—using Node.js to cement it together.

Day 1: CRUD and Datatypes

Because the command-line interface (CLI) is of such primary importance to the Redis development team—and loved by users everywhere—we're going to spend Day 1 looking at many of the 160+ commands available. Of primary importance are Redis's sophisticated datatypes and how they can query in ways that go far beyond simply "retrieve the value of this key."

Getting Started

Redis is available through a few package builders such as Homebrew for Mac but is also rather painless to build from source.[1] We'll be working off version 3.2.8. Once you have it installed, you can start up the server by calling this:

```
$ redis-server
```

It won't run in the background by default, but you can make that happen by appending &, or you can just open another terminal. Next, run the command-line tool, which should connect to the default port 6379 automatically.

```
$ redis-cli
```

After you connect, let's try to ping the server.

---

1.   http://redis.io

```
redis 127.0.0.1:6379> PING
PONG
```

If you cannot connect, you'll receive an error message. Typing help will display a list of help options. Type help followed by a space and then start typing any command. If you don't know any Redis commands, just start pressing Tab to cycle through your options.

```
redis 127.0.0.1:6379> help
redis-cli 3.2.8
To get help about Redis commands type:
      "help @<group>" to get a list of commands in <group>
      "help <command>" for help on <command>
      "help <tab>" to get a list of possible help topics
      "quit" to exit
```

Today we're going to use Redis to build the back end for a URL shortener, such as tinyurl.com or bit.ly. A URL shortener is a service that takes a really long URL and maps it to a shorter version on their own domain—like mapping http://supercalifragilisticexpialidocious.com to http://bit.ly/VLD. Visiting that short URL redirects users to the longer, mapped URL, which saves the visitors from text messaging long strings and also provides the short URL creator with some statistics, such as a count of visits.

In Redis, we can use SET to key a shortcode like 7wks to a value like http://www.sevenweeks.org. SET always requires two parameters: a key and a value. Retrieving the value just needs GET and the key name.

```
redis 127.0.0.1:6379> SET 7wks http://www.sevenweeks.org/
OK
redis 127.0.0.1:6379> GET 7wks
"http://www.sevenweeks.org/"
```

To reduce traffic, we can also set multiple values with MSET, like any number of key-value pairs. Here we map Google.com to gog and Yahoo.com to yah.

```
redis 127.0.0.1:6379> MSET gog http://www.google.com yah http://www.yahoo.com
OK
```

Correlatively, MGET grabs multiple keys and returns values as an ordered list.

```
redis 127.0.0.1:6379> MGET gog yah
1) "http://www.google.com/"
2) "http://www.yahoo.com/"
```

Although Redis stores strings, it recognizes integers and provides some simple operations for them. If we want to keep a running total of how many short keys are in our dataset, we can create a count and then increment it with the INCR command.

```
redis 127.0.0.1:6379> SET count 2
OK
redis 127.0.0.1:6379> INCR count
(integer) 3
redis 127.0.0.1:6379> GET count
"3"
```

Although GET returns count as a string, INCR recognized it as an integer and added one to it. Any attempt to increment a non-integer ends poorly.

```
redis 127.0.0.1:6379> SET bad_count "a"
OK
redis 127.0.0.1:6379> INCR bad_count
(error) ERR value is not an integer or out of range
```

If the value can't be resolved to an integer, Redis rightly complains. You can also increment by any integer (INCRBY) or decrement (DECR, DECRBY).

Transactions

You've seen transactions in previous databases (Postgres and Neo4j), and Redis's MULTI block atomic commands are a similar concept. Wrapping two operations like SET and INCR in a single block will complete either successfully or not at all. But you will never end up with a partial operation.

Let's key another shortcode to a URL and also increment the count all in one transaction. We begin the transaction with the MULTI command and execute it with EXEC.

```
redis 127.0.0.1:6379> MULTI
OK
redis 127.0.0.1:6379> SET prag http://pragprog.com
QUEUED
redis 127.0.0.1:6379> INCR count
QUEUED
redis 127.0.0.1:6379> EXEC
1) OK
2) (integer) 4
```

When using MULTI, the commands aren't actually executed when we define them (similar to Postgres transactions). Instead, they are queued and then executed in sequence.

Similar to ROLLBACK in SQL, you can stop a transaction with the DISCARD command, which will clear the transaction queue. Unlike ROLLBACK, it won't revert the database; it will simply not run the transaction at all. The effect is identical, although the underlying concept is a different mechanism (transaction rollback vs. operation cancellation).

Complex Datatypes

So far, we haven't seen much complex behavior. Storing string and integer values under keys—even as transactions—is all fine and good, but most programming and data storage problems deal with many types of data. Storing lists, hashes, sets, and sorted sets natively helps explain Redis's popularity, and after exploring the complex operations you can enact on them, you may find you agree.

These collection datatypes can contain a huge number of values (up to 2^32 elements or more than 4 billion) per key. That's more than enough for all Facebook accounts to live as a list under a single key (though maybe not for much longer!).

While some Redis commands may appear cryptic, they generally follow a repeated pattern. SET commands begin with S, hashes with H, and sorted sets with Z. List commands generally start with either an L (for left) or an R (for right), depending on the direction of the operation (such as LPUSH).

Hashes

Hashes are like nested Redis objects that can take any number of key-value pairs. Let's use a hash to keep track of users who sign up for our URL-shortening service.

Hashes are nice because they help you avoid storing data with artificial key prefixes. (Note that we will use colons [:] within our keys. This is a valid character that often logically separates a key into segments. It's merely a matter of convention, with no deeper meaning in Redis.)

```
redis 127.0.0.1:6379> MSET user:luc:name "Luc" user:luc:password s3cret
OK
redis 127.0.0.1:6379> MGET user:luc:name user:luc:password
1) "Luc"
2) "s3cret"
```

Instead of separate keys, we can create a hash that contains its own key-value pairs.

```
redis 127.0.0.1:6379> HMSET user:luc name "Luc" password s3cret
OK
```

We only need to keep track of the single Redis key to retrieve all values of the hash.

```
redis 127.0.0.1:6379> HVALS user:luc
1) "Luc"
2) "s3cret"
```

Or we can retrieve all hash keys.

```
redis 127.0.0.1:6379> HVALS user:luc
1) "name"
2) "password"
```

Or we can get a single value by passing in the Redis key followed by the hash key. Here we get just the password.

```
redis 127.0.0.1:6379> HGET user:luc password
"s3cret"
```

Unlike the document databases MongoDB and CouchDB, hashes in Redis cannot nest (nor can any other complex datatype such as lists). In other words, hashes can store only string values and not, say, sets or nested hashes.

More hash-specific commands exist to delete hash fields (HDEL), increment an integer field value by some count (HINCRBY), retrieve the number of fields in a hash (HLEN), get all keys *and* values (HGETALL), set a value only if the key doesn't yet exist (HSETNX), and more.

Lists

Lists contain multiple ordered values that can act both as queues (first value in, first value out) and as stacks (last value in, first value out). They also have more sophisticated actions for inserting somewhere in the middle of a list, constraining list size, and moving values between lists.

Because our URL-shortening service can now track users, we want to allow them to keep a wishlist of URLs they'd like to visit. To create a list of short-coded websites we'd like to visit, we set the key to USERNAME:wishlist and push any number of values to the right (end) of the list.

```
redis 127.0.0.1:6379> RPUSH eric:wishlist 7wks gog prag
(integer) 3
```

Like most collection value insertions, the Redis command returns the number of values pushed. In other words, we pushed three values into the list so it returns 3. You can get the list length at any time with LLEN.

Using the list range command LRANGE, we can retrieve any part of the list by specifying the first and last positions. All list operations in Redis use a zero-based index. A negative position means the number of steps from the end.

```
redis 127.0.0.1:6379> LRANGE eric:wishlist 0 -1
1) "7wks"
2) "gog"
3) "prag"
```

LREM removes from the given key some matching values. It also requires a number to know how many matches to remove. Setting the count to 0 as we do here just removes them all:

```
redis 127.0.0.1:6379> LREM eric:wishlist 0 gog
```

Setting the count greater than 0 will remove only that number of matches, and setting the count to a negative number will remove that number of matches but scan the list from the end (right side).

To remove and retrieve each value in the order we added them (like a queue), we can pop them off from the left (head) of the list.

```
redis 127.0.0.1:6379> LPOP eric:wishlist
"7wks"
```

To act as a stack, after you RPUSH the values, you would RPOP from the end of the list. All of these operations are performed in constant time (meaning that the size of the list shouldn't impact performance).

On the previous combination of commands, you can use LPUSH and RPOP to similar effect (a queue) or LPUSH and LPOP to be a stack.

Suppose we wanted to remove values from our wishlist and move them to another list of visited sites. To execute this move atomically, we might try wrapping pop and push actions within a multiblock. In Ruby, these steps might look something like this (you can't use the CLI here because you must save the popped value, so we'll use the redis-rb gem):

```ruby
redis.multi do
  site = redis.rpop('eric:wishlist')
  redis.lpush('eric:visited', site)
end
```

Because the multi block queues requests, the above won't work. This is really a feature of lists, not a bug because it prevents concurrent access to list members. Fortunately, Redis provides a single command for popping values from the tail of one list and pushing to the head of another. It's called RPOPLPUSH (right pop, left push).

```
redis 127.0.0.1:6379> RPOPLPUSH eric:wishlist eric:visited
"prag"
```

If you find the range of the wishlist, prag will be gone; it now lives under visited. This is a useful mechanism for queuing commands.

If you looked through the Redis docs to find RPOPRPUSH, LPOPLPUSH, and LPOPRPUSH commands, you may be dismayed to learn they don't exist. RPOPLPUSH is your only option, and you must build your list accordingly.

Blocking Lists

Now that our URL shortener is taking off, let's add some social activities—like a real-time commenting system—where people can post about the websites they have visited.

Let's write a simple messaging system where multiple clients can push comments and one client (the digester) pops messages from the queue. We'd like the digester to just listen for new comments and pop them as they arrive. Redis provides a few blocking commands for this sort of purpose.

First, open another terminal and start another redis-cli client. This will be our digester. The command to block until a value exists to pop is BRPOP. It requires the key to pop a value from and a timeout in seconds, which we'll set to five minutes.

```
redis 127.0.0.1:6379> BRPOP comments 300
```

Then switch back to the first console and push a message to comments.

```
redis 127.0.0.1:6379> LPUSH comments "Prag is a great publisher!"
```

If you switch back to the digester console, two lines will be returned: the key and the popped value. The console will also output the length of time it spent blocking.

```
1) "comments"
2) "Prag is a great publisher!"
(7.88s)
```

There's also a blocking version of left pop (BLPOP) and left push (BRPOPLPUSH). BLPOP will remove the first element in a list or block (just like BRPOP removed the last element) while BRPOPLPUSH is a blocking version of RPOPLPUSH.

Sets

Our URL shortener is shaping up nicely, but it would be nice to be able to group common URLs in some way.

Sets are unordered collections with no duplicate values and are an excellent choice for performing complex operations between two or more key values, such as unions or intersections.

If we wanted to categorize sets of URLs with a common key, we could add multiple values with SADD.

```
redis 127.0.0.1:6379> SADD news nytimes.com pragprog.com
(integer) 2
```

Redis added two values. We can retrieve the full set, in no particular order, using the SMEMBERS command.

```
redis 127.0.0.1:6379> SMEMBERS news
1) "pragprog.com"
2) "nytimes.com"
```

Let's add another category called *tech* for technology-related sites.

```
redis 127.0.0.1:6379> SADD tech pragprog.com apple.com
(integer) 2
```

To find the intersection of websites that both provide news and are technology focused, we use the SINTER command.

```
redis 127.0.0.1:6379> SINTER news tech
1) "pragprog.com"
```

Just as easily, we can remove any matching values in one set from another. To find all news sites that are not tech sites, use SDIFF:

```
redis 127.0.0.1:6379> SDIFF news tech
1) "nytimes.com"
```

We can also build a union of websites that are either news or tech. Because it's a set, any duplicates are dropped.

```
redis 127.0.0.1:6379> SUNION news tech
1) "apple.com"
2) "pragprog.com"
3) "nytimes.com"
```

That set of values can also be stored directly into a new set (SUNIONSTORE destination key [key ...]).

```
redis 127.0.0.1:6379> SUNIONSTORE websites news tech
redis 127.0.0.1:6379> SMEMBERS websites
1) "pragprog.com"
2) "nytimes.com"
3) "apple.com"
```

This also provides a useful trick for cloning a single key's values to another key, such as SUNIONSTORE news_copy news. Similar commands exist for storing intersections (SINTERSTORE) and diffs (SDIFFSTORE).

Just as RPOPLPUSH moved values from one list to another, SMOVE does the same for sets; it's just easier to remember. And like LLEN finds the length of a list, SCARD (set cardinality) counts the set; it's just harder to remember.

Because sets are not ordered, there are no left, right, or other positional commands. Popping a random value from a set just requires SPOP key, and removing values is SREM key value [value ...].

Unlike lists, there are no blocking commands for sets. With no blocking or positional commands, sets are a subpar choice for some Redis use cases such as message queues, but they're nonetheless great for all kinds of operations over collections.

Sorted Sets

Whereas other Redis datatypes we've looked at so far easily map to common programming language constructs, sorted sets take something from each of the previous datatypes. They are ordered like lists and are unique like sets. They have field-value pairs like hashes, but their fields are numeric scores that denote the order of the values rather than plain strings. You can think of sorted sets as similar to a random access priority queue. This power has a trade-off, however. Internally, sorted sets keep values in order, so inserts can take log(N) time to insert (where N is the size of the set), rather than the constant time complexity of hashes or lists.

Next, we want to keep track of the popularity of specific shortcodes. Every time someone visits a URL, the score gets increased. Like a hash, adding a value to a sorted set requires two values after the Redis key name: the score and the member.

```
redis 127.0.0.1:6379> ZADD visits 500 7wks 9 gog 9999 prag
(integer) 3
```

To increment a score, we can either re-add it with the new score, which just updates the score but does not add a new value, or increment by some number, which will return the new value.

```
redis 127.0.0.1:6379> ZINCRBY visits 1 prag
"10000"
```

You can decrement also by setting a negative number for ZINCRBY.

Ranges

To get values from our visits set, we can issue a range command, ZRANGE, which returns by position, just like the list datatype's LRANGE command. Except in the case of a sorted set, the position is ordered by score from lowest to highest. So, to get the top two scoring visited sites (zero-based), use this:

```
redis 127.0.0.1:6379> ZRANGE visits 0 1
1) "gog"
2) "7wks"
```

To get the scores of each element as well, append WITHSCORES to the previous code. To get them in reverse, insert the word REV, as in ZREVRANGE.

```
redis 127.0.0.1:6379> ZREVRANGE visits 0 -1 WITHSCORES
1) "prag"
2) "10000"
3) "7wks"
4) "500"
5) "gog"
6) "9"
```

But if we're using a sorted set, it's more likely we want to range by score, rather than by position. ZRANGEBYSCORE has a slightly different syntax from ZRANGE. Because the low and high range numbers are *inclusive* by default, we can make a score number *exclusive* by prefixing it with an opening paren: (. So this will return all scores where 9 <= score <= 10,000:

```
redis 127.0.0.1:6379> ZRANGEBYSCORE visits 9 9999
1) "gog"
2) "7wks"
```

But the following will return 9 < score <= 10,000:

```
redis 127.0.0.1:6379> ZRANGEBYSCORE visits (9 9999
1) "7wks"
```

We can also range by both positive and negative values, including infinities. This returns the entire set.

```
redis 127.0.0.1:6379> ZRANGEBYSCORE visits -inf inf
1) "gog"
2) "7wks"
3) "prag"
```

You can list them in reverse, too, with ZREVRANGEBYSCORE.

```
redis 127.0.0.1:6379> ZREVRANGEBYSCORE visits inf -inf
1) "prag"
2) "7wks"
3) "gog"
```

Along with retrieving a range of values by rank (index) or score, ZREMRANGE-BYRANK and ZREMRANGEBYSCORE, respectively, remove values by rank or score.

Unions

Just like the set datatype, we can create a destination key that contains the union or intersection of one or more keys. This is one of the more complex commands in Redis because it must not only join the keys—a relatively simple operation—but also merge (possibly) differing scores. The union operation looks like this:

```
ZUNIONSTORE destination numkeys key [key ...]
  [WEIGHTS weight [weight ...]] [AGGREGATE SUM|MIN|MAX]
```

destination is the key to store into, and key is one or more keys to union. numkeys is simply the number of keys you're about to join, while weight is the optional number to multiply each score of the relative key by (if you have two keys, you can have two weights, and so on). Finally, aggregate is the optional rule for resolving each weighted score and summing by default, but you can also choose the min or max between many scores.

Let's use this command to measure the importance of a sorted set of short-codes. First, we'll create another key that scores our shortcodes by votes. Each visitor to a site can vote if they like the site or not, and each vote adds a point.

```
redis 127.0.0.1:6379> ZADD votes 2 7wks 0 gog 9001 prag
(integer) 3
```

We want to figure out the most important websites in our system as some combination of votes and visits. Votes are important, but to a lesser extent, website visits also carry some weight (perhaps people are so enchanted by the website, they simply forget to vote). We want to add the two types of scores together to compute a new importance score while giving votes a weight of double importance—multiplied by two.

```
redis 127.0.0.1:6379> ZUNIONSTORE imp 2 visits votes WEIGHTS 1 2 AGGREGATE SUM
(integer) 3
redis 127.0.0.1:6379> ZRANGEBYSCORE imp -inf inf WITHSCORES
1) "gog"
2) "9"
3) "7wks"
4) "504"
5) "prag"
6) "28002"
```

This command is powerful in other ways, too. For example, if you need to double all scores of a set, you can union a single key with a weight of 2 and store it back into itself.

```
redis 127.0.0.1:6379> ZUNIONSTORE votes 1 votes WEIGHTS 2
(integer) 2
redis 127.0.0.1:6379> ZRANGE votes 0 -1 WITHSCORES
1) "gog"
2) "0"
3) "7wks"
4) "4"
5) "prag"
6) "18002"
```

Sorted sets contain a similar command (ZINTERSTORE) to perform intersections.

Expiry

Another common use case for a key-value system like Redis is as a fast-access cache for data that's more expensive to retrieve or compute. In just about any cache, ensuring that keys expire after a designated time period is essential to keeping the key set from growing unboundedly.

Marking a key for expiration requires the EXPIRE command, an existing key, and a time to live (in seconds). Here we set a key and set it to expire in ten seconds. We can check whether the key EXISTS within ten seconds and it returns a 1 (true). If we wait to execute, it will eventually return a 0 (false).

```
redis 127.0.0.1:6379> SET ice "I'm melting..."
OK
redis 127.0.0.1:6379> EXPIRE ice 10
(integer) 1
redis 127.0.0.1:6379> EXISTS ice
(integer) 1
redis 127.0.0.1:6379> EXISTS ice
(integer) 0
```

Setting and expiring keys is so common that Redis provides a shortcut command called SETEX.

```
redis 127.0.0.1:6379> SETEX ice 10 "I'm melting..."
```

You can query the time a key has to live with TTL. Setting ice to expire as shown earlier and checking its TTL will return the number of seconds left (or -2 if the key has already expired or doesn't exist, which is the same thing).

```
redis 127.0.0.1:6379> TTL ice
(integer) 4
```

At any moment before the key expires, you can remove the timeout by running PERSIST key.

```
redis 127.0.0.1:6379> PERSIST ice
```

For marking a countdown to a specific time, EXPIREAT accepts a Unix timestamp (as seconds since January 1, 1970) rather than a number of seconds to count up to. In other words, EXPIREAT is for absolute timeouts, and EXPIRE is for relative timeouts.

A common trick for keeping only recently used keys is to update the expire time whenever you retrieve a value. This is the most recently used (MRU) caching algorithm to ensure that your most recently used keys will remain in Redis, while the unused keys will just expire as normal.

Database Namespaces

So far, we've interacted only with a single namespace. Sometimes we need to separate keys into multiple namespaces. For example, if you wrote an internationalized key-value store, you could store different translated responses in different namespaces. The key greeting could be set to "guten Tag" in a German namespace and "bonjour" in French. When a user selects their language, the application just pulls all values from the namespace assigned.

In Redis nomenclature, a namespace is called a *database* and is keyed by number. So far, we've always interacted with the default namespace 0 (also known as database 0). Here we set greeting to the English hello.

```
redis 127.0.0.1:6379> SET greeting hello
OK
redis 127.0.0.1:6379> GET greeting
"hello"
```

But if we switch to another database via the SELECT command, that key is unavailable.

```
redis 127.0.0.1:6379> SELECT 1
OK
redis 127.0.0.1:6379[1]> GET greeting
(nil)
```

And setting a value to this database's namespace will not affect the value of the original.

```
redis 127.0.0.1:6379[1]> SET greeting "guten Tag"
OK
redis 127.0.0.1:6379[1]> SELECT 0
OK
redis 127.0.0.1:6379> GET greeting
"hello"
```

Because all databases are running in the same server instance, Redis lets us shuffle keys around with the MOVE command. Here we move greeting to database 2:

```
redis 127.0.0.1:6379> MOVE greeting 2
(integer) 2
redis 127.0.0.1:6379> SELECT 2
OK
redis 127.0.0.1:6379[2]> GET greeting
"hello"
```

This can be useful for running different applications against a single Redis server while still allowing these multiple applications to trade data between each other.

And There's More

Redis has plenty of other commands for actions such as renaming keys (RENAME), determining the type of a key's value (TYPE), and deleting a key-value (DEL). There's also the painfully dangerous FLUSHDB, which removes all keys from this Redis database, and its apocalyptic cousin, FLUSHALL, which removes all keys from all Redis databases. We won't cover all commands here, but we recommend checking out the online documentation for the full list of Redis commands (and we must say, the Redis documentation is truly a joy to read and interact with).

Day 1 Wrap-Up

The datatypes of Redis and the complex queries it can perform make it much more than a standard key-value store. It can act as a stack, queue, or priority queue; you can interact with it as you would an object store (via hashes); and Redis even can perform complex set operations such as unions, intersections, and subtractions (diff). It provides many atomic commands as well as a transaction mechanism for multistep commands. Plus, it has a built-in ability to expire keys, which is useful as a cache.

Day 1 Homework

Find

Find the complete Redis commands documentation, as well as the Big-O notated (O(x)) time complexity under the command details.

Do

1. Install your favorite programming language driver and connect to the Redis server. Insert and increment a value within a transaction.

2. Using your driver of choice, create a program that reads a blocking list and outputs somewhere (console, file, Socket.io, and so on) and another that writes to the same list.

Day 2: Advanced Usage, Distribution

Day 1 introduced us to Redis as a data structure server. Today, we'll build on that foundation by looking at some of the advanced functions provided by Redis, such as pipelining, the publish-subscribe model, system configuration, and replication. Beyond that, we'll look at how to create a Redis cluster, store a lot of data quickly, and use an advanced technique involving Bloom filters.

A Simple Interface

At 80,000 lines of source code, Redis is a fairly small project compared to most databases. But beyond code size, it has a simple interface that accepts the very strings we have been writing in the console.

Telnet

We can interact without the command-line interface by streaming commands through TCP on our own via telnet and terminating the command with a carriage return line feed (CRLF, or \r\n). Run Ctrl+] at any time to exit.

redis/telnet.sh
```
$ telnet localhost 6379
Trying 127.0.0.1...
Connected to localhost.
Escape character is '^]'.
SET test hello
+OK
GET test
```

```
$5
hello
SADD stest 1 99
:2
SMEMBERS stest
*2
$1
1
$2
99
```

Here we see four Redis commands as inputs (you should be able to identify them quickly) and their corresponding outputs. We can see that our input is the same as we provided in the Redis console, but the console has cleaned up the responses a bit. To give a few examples:

- Redis streams the OK status prefixed by a + sign.

- Before it returned the string *hello*, it sent $5, which means "the following string is five characters."

- After we add two set items to the test key, the number 2 is prefixed by : to represent an integer (two values were added successfully).

Finally, when we requested two items, the first line returned begins with an asterisk and the number 2—meaning there are two complex values about to be returned. The next two lines are just like the *hello* string but contain the string *1*, followed by the string *99*.

Pipelining

We can also stream our own strings one at a time by using the BSD netcat (nc) command, which is already installed on many Unix machines. With netcat, we must specifically end a line with CRLF (telnet did this for us implicitly). We also sleep for a second after the ECHO command has finished to give some time for the Redis server to return. Some nc implementations have a -q option, thus negating the need for a sleep, but not all do, so feel free to try it.

```
$ (echo -en "ECHO hello\r\n"; sleep 1) | nc localhost 6379
$5
hello
```

We can take advantage of this level of control by *pipelining* our commands, or streaming multiple commands in a single request.

```
$ (echo -en "PING\r\nPING\r\nPING\r\n"; sleep 1) | nc localhost 6379
+PONG
+PONG
+PONG
```

This can be far more efficient than pushing a single command at a time and should always be considered if it makes sense to do so—especially in transactions. Just be sure to end every command with \r\n, which is a required delimiter for the server.

publish-subscribe

On Day 1, we were able to implement a rudimentary blocking queue using the list datatype. We queued data that could be read by a blocking pop command. Using that queue, we made a very basic queue according to a publish-subscribe model. Any number of messages could be pushed to this queue, and a single queue reader would pop messages as they were available. This is powerful but limited. Under many circumstances we want a slightly inverted behavior, where several subscribers want to read the announcements of a single publisher who sends a message to all subscribers, as shown in the following figure. Redis provides some specialized publish-subscribe (or pub-sub) commands.

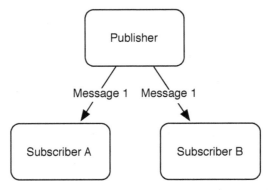

Let's improve on the commenting mechanism we made before using blocking lists, by allowing a user to post a comment to multiple subscribers (as opposed to just one). We start with a subscriber that listens on a key for messages (the key will act as a *channel* in pub-sub nomenclature). This will cause the CLI to output Reading messages... and then block while the subscriber listens for incoming messages.

```
redis 127.0.0.1:6379> SUBSCRIBE comments
Reading messages... (press Ctrl-C to quit)
1) "subscribe"
2) "comments"
3) (integer) 1
```

With two subscribers, we can publish any string we want as a message to the comments channel. The PUBLISH command will return the integer 2, meaning two subscribers received it.

```
redis 127.0.0.1:6379> PUBLISH comments "Check out this shortcoded site! 7wks"
(integer) 2
```

Both of the subscribers will receive a *multibulk reply* (a list) of three items: the string "message," the channel name, and the published message value.

```
1) "message"
2) "comments"
3) "Check out this shortcoded site! 7wks"
```

When your clients no longer want to receive correspondence, they can execute the UNSUBSCRIBE comments command to disconnect from the comments channel or simply UNSUBSCRIBE alone to disconnect from all channels. However, note that in the redis-cli console you will have to press Ctrl+C to break the connection.

Server Info

Before getting into changing Redis's system settings, it's worth taking a quick look at the INFO command because changing settings values will alter some of these values as well. INFO outputs a list of server data, including version, process ID, memory used, and uptime.

```
redis 127.0.0.1:6379> INFO
# Server
redis_version:3.2.8
redis_git_sha1:00000000
redis_git_dirty:0
redis_build_id:b533f811ec736a0c
redis_mode:standalone
...
```

You may want to revisit this command again in this chapter because it provides a useful snapshot of this server's global information and settings. It even provides information on durability, memory fragmentation, and replication server status.

Redis Configuration

So far, we've only used Redis with its out-of-the-box configuration. But much of Redis's power comes from its configurability, allowing you to tailor settings to your use case. The redis.conf file that comes with the distribution—found in /etc/redis on *nix systems or /usr/local/etc on Mac OS—is fairly self-explanatory, so we're going to cover only a portion of the file. We'll go through a few of the common settings in order.

```
daemonize no
port 6379
loglevel verbose
logfile stdout
database 16
```

By default, daemonize is set to *no*, which is why the server always starts up in the foreground. This is nice for testing but not very production friendly. Changing this value to *yes* will run the server in the background while setting the server's process ID in a pid file.

The next line is the default port number for this server, port 6379. This can be especially useful when running multiple Redis servers on a single machine.

loglevel defaults to verbose, but it's good to set it to notice or warning in production to cut down on the number of log events. logfile outputs to stdout (standard output, the console), but a filename is necessary if you run in daemonize mode.

database sets the number of Redis databases we have available. We saw how to switch between databases. If you plan to only ever use a single database namespace, it's not a bad idea to set this to 1 to prevent unwanted databases from being accidentally created.

Durability

Redis has a few persistence options. First is no persistence at all, which will simply keep all values in main memory. If you're running a basic caching server, this is a reasonable choice since durability always increases latency.

One of the things that sets Redis apart from other fast-access caches like memcached[2] is its built-in support for storing values to disk. By default, key-value pairs are only occasionally saved. You can run the LASTSAVE command to get a Unix timestamp of the last time a Redis disk write succeeded, or you can read the last_save_time field from the server INFO output.

You can force durability by executing the SAVE command (or BGSAVE, to asynchronously save in the background).

```
redis 127.0.0.1:6379> SAVE
```

If you read the redis-server log, you will see lines similar to this:

```
[46421] 10 Oct 19:11:50 * Background saving started by pid 52123
[52123] 10 Oct 19:11:50 * DB saved on disk
[46421] 10 Oct 19:11:50 * Background saving terminated with success
```

---

2.   http://www.memcached.org/

Another durability method is to alter the snapshotting settings in the configuration file.

Snapshotting

We can alter the rate of storage to disk by adding, removing, or altering one of the save fields. By default, there are three, prefixed by the save keyword followed by a time in seconds and a minimum number of keys that must change before a write to disk occurs. For example, to trigger a save every 5 minutes (300 seconds) if any keys change at all, you would write the following:

```
save 300 1
```

The configuration has a good set of defaults. The set means if 10,000 keys change, save in 60 seconds; if 10 keys change, save in 300 seconds, and any key changes will be saved in at least 900 seconds (15 minutes).

```
save 900 1
save 300 10
save 60 10000
```

You can add as many or as few save lines as necessary to specify precise thresholds.

Append-Only File

Redis is *eventually durable* by default, in that it asynchronously writes values to disk in intervals defined by our save settings, or it is forced to write by client-initiated commands. This is acceptable for a second-level cache or session server but is insufficient for storing data that you need to be durable, like financial data. If a Redis server crashes, our users might not appreciate having lost money.

Redis provides an append-only file (appendonly.aof) that keeps a record of all write commands. This is like the write-ahead logging we saw in Chapter 3, *HBase*, on page 53. If the server crashes before a value is saved, it executes the commands on startup, restoring its state; appendonly must be enabled by setting it to yes in the redis.conf file.

```
appendonly yes
```

Then we must decide how often a command is appended to the file. Setting always is the more durable because every command is saved. It's also slow, which often negates the reason people have for using Redis. By default, everysec is enabled, which saves up and writes commands only once a second. This is a decent trade-off because it's fast enough, and worst case you'll lose only the last one second of data. Finally, no is an option, which just lets the

OS handle flushing. It can be fairly infrequent, and you're often better off skipping the append-only file altogether rather than choosing it.

```
# appendfsync always
appendfsync everysec
# appendfsync no
```

Append-only has more detailed parameters, which may be worth reading about in the config file when you need to respond to specific production issues.

Security

Although Redis is not natively built to be a fully secure server, you may run across the requirepass setting and AUTH command in the Redis documentation. These can be safely ignored because they are merely a scheme for setting a plaintext password. Because a client can try nearly 100,000 passwords a second, it's almost a moot point, beyond the fact that plaintext passwords are inherently unsafe anyway. If you want Redis security, you're better off with a good firewall and SSH security.

Interestingly, Redis provides command-level security through obscurity, by allowing you to hide or suppress commands. Adding this to your config will rename the FLUSHALL command (remove all keys from the system) into some hard-to-guess value like c283d93ac9528f986023793b411e4ba2:

```
rename-command FLUSHALL c283d93ac9528f986023793b411e4ba2
```

If you attempt to execute FLUSHALL against this server, you'll be hit with an error. The secret command works instead.

```
redis 127.0.0.1:6379> FLUSHALL
(error) ERR unknown command 'FLUSHALL'
redis 127.0.0.1:6379> c283d93ac9528f986023793b411e4ba2
OK
```

Or better yet, we can disable the command entirely by setting it to a blank string in the configuration.

```
rename-command FLUSHALL ""
```

You can set any number of commands to a blank string, allowing you a modicum of customization over your command environment.

Tweaking Parameters

There are several more advanced settings for speeding up slow query logs, encoding details, making latency tweaks, and importing external config files. Keep in mind, though, if you run across some documentation about Redis virtual memory, simply ignore it, as that feature was removed in version 2.6.

To aid in testing your server configuration, Redis provides an excellent benchmarking tool. It connects locally to port 6379 by default and issues 10,000 requests using 50 parallel clients. We can execute 100,000 requests with the -n argument.

```
$ redis-benchmark -n 100000
====== PING (inline) ======
  100000 requests completed in 0.89 seconds
  50 parallel clients
  3 bytes payload
  keep alive: 1
99.91% <= 1 milliseconds
100.00% <= 1 milliseconds
32808.40 requests per second
...
```

Other commands are tested as well, such as SADD and LRANGE, with the more complex commands generally taking more time.

Master-Slave Replication

As with other NoSQL databases we've seen (such as MongoDB and Neo4j), Redis supports master-slave replication. One server is the master by default if you don't set it as a slave of anything. Data will be replicated to any number of slave servers.

Making slave servers is easy. We first need a copy of our redis.conf file.

```
$ cp redis.conf redis-s1.conf
```

The file will remain largely the same but with the following changes:

```
port 6380
slaveof 127.0.0.1 6379
```

If all went according to plan, you should see something similar to the following in the slave server's log when you start it:

```
$ redis-server redis-s1.conf
```

```
34648:S 28 Apr 06:42:22.496 * Connecting to MASTER 127.0.0.1:6379
34648:S 28 Apr 06:42:22.496 * MASTER <-> SLAVE sync started
34648:S 28 Apr 06:42:22.497 * Non blocking connect for SYNC fired the event.
34648:S 28 Apr 06:42:22.497 * Master replied to PING, replication can...
34648:S 28 Apr 06:42:22.497 * Partial resynchronization not possible...
34648:S 28 Apr 06:42:22.497 * Full resync from master: 4829...1f88a68bc:1
34648:S 28 Apr 06:42:22.549 * MASTER <-> SLAVE sync: receiving 76 bytes...
34648:S 28 Apr 06:42:22.549 * MASTER <-> SLAVE sync: Flushing old data
34648:S 28 Apr 06:42:22.549 * MASTER <-> SLAVE sync: Loading DB in memory
34648:S 28 Apr 06:42:22.549 * MASTER <-> SLAVE sync: Finished with success
```

And you should see the string 1 slaves output in the master log.

```
redis 127.0.0.1:6379> SADD meetings "StarTrek Pastry Chefs" "LARPers Intl."
```

If we connect the command line to our slave, we should receive our meeting list.

```
redis 127.0.0.1:6380> SMEMBERS meetings
1) "StarTrek Pastry Chefs"
2) "LARPers Intl."
```

In production, you'll generally want to implement replication for availability or backup purposes and thus have Redis slaves on different machines.

Data Dump

So far, we've talked a lot about how fast Redis is, but it's hard to get a feel for it without playing with a bit more data.

Let's insert a large dummy dataset into our Redis server. You can keep the slave running if you like, but a laptop or desktop might run quicker if you're running just a single master server. We're going to autogenerate a list of keys and values of arbitrary size, where the keys will be key1, key2, and so on, while the values will be value1, and so on.

You'll first need to install the redis Ruby gem.

```
$ gem install redis
```

There are several ways to go about inserting a large dataset, and they get progressively faster but more complex.

The simplest method is to simply iterate through a list of data and execute SET for each value using the standard redis-rb client. In our case, we don't really care what the data looks like, as we just want to look at performance, so we'll insert our randomized data.

```
redis/data_dump.rb
require 'redis'
#%w{hiredis redis/connection/hiredis}.each{|r| require r}

# the number of set operations to perform will be defined as a CLI arg
TOTAL_NUMBER_OF_ENTRIES = ARGV[0].to_i

$redis = Redis.new(:host => "127.0.0.1", :port => 6379)
$redis.flushall
count, start = 0, Time.now

(1..TOTAL_NUMBER_OF_ENTRIES).each do |n|
  count += 1
```

```
  key = "key#{n}"
  value = "value#{n}"

  $redis.set(key, value)

  # stop iterating when we reach the specified number
  break if count >= TOTAL_NUMBER_OF_ENTRIES
end
puts "#{count} items in #{Time.now - start} seconds"
```

Run the script, specifying the number of SET operations. Feel free to experiment with lower or higher numbers. Let's start with 100,000.

```
$ ruby data_dump.rb 100000
100000 items in 5.851211 seconds
```

If you want to speed up insertion—and are not running JRuby—you can optionally install the hiredis gem. It's a C driver that is considerably faster than the native Ruby driver. Just uncomment the %w{hiredis redis/connection/hiredis}.each{|r| require r} statement at the top in order to load the driver and then re-run the script. You may not see a large improvement for this type of CPU-bound operation, but we highly recommend hiredis for production Ruby use.

You will, however, see a big improvement with pipelinined operations. Here we batch 1,000 lines at a time and pipeline their insertion. You may see time reductions of 500 percent or more.

redis/data_dump_pipelined.rb
```
require 'redis'
#%w{hiredis redis/connection/hiredis}.each{|r| require r}

TOTAL_NUMBER_OF_ENTRIES = ARGV[0].to_i
BATCH_SIZE = 1000

# perform a single batch update for each number
def flush(batch)
  $redis.pipelined do
    batch.each do |n|
      key, value = "key#{n}", "value#{n}"
      $redis.set(key, value)
    end
  end
  batch.clear
end

$redis = Redis.new(:host => "127.0.0.1", :port => 6379)
$redis.flushall

batch = []
count, start = 0, Time.now
```

```
(1..TOTAL_NUMBER_OF_ENTRIES).each do |n|
  count += 1

  # push integers into an array
  batch << n

  # watch this number fluctuate between 1 and 1000
  puts "Batch size: #{batch.length}"

  # if the array grows to BATCH_SIZE, flush it
  if batch.size == BATCH_SIZE
    flush(batch)
  end

  break if count >= TOTAL_NUMBER_OF_ENTRIES
end
# flush any remaining values
flush(batch)

puts "#{count} items in #{Time.now - start} seconds"
```

```
$ ruby data_dump_pipelined.rb 100000
100000 items in 1.061089 seconds
```

This reduces the number of Redis connections required, but building the pipelined dataset has some overhead of its own. You should try it out with different numbers of batched operations when pipelining in production. For now, experiment with increasing the number of items and re-run the script using the hiredis gem for an even more dramatic performance increase.

Redis Cluster

Beyond simple replication, many Redis clients provide an interface for building a simple ad hoc distributed Redis cluster. The Ruby client supports a consistent-hashing managed cluster.

To get started with building out a managed cluster, we need another server. Unlike the master-slave setup, both of our servers will take the master (default) configuration. We copied the redis.conf file and changed the port to 6380. That's all that's required for the servers.

```
redis/data_dump_cluster.rb
require 'redis'
require 'redis/distributed'

TOTAL_NUMBER_OF_ENTRIES = ARGV[0].to_i

$redis = Redis::Distributed.new([
  "redis://localhost:6379/",
  "redis://localhost:6380/"
])
$redis.flushall
count, start = 0, Time.now
```

```ruby
(1..TOTAL_NUMBER_OF_ENTRIES).each do |n|
  count += 1

  key = "key#{n}"
  value = "value#{n}"

  $redis.set(key, value)

  break if count >= TOTAL_NUMBER_OF_ENTRIES
end
puts "#{count} items in #{Time.now - start} seconds"
```

Bridging between two or more servers requires only some minor changes to our existing data dump client. First, we need to require the redis/distributed file from the redis gem.

```ruby
require 'redis/distributed'
```

Then replace the Redis client with Redis::Distributed and pass in an array of server URIs. Each URI requires the redis scheme, server (localhost in our case), and port.

```ruby
$redis = Redis::Distributed.new([
  "redis://localhost:6379/",
  "redis://localhost:6380/"
])
```

Running the client is the same as before.

```
$ ruby data_dump_cluster.rb 10000
100000 items in 6.614907 seconds
```

We do see a performance decrease here because a lot more work is being done by the client, since it handles computing which keys are stored on which servers. You can validate that keys are stored on separate servers by attempting to retrieve the same key from each server through the CLI.

```
$ redis-cli -p 6379 --raw GET key537
$ redis-cli -p 6380 --raw GET key537
```

Only one client will be able to GET the value of value537. But as long as you retrieve keys set through the same Redis::Distributed configuration, the client will access the values from the correct servers.

Bloom Filters

A good way to improve the performance of just about *any* data retrieval system is to simply never perform queries that you *know* are doomed to fail and find no data. If you know that you dropped your car keys in your house, it's senseless to scour your neighbor's house in search of them. You should start your search operation at home, maybe starting with the couch cushions. What matters is that you can safely exclude some search avenues that you know will be fruitless.

A *Bloom filter* enables you to do something similar with database queries. These filters are probabilistic data structures that check for the nonexistence of an item in a set, first covered in *Compression and Bloom Filters*, on page 71. Although Bloom filters can return false positives, they cannot return a false negative. This is very useful when you need to quickly discover whether a value does not exist in a system. If only they made Bloom filters for lost car keys!

Bloom filters succeed at discovering nonexistence by converting a value to a very sparse sequence of bits and comparing that to a union of every value's bits. In other words, when a new value is added, it is OR'd against the current Bloom filter bit sequence. When you want to check whether the value is already in the system, you perform an AND against the Bloom filter's sequence. If the value has any true bits that aren't also true in the Bloom filter's corresponding buckets, then the value was never added. In other words, this value is definitely not in the Bloom filter. The following figure provides a graphic representation of this concept.

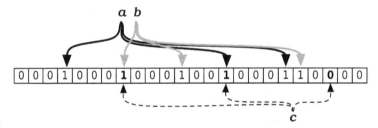

To get started writing our own Bloom filter, we need to install a new gem:

```
$ gem install bloomfilter-rb
```

Ruby wunderkind Ilya Grigorik created this Redis-backed Bloom filter, but the concepts are transferable to any language. Let's have a look at a script that looks a bit like our previous data dump script but with a few key differences.

For our example here, we'll download a text file containing the entire text of *Moby Dick* from Project Gutenberg[3] and assemble a list of all words in the text (including a *lot* of repeat words such as "the" and "a"). Then, we'll loop through each word, check if it's already in our Bloom filter, and insert it into the filter if it isn't there already.

---

3.   https://www.gutenberg.org/

```
redis/bloom_filter.rb
require 'bloomfilter-rb'

bloomfilter = BloomFilter::Redis.new(:size => 1000000)
bloomfilter.clear

# we'll read the file data and strip out all the non-word material
text_data = File.read(ARGV[0])
clean_text = text_data.gsub(/\n/, ' ').gsub(/[,-.;'?"()!*]/, '')

clean_text.split(' ').each do |word|
  word = word.downcase

  next if bloomfilter.include?(word)
  puts word
  bloomfilter.insert(word)
end

puts "Total number of words: #{text_data.length}"
puts "Number of words in filter: #{bloomfilter.size}"
```

Let's download the text using cURL and run the script:

```
$ curl -o moby-dick.txt https://www.gutenberg.org/files/2701/old/moby10b.txt
$ ruby bloom_filter.rb moby-dick.txt > output.txt
```

Open up the output.txt and scroll through the contents. Each word in this file has not yet been added to the filter. At the top of the list, you'll find a lot of common words like *the*, *a*, and *but*. At the bottom of the list, you'll see the word "orphan," which is the very last word in the Epilogue, which explains why it hadn't been added to the filter yet! Some other fairly esoteric words toward the end include "ixion," "sheathed," "dirgelike," and "intermixingly."

What essentially happened here is that the more frequently used words were more likely to get filtered out early, whereas less common words or words used only once were filtered out later. The upside with this approach is the ability to detect duplicate words. The downside is that a few false positives will seep through—the Bloom filter may flag a word we have never seen before. This is why in a real-world use case you would perform some secondary check, such as a slower database query to a system of record, which should happen only a small percentage of the time, presuming a large enough filter size, which is computable.[4]

SETBIT and GETBIT

As mentioned earlier, Bloom filters function by flipping certain bits in a sparse binary field. The Redis Bloom filter implementation we just used takes advantage of two Redis commands that perform just such actions: SETBIT and GETBIT.

---

4. http://en.wikipedia.org/wiki/Bloom_filter

Like all Redis commands, SETBIT is fairly descriptive. The command sets a single bit (either 1 or 0) at a certain location in a bit sequence, starting from zero. It's a common use case for high-performance multivariate flagging—it's faster to flip a few bits than write a set of descriptive strings.

If we want to keep track of the toppings on a hamburger, we can assign each type of topping to a bit position, such as ketchup = 0, mustard = 1, onion = 2, lettuce = 3. So, a hamburger with only mustard and onion could be represented as 0110 and set in the command line:

```
redis 127.0.0.1:6379> SETBIT my_burger 1 1
(integer) 0
redis 127.0.0.1:6379> SETBIT my_burger 2 1
(integer) 0
```

Later, a process can check whether my burger should have lettuce or mustard. If zero is returned, the answer is false—one if true.

```
redis 127.0.0.1:6379> GETBIT my_burger 3
(integer) 0
redis 127.0.0.1:6379> GETBIT my_burger 1
(integer) 1
```

The Bloom filter implementation takes advantage of this behavior by hashing a value as a multibit value. It calls SETBIT X 1 for each on position in an insert() (where X is the bit position) and verifies existence by calling GETBIT X on the include?() method—returning false if any GETBIT position returns 0.

Bloom filters are excellent for reducing unnecessary traffic to a slower underlying system, be it a slower database, limited resource, or network request. If you have a slower database of IP addresses and you want to track all new users to your site, you can use a Bloom filter to first check whether the IP address exists in your system. If the Bloom filter returns false, you know the IP address has yet to be added and can respond accordingly. If the Bloom filter returns true, this IP address may or may not exist on the back end and requires a secondary lookup to be sure. This is why computing the correct size is important—a well-sized Bloom filter can reduce (but not eliminate) the error rate or the likelihood of a false positive.

Day 2 Wrap-Up

Today we rounded out our Redis investigation by moving beyond simple operations into squeezing every last bit of speed out of an already very fast system. Redis provides for fast and flexible data structure storage and simple manipulations as we saw in Day 1, but it's equally adept at more complex behaviors by way of built-in publish-subscribe functions and bit operations.

It's also highly configurable, with many durability and replication settings that conform to whatever your needs may be. Finally, Redis also supports some nice third-party enhancements, such as Bloom filters and clustering.

This concludes major operations for the Redis data structure store. Tomorrow we're going to do something a bit different, by using Redis as the cornerstone of a polyglot persistence setup along with CouchDB and Neo4j.

Day 2 Homework

Find

1. Find out what messaging patterns are, and discover how many Redis can implement.

2. Read some documentation on Sentinel,[5] a system used to manage high-availability Redis clusters.

Do

1. Run the data dump script with all snapshotting and the append-only file turned off. Then try running with appendfsync set to always, noting the speed difference.

2. Using your favorite programming language's web framework, try to build a simple URL-shortening service backed by Redis with an input box for the URL and a simple redirect based on the URL. Back it up with a Redis master-slave replicated cluster across multiple nodes as your back end.

Day 3: Playing with Other Databases

Today we're wrapping up our final database chapter by inviting some other databases from the book to the Redis party. Amongst the databases we've gone over in this book, Redis is the most lightweight and modular, capable of enhancing just about any complex data setup without imposing a ton of engineering and ops overhead. Redis will hold a starring role in today's exercise by making our interaction with other databases faster and easier.

We've learned throughout this book that different databases have different strengths, so many modern systems have moved toward a *polyglot persistence model*, where many databases each play a role in the system. You will learn how to build one of these projects using CouchDB as the system of record (the canonical data source), Neo4j to handle data relationships, and Redis

---

5. http://objectrocket.com/blog/how-to/introduction-to-redis-sentinel

to help with data population and caching. Consider this your final exam for the book.

Note that our choice of databases for this last project should not be seen as the authors' endorsement of any specific set of databases, languages, or frameworks over another but rather a showcase of how multiple databases can work together, leveraging the capabilities of each in pursuit of a single goal.

A Polyglot, Persistent Service

Our polyglot persistence service will act as the backend for a web interface that provides information about bands. We want to store a list of musical band names, the artists who performed in those bands, and any number of roles each artist played in the band, from lead singer to backup keytar player to people who just dance (like the guy in Mighty Mighty Bosstones). Each of the three databases—Redis, CouchDB, and Neo4j—will handle a different aspect of our band data management system.

Redis plays three important roles in our system: It assists in populating data to CouchDB, it acts as a cache for recent Neo4j changes, and it enables quick lookup for partial value searches. Its speed and ability to store multiple data formats make it well suited for data population, and its built-in expiry policies are perfect for handling cached data.

CouchDB is our system of record (SOR), or authoritative data source. CouchDB's document structure is an easy way to store band data because it allows for nested artist and role information, and we will take advantage of the changes API[6] in CouchDB to keep our third data source in sync.

Neo4j is our relationship store. Although querying the CouchDB SOR directly is perfectly reasonable, a graph database affords us a simplicity and speed in walking node relationships that other databases have a difficult time matching. We'll store relationships between bands, band members, and the roles the members play.

Each database has a specific role to play in our system, but they don't natively communicate with another, which means that we need to build a translation layer between them. We'll use Node.js to populate the databases, communicate between them, and act as a simple front-end server. Because gluing multiple databases together requires a bit of code, this last day will include much more code than we have seen so far in this book.

---

6. http://docs.couchdb.org/en/latest/api/database/changes.html

The Rise of Polyglot Persistence

Like the growing phenomenon of polyglot programming, polyglot persistence is now well established in most corners of the database universe.

If you are unfamiliar with the practice, polyglot programming is what happens when a team uses more than one programming language in a single project. Contrast this with the convention of using one general-purpose language throughout a project or even an entire company (you may have heard of "Java shops" or "Ruby shops"). Polyglot programming is useful because each language has different inherent strengths. A language like Scala may be better suited for large "Big Data" processing tasks, whereas a language like Ruby may be friendlier for shell scripts. Used together, they create a synergy. The rise of so-called *microservice* architectures, in which services written in different languages interact with each other to form complex, unified systems, is a logical outcome of polyglot programming.

Similar to its language-centric cousin, polyglot persistence happens when you use the strengths of many kinds of database in the same system, as opposed to relying on a single database (often a relational database). A basic variant of this is already quite common: using a key-value store (such as Redis) that acts as a cache for queries against a relatively slower relational database (such as PostgreSQL). Relational models, as we've seen in previous chapters, are ill-suited for a growing host of problems, such as graph traversal. But even these new databases shine only as a few stars in the full galaxy of requirements.

Why the sudden interest in polyglot everything? Nearly a decade ago, Martin Fowler noted[a] that having a single central database that multiple applications could use as a source of truth was a common pattern in software design. This once-popular database integration pattern has given way to a *middleware layer* pattern, where multiple applications instead communicate to a service layer over HTTP or a lighter protocol, such as Thrift or Protocol Buffers. This frees up the middleware service itself to rely on any number of databases or, in the case of polyglot persistence, many types of database.

---

a.   http://martinfowler.com/bliki/DatabaseThaw.html

Population

The first item of business is to populate our databases with the necessary data. We take a two-phased approach here, by first populating Redis and then populating our CouchDB SOR. We'll be using a large dataset holding information about bands, including the names of those bands, band members, which role each band member played, and more. This dataset contains a lot of information, but we're interested only in extracting the member or artist name, the group or band name, and their roles in that band stored as a comma-separated list. For example, *John Cooper* played in the band *Skillet* as the *Lead vocalist, Acoustic guitar* player, and *Bassist*.

First, download the file holding the dataset:

```
$ curl -O [data-file-url]
```

Replace [data-file-url] with the URL in the footnote below.[7]

This file contains a lot of information, but we are interested only in extracting the member or artist name, the group or band name, and their roles in that band stored as a comma-separated list. For example, *John Cooper* played in the band *Skillet* as the *Lead vocalist, Acoustic guitar* player, and *Bassist*.

```
/m/0654bxy   John Cooper Skillet Lead vocalist,Acoustic guitar,Bass   1996
```

Ultimately we want to structure John Cooper and the other members of Skillet into a single CouchDB document like the following, stored at the URL http://localhost:5984/bands/Skillet:

```
{
  "_id": "Skillet",
  "name": "Skillet"
  "artists": [
    {
      "name": "John Cooper",
      "role": [
        "Acoustic guitar",
        "Lead vocalist",
        "Bass"
      ]
    },
    ...
    {
      "name": "Korey Cooper",
      "role": [
        "backing vocals",
        "Synthesizer",
        "Guitar",
        "Keyboard instrument"
      ]
    }
  ]
}
```

This file contains well over 100,000 band members and more than 30,000 bands. That's not many, but it's a good starting point to build your own system. Note that not all roles are documented for each artist. This is an incomplete dataset, but we can deal with that later.

---

7.   https://raw.githubusercontent.com/coderoshi/NCNRCSBuzzSpec/master/group_membership.tsv

Phase 1: Data Transformation

You may wonder why we bother populating Redis and don't just dive right into populating CouchDB. Acting as an intermediary, Redis adds structure to the flat TSV data so that subsequent insertion into another database is fast. Because our plan is to create a single record per band name, Redis allows us to make a single pass through our TSV file (which lists the same band for each band member—each band member is represented in a line). Adding single members directly to CouchDB for each line in the file can cause update thrashing, where two band member lines attempt to create/update the same band document at the same time, forcing the system to reinsert when one of them fails CouchDB's version check.

The catch with this strategy is that you're limited to the constraints of Redis to hold an entire dataset in RAM—though this limit could be overcome by the simple consistent-hashing cluster you saw on Day 2.

With our data file in hand, ensure you have Node.js installed as well as the Node Package Manager (npm). Once that's all done, we need to install three NPM projects: redis, csv, and hiredis (the optional Redis C-driver you learned about on Day 2 that can greatly speed up Redis interactions).

```
$ npm install hiredis redis csv-parser cradle
```

Then, check that your Redis server is running on the default port 6379, or alter each script's createClient() function to point to your Redis port.

You can populate Redis by running the following Node.js script in the same directory as your TSV file, which we assume is named group_membership.tsv. (All of the JavaScript files we'll look at are fairly verbose, so we don't show them in their entirety. All of the code can be downloaded from the Pragmatic Bookshelf website. Here we'll just stick to the meat of each file.) Download and run the following file:

```
$ node prePopulate.js
```

This script basically iterates through each line of the TSV and extracts the artist name, the band name, and the roles they play in that band. Then it adds those values to Redis (skipping any blank values).

The format of each Redis band key is "band:Band Name". The script will add this artist name to the set of artist names. So, the key "band:Beatles" will contain the set of values ["John Lennon", "Paul McCartney", "George Harrison", "Ringo Starr"]. The artist keys will also contain the band name and similarly contain a set of roles. "artist:Beatles:Ringo Starr" will contain the set ["Drums"].

The other code just keeps track of how many lines we've processed and outputs the results to the screen.

```
redis/prePopulate.js
var stream = csv({
  separator: '\t',
  newline: '\n'
});

fs.createReadStream(tsvFilename)
  .pipe(stream)
  .on('data', function(data) {
    var
      artist = data['member'],
      band = data['group'],
      roles = buildRoles(data['role']);

    if (artist === '' || band === '') {
      trackLineCount();
      return true;
    }

    redisClient.sadd('band:' + band, artist);

    if (roles.length > 0) {
      roles.forEach(function(role) {
        redisClient.sadd(`artist:${band}:${artist}`, role);
      });
    }

    trackLineCount();
  })
  .on('end', function(totalLines) {
    console.log(`Total lines processed: ${processedLines}`);
    redisClient.quit();
  });
```

You can test that the code has been populating Redis by launching redis-cli and executing RANDOMKEY. We should expect a key prefixed by band: or artist: ... any value but (nil) is good.

Now that Redis is populated, proceed immediately to the next section. You could lose data if you turn Redis off, *unless* you chose to set a higher durability than the default or initiated a SAVE command.

Phase 2: SOR Insertion

CouchDB will play the role of our system of record (SOR). If any data conflicts arise between Redis, CouchDB, or Neo4j, CouchDB wins. A good SOR should contain all of the data necessary to rebuild any other data source in its domain.

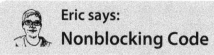

Eric says:

Nonblocking Code

Before starting this book, we were only passingly familiar with writing event-driven nonblocking applications. *Nonblocking* means precisely that: rather than waiting for a long-running process to complete, the main code will continue executing. Whatever you need to do in response to a blocking event you put inside a function or code block to be executed later. This can be by spawning a separate thread or, in our case, implementing a reactor pattern event-driven approach.

In a blocking program, you can write code that queries a database, waits, and loops through the results.

```
results = database.some_query()
for value in results
  # do something with each value
end
# this is not executed until after the results are looped...
```

In an event-driven program, you would pass in the loop as a function/code block. While the database is doing its thing, the rest of the program can continue running. Only after the database returns the result does the function/code block get executed.

```
database.some_query do |results|
  for value in results
    # do something with each value
  end
end
# this continues running while the database performs its query...
```

It took us quite some time to realize the benefits here. The rest of the program can run rather than sitting idle while it waits on the database, sure, but is this common? Apparently so, because when we began coding in this style, we noticed an order-of-magnitude decrease in latency.

We try to keep the code as simple as we can, but interacting with databases in a non-blocking way is an inherently complex process. But as we learned, it's generally a very good method when dealing with databases. Nearly every popular programming language has some sort of nonblocking library. Ruby has EventMachine, Python has Twisted, Java has the NIO library, C# has Interlace, and, of course, JavaScript has Node.js.

Ensure CouchDB is running on the default port 5984, or change the require ('http').createClient(5984, 'localhost') line in the following code to the port number you require. Redis should also still be running from the previous section. Download and run the following file:

```
$ node populateCouch.js
```

Because phase 1 was all about pulling data from a TSV and populating Redis, this phase is all about pulling data from Redis and populating CouchDB. You don't use any special drivers for CouchDB because it's a simple REST interface and Node.js has a simple built-in HTTP library.

In the following block of code, we perform a Redis KEYS bands:* to get a list of all band names in our system. If we had a *really* big dataset, we could add more scoping (for example, bands:A* to get only band names starting with *a*, and so on). Then, for each of those bands we fetch the set of artists and extract the band name from the key by removing the prefix *bands:* from the key string.

```
redis/populateCouch.js
redisClient.keys('band:*', function(err, bandKeys) {
  totalBands = bandKeys.length;
  var
    readBands = 0,
    bandsBatch = [];

  bandKeys.forEach(function(bandKey) {
    // substring of 'band:'.length gives us the band name
    var bandName = bandKey.substring(5);
    redisClient.smembers(bandKey, function(err, artists) {
```

Next, we get all of the roles for every artist in this band, which Redis returns as an array of arrays (each artists role is its own array). You can do this by batching up Redis SMEMBERS commands into an array called roleBatch and executing them in a single MULTI batch. Effectively, that would be executing a single pipelined request like this:

```
MULTI
  SMEMBERS "artist:Beatles:John Lennon"
  SMEMBERS "artist:Beatles:Ringo Starr"
EXEC
```

From there, a batch of 50 CouchDB documents is made. We build a batch of 50 because we then send the entire set to CouchDB's /_bulk_docs command, allowing us very, very fast insertion.

```
redis/populateCouch.js
redisClient.
  multi(roleBatch).
  exec(function(err, roles) {
    var
      i = 0,
      artistDocs = [];

    // build the artists sub-documents
    artists.forEach(function(artistName) {
      artistDocs.push({ name: artistName, role : roles[i++] });
    });
```

```
// add this new band document to the batch to be executed later
bandsBatch.push({
  _id: couchKeyify(bandName),
  name: bandName,
  artists: artistDocs
});
```

With the population of the bands database, we now have in a single location all of the data our system requires. We know the names of many bands, the artists who performed in them, and the roles they played in those bands.

Now would be a good time to take a break and play around with our newly populated bands system of record in CouchDB at http://localhost:5984/_utils/ database.html?bands.

Relationship Store

Next on the docket is our Neo4j service that we'll use to track relationships between artists and the roles they play. We could certainly query CouchDB outright by creating views, but we are rather limited on complex queries based on relationships. If Wayne Coyne from the Flaming Lips loses his theremin before a show, he could ask Charlie Clouser from Nine Inch Nails, who also plays a theremin. Or we could discover artists who have many overlapping talents, even if they performed different roles in different bands—all with a simple node walk.

With our initial data in place, now we need to keep Neo4j in sync with CouchDB should any data ever change on our system of record. So, we'll kill two birds by crafting a service that populates Neo4j with any changes to CouchDB since the database was created.

We also want to populate Redis with keys for our bands, artists, and roles so we can quickly access this data later. Happily, this includes all data that we've already populated in CouchDB, thus saving us a separate initial Neo4j and Redis population step.

Ensure that Neo4j is running on port 7474, or change the appropriate create-Client() function to use your correct port. CouchDB and Redis should still be running. Download and run the following file. This file will continue running until you shut it down.

```
$ node graphSync.js
```

This server just uses the continuous polling example we saw in the CouchDB chapter to track all CouchDB changes. Whenever a change is detected, we do two things: populate Redis and populate Neo4j. This code populates Redis by cascading callback functions. First it populates the band as "band-name:Band Name". It follows this pattern for artist name and roles.

This way, we can search with partial strings. For example, KEYS band-name:Bea* could return this: Beach Boys, Beastie Boys, Beatles, and so on.

redis/graphSync.js
```
function feedBandToRedis(band) {
  redisClient.set(`band-name:${band.name}`, 1);
  band.artists.forEach(function(artist) {
    redisClient.set(`artist-name:${artist.name}`, 1);
    artist.role.forEach(function(role){
      redisClient.set(`role-name:${role}`, 1);
```

The next block is how we populate Neo4j. We created a driver that you can download as part of this book's code, named neo4jCachingClient.js. It just uses Node.js's HTTP library to connect to the Neo4j REST interface with a bit of rate-limiting built in so the client doesn't open too many connections at once. Our driver also uses Redis to keep track of changes made to the Neo4j graph without having to initiate a separate query. This is our third separate use for Redis—the first being as a data transformation step for populating CouchDB, and the second we just saw earlier, to quickly search for band values.

This code creates band nodes (if they need to be created), then artist nodes (if they need to be created), and then roles. Each step along the way creates a new relationship, so The Beatles node will relate to John, Paul, George, and Ringo nodes, who in turn each relate to the roles they play.

redis/graphSync.js
```
function feedBandToNeo4j(band, progress) {
  var
    lookup = neo4jClient.lookupOrCreateNode,
    relate = neo4jClient.createRelationship;

  lookup('bands', 'name', band.name, 'Band', function(bandNode) {
    progress.emit('progress', 'band');
    band.artists.forEach(function(artist) {
      lookup('artists', 'name', artist.name, 'Artist', function(artistNode) {
        progress.emit('progress', 'artist');
        relate(bandNode.metadata.id, artistNode.self, 'member', function() {
          progress.emit('progress', 'member');
        });
        artist.role.forEach(function(role){
          lookup('roles', 'role', role, 'Role', function(roleNode) {
            progress.emit('progress', 'role');
            relate(artistNode.metadata.id, roleNode.self, 'plays', function() {
              progress.emit('progress', 'plays');
```

Let this service keep running in its own window. Every update to CouchDB that adds a new artist or role to an existing artist will trigger a new relationship in Neo4j and potentially new keys in Redis. As long as this service runs, they should be in sync.

Open your CouchDB web console and open a band. Make any data change you want to the database: add a new band member (make yourself a member of the Beatles!), or add a new role to an artist. Keep an eye on the graphSync output. Then fire up the Neo4j console and try finding any new connections in the graph. If you added a new band member, they should now have a relationship with the band node or new role if that was altered. The current implementation does not remove relationships—though it would not be a complete modification to add a Neo4j DELETE operation to the script.

The Service

This is the part we've been building up to. We're going to create a simple web application that allows users to search for a band. Any band in the system will list all of the band members as links, and any clicked band member link will list some information about the artist—namely, the roles they play. In addition, each role the artist plays will list every other artist in the system who also plays that role.

For example, searching for Led Zeppelin would give you Jimmy Page, John Paul Jones, John Bonham, and Robert Plant. Clicking Jimmy Page will list that he plays guitar and also many other artists who play guitar, like The Edge from U2.

To simplify our web app creation a bit, we'll need two more node packages: bricks (a simple web framework) and mustache (a templating library).

```
$ npm install bricks mustache neo4j-driver
```

As in the previous sections, ensure you have all of the databases running, and then start up the server. Download and run the following code:

```
$ node band.js
```

The server is set to run on port 8080, so if you point your browser to http://localhost:8080/, you should see a simple search form.

Let's take a look at the code that will build a web page that lists band information. Each URL performs a separate function in our little HTTP server. The first is at http://localhost:8080/band and accepts any band name as a parameter.

```
redis/bands.js
appServer.addRoute("^/band$", function(req, res) {
  var
    bandName = req.param('name'),
    bandNodePath = couchUtil.couchKeyify(bandName),
    membersCypherQuery =
      `MATCH (Band {name: "${bandName}"})-[:member*1..3]-(b:Band)` +
      `RETURN DISTINCT b LIMIT 10`;

  getCouchDoc(bandNodePath, res, function(couchDoc) {
    var artists = couchDoc && couchDoc['artists'];

    cypher(membersCypherQuery, function(bandsGraphData) {
      var bands = [];
      bandsGraphData.data.forEach(function(band) {
        bands.push(band[0].data.name);
      });

      var values = { band: bandName, artists: artists, bands: bands };

      var template = `
        <h2>{{band}} Band Members</h2>
        <ul>
          {{#artists}}
          <li><a href="/artist?name={{name}}">{{name}}</a></li>
          {{/artists}}
        </ul>
        <h3>You may also like</h3>
        <ul>
          {{#bands}}
          <li><a href="/band?name={{.}}">{{.}}</a></li>
          {{/bands}}
        </ul>
      `;

      writeTemplate(res, template, values);
    });
```

If you enter the band Nirvana in the search form, your URL request will be
http://localhost:8080/band?name=Nirvana. This function will render an HTML page
(the overall template is in an external file named template.html). This web page
lists all artists in a band, which it pulls directly from CouchDB. It also lists
some suggested bands, which it retrieves from a Gremlin query against the
Neo4j graph. The Gremlin query is like this for Nirvana:

```
g.V.filter{it.name=="Nirvana"}.out("member").in("member").dedup.name
```

Or in other words, from the Nirvana node, get all unique names whose
members are connected to Nirvana members. For example, Dave Grohl played
in Nirvana and the Foo Fighters, so Foo Fighters will be returned in this list.

The next action is the http://localhost:8080/artist URL. This page will output information about an artist.

```
redis/bands.js
appServer.addRoute("^/artist$", function(req, res) {
  var
    artistName = req.param('name'),
    rolesCypherQuery = `MATCH (Artist {name: "${artistName}"})` +
      `-[:plays]-(r:Role) RETURN r`,
    bandsCypherQuery = `MATCH (Artist {name: "${artistName}"})` +
      `-[:member]-(b:Band) RETURN b`;

  cypher(rolesCypherQuery, function(rolesGraphData) {
    cypher(bandsCypherQuery, function(bandsGraphData) {
      var
        roles = [],
        bands = [];

      rolesGraphData.data.forEach(function(role) {
        roles.push(role[0].data.role);
      });

      bandsGraphData.data.forEach(function(band) {
        bands.push(band[0].data.name);
      });

      var values = { artist: artistName, roles: roles, bands: bands };

      var template = `
        <h3>{{artist}} Performs these Roles</h3>
        <ul>
          {{#roles}}
          <li>{{.}}</li>
          {{/roles}}
        </ul>
        <h3>Play in Bands</h3>
        <ul>
          {{#bands}}
          <li><a href="/band?name={{.}}">{{.}}</a></li>
          {{/bands}}
        </ul>
        `;
      writeTemplate(res, template, values);
    });
  });
```

Two Gremlin queries are executed here. This first outputs all roles a member plays, and the second is a list of bands that person played in. For example, Jeff Ward (http://localhost:8080/artist?name=Jeff%20Ward) would be listed as playing the role Drummer and in the bands Nine Inch Nails and Ministry.

A cool feature of the previous two pages is that we render links between these values. The artist list in the /bands page links to the chosen /artist page, and vice versa. But we could make searching a bit easier.

```
redis/bands.js
appServer.addRoute("^/search$", function(req, res) {
  var query = req.param('term');

  redisClient.keys(`band-name:${query}*`, function(error, keys) {
    var bands = [];
    keys.forEach(function(key){
      bands.push(key.replace("band-name:", ''));
    });
    res.write(JSON.stringify(bands));
    res.end();
```

Here we just pull all keys from Redis that match the first part of the string, such as "Bea*" as described previously. The function then outputs the data as JSON. The template.html file links to the jQuery code necessary to make this function as an autocomplete feature on the rendered search box.

Expanding the Service

This is a fairly little script for all of the bare-bones work we're doing here. You may find many places you want to extend. Notice that the band suggestion is only first-order bands (bands the current band's members have performed in); you can get interesting results by writing a query to traverse second-order bands, like this: g.V.filter{it.name=='Nine Inch Nails'}.out('member').in('member').dedup. loop(3){ it.loops <= 2 }.name.

You may also note that we do not have a form where someone can update band information. Adding this functionality could be fairly simple because we already wrote CouchDB population code in the populateCouch.js script, and populating CouchDB will automatically keep Neo4j and Redis eventually consistent as long as the graph_sync.js service is running.

If you enjoy playing with this kind of polyglot persistence, you could take this even further. You could add a PostgreSQL data warehouse[8] to transform this data into a star schema—allowing for different dimensions of analysis, such as most commonly played instrument or average numbers of total members in a band vs. total instruments. You could add a CouchDB server to store information about the music associated with each band, an HBase server to build a messaging system that enables users to keep track of their historical likes/dislikes, or a MongoDB extension to add a geographic element to this service.

---

8. http://en.wikipedia.org/wiki/Data_warehouse

Or, redesign this project entirely with a different language, web framework, or dataset. There are as many opportunities to extend this project as there are combinations of databases and technologies to create it—a Cartesian product of all open source.

Day 3 Wrap-Up

Today was a big day—so big, in fact, we wouldn't be surprised if it took several days to complete. But this is a little taste of the future of data management systems, as the world strolls away from the *one large relational database* model to a *several specialized databases* model. We also glued these databases together with some nonblocking code, which, though not a focus of this book, also seems to be where database interaction is headed in the development space.

The importance of Redis in this model should not be missed. Redis certainly doesn't provide any functionality these databases don't supply individually, but it does supply speedy data structures. We were able to organize a flat file into a series of meaningful data structures, which is an integral part of both data population and transportation. And it did this in a fast and simple-to-use way.

Even if you're not sold on the whole polyglot persistence model, you should certainly consider Redis for any system.

Day 3 Homework

Do

1. Alter the importer steps to also track a band member's start and end dates with the band. Track that data in the artist's CouchDB subdocument. Display this information on the artist's page.

2. Add MongoDB into the mix by storing a few music samples into GridFS, whereby users can hear a song or two related to a band. If any song exists for a band, add a link to the web app.

Wrap-Up

The Redis key-value (or data structure) store is light and compact, with a variety of uses. It's akin to one of those multitools composed of a knife, can opener, and other bits and bobs like a corkscrew—Redis is good to have around for solving a variety of odd tasks. Above all, Redis is fast, simple, and as durable as you choose. While rarely a standalone database, Redis is a perfect complement to any polyglot ecosystem as an ever-present helper for transforming data, caching requests, or managing messages by way of its blocking commands.

Redis's Strengths

The obvious strength of Redis is speed, like so many key-value stores of its ilk. But more than most key-value stores, Redis provides the ability to store complex values such as lists, hashes, and sets, and retrieve them based on operations specific to those datatypes. Beyond even a data structure store, however, Redis's durability options allow you to trade speed for data safety up to a fairly fine point. Built-in master-slave replication is another nice way of ensuring better durability without requiring the slowness of syncing an append-only file to disk on every operation. Additionally, replication is great for very high-read systems.

Redis's Weaknesses

Redis is fast largely because it resides in memory. Some may consider this cheating because, of course, a database that never hits the disk will be fast. A main memory database has an inherent durability problem; namely, if you shut down the database before a snapshot occurs, you can lose data. Even if you set the append-only file to disk sync on every operation, you run a risk with playing back expiry values because time-based events can never be counted on to replay in exactly the same manner—though, in fairness, this case is more hypothetical than practical.

Redis also does not support datasets larger than your available RAM (Redis is removing virtual memory support), so its size has a practical limitation. Although there is a Redis Cluster currently in development to grow beyond a single machine's RAM requirements, anyone wanting to cluster Redis must currently roll their own with a client that supports it (like the Ruby driver we used in Day 2).

Parting Thoughts

Redis is chock-full of commands—more than 120 of them. Most commands are straightforward enough to understand by their names alone, once you get used to the idea that seemingly random letters will be removed (for example, INCRBY) or that mathematical precision can sometimes be more confusing than helpful (for example, ZCOUNT, or sorted set count, vs. SCARD, or set cardinality).

Redis is already becoming an integral part of many systems. Several open source projects rely on Redis, from Resque, a Ruby-based asynchronous job queueing service, to session management in the Node.js project SocketStream. Regardless of the database you choose as your SOR, you should certainly add Redis to the mix.

## CHAPTER 9

Wrapping Up

Now that we've made it through the databases, congratulations are in order! We hope that you've gained an appreciation for these seven challenging databases and their unique worldviews. If you use one in a project, we'll be happy. And if you decide to use multiple databases, as you saw at the end of the Redis chapter, we'll be ecstatic. We believe that the future of data management lies in the polyglot persistence model (using more than one database in a project), while the approach that sees a single general-purpose RDBMS as the only available design pattern slowly drifts away.

Let's take this opportunity to see where our seven databases fit together in the greater database ecosystem. By this point, we have explored the details of each and mentioned a few commonalities and differences. You'll see how they contribute to the vast and expanding landscape of data storage options.

Genres Redux

You've seen that how databases store their data can be largely divided into five genres: relational, key-value, columnar, document, and graph. Let's take a moment and recap their differences and see what each style is good for and not so good for—when you'd want to use them and when to avoid them.

Relational

This is the most common classic database pattern. Relational database management systems (RDBMSs) are set-theory-based systems implemented as two-dimensional tables with rows and columns. Relational databases strictly enforce type and are generally numeric, strings, dates, and uninterpreted blobs, but as you saw, PostgreSQL provides extensions such as array or cube.

Good For:

Because of the structured nature of relational databases, they make sense when the layout of the data is known in advance but how you plan to use that data later may not be. Or, in other words, you pay the organizational complexity up front to achieve query flexibility later. Many business problems are aptly modeled this way, from orders to shipments and from inventory to shopping carts. You may not know in advance how you'll want to query the data later—how many orders did we process in February?—but the data is quite regular in nature, so enforcing that regularity is helpful.

Not-So-Good For:

When your data is highly variable or deeply hierarchical, relational databases aren't the best fit. Because you must specify a schema up front, data problems that exhibit a high degree of record-to-record variation will be problematic. Consider developing a database to describe all the creatures in nature. Creating a full list of all features to account for (hasHair, numLegs, laysEggs, and so on) would be intractable. In such a case, you'd want a database that places fewer restrictions in advance on what you can put into it.

Key-Value

The key-value (KV) store was the simplest model we covered. KV maps simple keys—sometimes to simple values like strings, and sometimes to more complex values, like a huge hashtable. Because of their relative simplicity, this genre of database has the most flexibility of implementation. Hash lookups are fast, so in the case of Redis, speed was its primary concern. Hash lookups are also easily distributed, and so DynamoDB took advantage of this in its partitioning scheme. Of course, its simplicity can be a downside for any data with strict or complex modeling requirements.

Good For:

With little or no need to maintain indexes, key-value stores are often designed to be horizontally scalable, extremely fast, or both. They're particularly suited for problems where the data are not highly related. For example, in a web application, users' session data meet this criteria; each user's session activity will be different and largely unrelated to the activity of other users.

Not-So-Good For:

Often lacking indexes and scanning capabilities, KV stores won't help you if you need to be able to perform queries on your data, other than basic CRUD operations (Create, Read, Update, Delete).

Columnar

Columnar databases (aka *column-oriented* or *column family*) share many similarities with both KV and RDBMS stores. As with a key-value database, values are queried by matching keys. Like relational, their values are groups of zero or more columns, though each row is capable of populating however many it wants. Unlike either, columnar databases store like data by columns, rather than keeping data together by rows. Columns are inexpensive to add, versioning is trivial, and there is no real storage cost for unpopulated values. You saw how HBase is a classic implementation of this genre.

Good For:

Columnar databases have been traditionally developed with horizontal scalability as a primary design goal. As such, they're particularly suited to "Big Data" problems, living on clusters of tens, hundreds, or thousands of nodes. They also tend to have built-in support for features such as compression and versioning. The canonical example of a good columnar data storage problem is indexing web pages. Pages on the web are highly textual (which means that they benefit from compression), they tend to be somewhat interrelated, and they change over time (which means that they benefit from versioning).

Not-So-Good For:

Different columnar databases have different features and therefore different drawbacks. But one thing they have in common is that it's best to design your schema based on how you plan to query the data. This means you should have some idea in advance of how your data will be used, not just what it'll consist of. If data usage patterns can't be defined in advance—for example, fast ad hoc reporting—then a columnar database may not be the best fit.

Document

Document databases allow for any number of fields per object and even allow objects to be nested to any depth as values of other fields. The common representation of these objects is as JavaScript Object Notation (JSON), adhered to by both MongoDB and CouchDB—though this is by no means a conceptual requirement. Because documents don't relate to each other like relational databases, they are relatively easy to shard and replicate across several servers, making distributed implementations fairly common. MongoHQ tends to tackle availability by supporting the creation of datacenters that manage huge datasets for the web. Meanwhile, CouchDB focuses on being simple and durable, where availability is achieved by master-master replication of fairly autonomous nodes. There is high overlap between these projects.

Good For:

Document databases are suited to problems involving highly variable domains. When you don't know in advance what exactly your data will look like, document databases are a good bet. Also, because of the nature of documents, they often map well to object-oriented programming models. This means less impedance mismatch when moving data between the database model and application model.

Not-So-Good For:

If you're used to performing elaborate join queries on highly normalized relational database schemas, you'll find the capabilities of document databases lacking. A document should generally contain most or all of the relevant information required for normal use. So while in a relational database you'd naturally normalize your data to reduce or eliminate copies that can get out of sync, with document databases, denormalized data is the norm.

Graph

Graph databases are an emerging class of database that focuses more on the interrelation between data nodes than on the actual values stored in those nodes. Neo4j, our open source example, is growing in popularity for many social network applications. Unlike other database styles that group collections of like objects into common buckets, graph databases are more free-form—queries consist of following edges shared by two nodes or, aka *traversing* nodes. As more projects use them, graph databases are growing the straightforward social examples to occupy more nuanced use cases, such as recommendation engines, access control lists, and geographic data.

Good For:

Graph databases seem to be tailor-made for networking applications. The prototypical example is a social network, where nodes represent users who have various kinds of relationships to each other. Modeling this kind of data using any of the other styles is often a tough fit, but a graph database would accept it with relish. They are also perfect matches for an object-oriented system. If you can model your data on a whiteboard, you can model it in a graph.

Not-So-Good For:

Because of the high degree of interconnectedness between nodes, graph databases are generally not suitable for network partitioning. Spidering the graph quickly means you can't afford network hops to other database nodes, so graph databases don't scale out well. It's likely that if you use a graph database, it'll be one piece of a larger system, with the bulk of the data stored elsewhere and only the relationships maintained in the graph.

Making a Choice

As we said at the beginning, data is like oil. We sit upon a vast ocean of data, yet until it's refined into *information*, it's unusable (and with a more crude comparison, no pun intended, there's a lot of money in data these days). The ease of collecting and ultimately storing, mining, and refining the data out there starts with the database you choose.

Deciding which database to choose is often more complex than merely considering which genre maps best to a given domain's data. Though a social graph may seem to clearly function best with a graph database, if you're Facebook, you simply have far too much data to choose one. You are more likely going to choose a "Big Data" implementation, such as HBase or DynamoDB. This will force your hand into choosing a columnar or key-value store. In other cases, though you may believe a relational database is clearly the best option for bank transactions, it's worth knowing that Neo4j also supports ACID transactions, expanding your options.

These examples serve to point out that there are other avenues beyond genre to consider when choosing which database—or databases—best serve your problem scope. As a general rule, as the size of data increases, the capacity of certain database styles wane. Column-oriented database implementations are often built to scale across datacenters and support the largest "Big Data" sets, while graphs generally support the smallest. This is not always the case, however. DynamoDB is a large-scale key-value store meant to automatically shard data across hundreds or thousands of nodes without any need for user administration, while Redis was built to run on one—with the possibility of a few master-slave replicas or client-managed shards.

There are several more dimensions to consider when choosing a database, such as durability, availability, consistency, scalability, and security. You have to decide whether ad hoc queryability is important or if mapreduce will suffice. Do you prefer to use an HTTP/REST interface, or are you willing to require a driver for a custom binary protocol? Even smaller scope concerns, such as the existence of bulk data loaders, might be important for you to think about.

Where Do We Go from Here?

Scaling problems associated with modern applications now fall largely in the realm of data management. We have reached a point in the evolution of applications where the choice of framework, operating system, programming language, and so on matters less than ever. Hardware and storage get cheaper by the day and tools like virtual machines, the cloud, and containers make interoperation between servers and runtime operations ever more seamless, to the point where once-epochal decisions about languages and platforms are often driven as much by preference as by necessity.

But for reasons we've laid out throughout this book, database choices are different. Someday those choices may revolve around whims and preferences, but we won't get there for quite some time. If you want to scale your application in this day and age, you should think long and hard about which database, or databases, you choose, as that aspect of your application could end up being more of a bottleneck and break point than the languages, platforms, operating systems, and other tools you use. One of the core purposes of this book was to help you make this choice wisely.

Although the book has come to a close, we trust your interest in polyglot persistence and the world of non-relational databases is wide open. The next steps from here are to pursue in detail the databases that piqued your interest or continue learning about other NoSQL options, such as Cassandra, ArangoDB, Titan, or Google Cloud Datastore.

It's time to get your hands dirty.

Database Overview Tables

This book contains a wealth of information about each of the seven databases we discuss: PostgreSQL, HBase, MongoDB, CouchDB, Neo4j, DynamoDB, and Redis. In the pages that follow, you'll find tables that tally up these databases along a number of dimensions to present an overview of what's covered in more detail elsewhere in the book. Although the tables are not a replacement for a true understanding, they should provide you with an at-a-glance sense of what each database is capable of, where it falls short, and how it fits into the modern database landscape.

	Genre	Version	Datatypes	Data Relations
PostgreSQL	Relational	9.1	Predefined and typed	Predefined
HBase	Columnar	1.4.1	Predefined and typed	None
MongoDB	Document	3.6	Typed	None
CouchDB	Document	2.1.1	Typed	None
Neo4j	Graph	3.1.4 Enterprise	Untyped	Ad hoc (Edges)
DynamoDB	Key-value (or "key-value plus," for reasons explained in chapter 7)	API version 2012-08-10	Typed	Predefined tables (plus support for arbitrary fields)
Redis	Key-value	4.0	Semi-typed	None

	Standard Object	Written in Language	Interface Protocol	HTTP/REST
PostgreSQL	Table	C	Custom over TCP	No
HBase	Columns	Java	Thrift, HTTP	Yes
MongoDB	JSON	C++	Custom over TCP	Simple
CouchDB	JSON	Erlang	HTTP	Yes
Neo4j	Hash	Java	HTTP	Yes
DynamoDB	Table	Unknown	JSON over HTTP	Yes
Redis	String	C/C++	Simple text over TCP	No

	Ad Hoc Query	Mapreduce	Scalable	Durability
PostgreSQL	SQL	No	Cluster (via add-ons)	ACID
HBase	Weak	Hadoop	Datacenter	Write-ahead logging
MongoDB	Commands, mapreduce	JavaScript	Datacenter	Write-ahead journaling, Safe mode
CouchDB	Temporary views	JavaScript	Datacenter (via BigCouch)	Crash-only
Neo4j	Graph walking, Cypher, search	No (in the distributed sense)	Cluster (via HA)	ACID
DynamoDB	Limited range of SQL-style queries	No	Multi-datacenter	ACID
Redis	Commands	No	Cluster (via master-slave)	Append-only log

	Secondary Indexes	Versioning	Bulk Load	Very Large Files
PostgreSQL	Yes	No	COPY command	BLOBs
HBase	No	Yes	No	No
MongoDB	Yes	No	mongoimport	GridFS
CouchDB	Yes	Yes	Bulk Doc API	Attachments
Neo4j	Yes (via Lucene)	No	No	No
DynamoDB	Yes	Yes	No	Lewak (deprecated)
Redis	No	No	No	No

	Requires Compaction	Replication	Sharding	Concurrency
PostgreSQL	No	Master-slave	Add-ons (e.g., PL/Proxy)	Table/row writer lock
HBase	No	Master-slave	Yes via HDFS	Consistent per row
MongoDB	No	Master-slave (via replica sets)	Yes	Write lock
CouchDB	File rewrite	Master-master	Yes (with filters in BigCouch)	Lock-free MVCC
Neo4j	No	Master-slave (in Enterprise Edition)	No	Write lock
DynamoDB	No	Peer-based, master-master	Yes	Vector-clocks
Redis	Snapshot	Master-slave	Add-ons (e.g., client)	None

	Transactions	Triggers	Security	Multitenancy
PostgreSQL	ACID	Yes	Users/groups	Yes
HBase	Yes (when enabled)	No	Kerberos via Hadoop security	No
MongoDB	No	No	Users	Yes
CouchDB	No	Update validation or Changes API	Users	Yes
Neo4j	ACID	Transaction event handlers	None	No
DynamoDB	No	Pre/post-commits	None	No
Redis	Multi opera-tion queues	No	Passwords	No

	Main Differentiator	Weaknesses
PostgreSQL	Best of OSS RDBMS model	Distributed availability
HBase	Very large-scale, Hadoop infrastructure	Flexible growth, query-ability
MongoDB	Easily query *Big Data*	Embed-ability
CouchDB	Durable and embeddable clusters	Query-ability
Neo4j	Flexible graph	BLOBs or terabyte scale
DynamoDB	Highly available	Query-ability
Redis	Very, very fast	Complex data

The CAP Theorem

Understanding the five database genres is important when deciding on which database to use in a particular case, but there's one other major thing that you should always bear in mind. A recurring theme in this book has been the CAP theorem, which lays bare an unsettling truth about how distributed database systems behave in the face of network instability.

CAP proves that you can create a distributed database that can have one or more of the following qualities: It can be *consistent* (writes are atomic and all subsequent requests retrieve the new value), *available* (the database will always return a value as long as a single server is running), and/or *partition tolerant* (the system will still function even if server communication is temporarily lost—that is, a network partition). But the catch is that any given system can be *at most* two of these things at once, and *never* all three.

In other words, you can create a distributed database system that is *consistent* and *partition tolerant* (a "CP" system), a system that is *available* and *partition tolerant* (an "AP" system), or a system that is *consistent* and *available* (the much more rare CA system that is not *partition tolerant*—which basically means not distributed). Or a system can have only one of those qualities (this book doesn't cover any databases like that, and you're unlikely to encounter such a database in wide use). But at the end of the day it simply isn't possible to create a distributed database that is consistent and available and partition tolerant at the same time, and anyone who says that they've "solved CAP" is saying that they've defied the laws of physics and thus should not be trusted.

The CAP theorem is pertinent when considering a distributed database because it forces you to decide what you are willing to give up. The database you choose will lose either availability or consistency. Partition tolerance is strictly an architectural decision (depending on whether you want a distributed database). It's important to understand the CAP theorem to fully grok your options. The trade-offs made by the database implementations in this book are largely influenced by it.

> ### A CAP Adventure, Part I: CAP
>
> Imagine the world as a giant distributed database system. All of the land in the world contains information about certain topics, and as long as you're *somewhere* near people or technology, you can find an answer to your questions.
>
> Now, for the sake of argument, imagine you are a passionate Beyoncé fan and the date is September 5, 2016. Suddenly, while at your friend's beach house party celebrating the release of Beyoncé's hot new studio album, a freak tidal wave sweeps across the dock and drags you out to sea. You fashion a makeshift raft and wash up on a desert island days later. Without any means of communication, you are effectively *partitioned* from the rest of the system (the world). There you wait for five long years...
>
> One morning in 2021, you are awakened by shouts from the sea. A salty old schooner captain has discovered you! After five years alone, the captain leans over the bow and bellows: "How many studio albums does Beyoncé have?"
>
> You now have a decision to make. You can answer the question with the most recent value you have (which is now five years old). If you answer his query, you are *available*. Or, you can decline to answer the question, knowing that because you are partitioned, your answer may not be *consistent* with the current state of the world. The captain won't get his answer, but the state of the world remains consistent (if he sails back home, he can get the correct answer). In your role of queried node, you can either help keep the world's data *consistent* or be *available*, but *not both*.

Eventual Consistency

Distributed databases must be partition tolerant, so the choice between availability and consistency can be difficult. However, while CAP dictates that if you pick availability you cannot have true consistency, you can still provide *eventual consistency*.

The idea behind eventual consistency is that each node is always available to serve requests. As a trade-off, data modifications are propagated in the background to other nodes. This means that at any time the system may be inconsistent, but the data is still largely accurate.

The Internet's Domain Name Service (DNS) is a prime example of an eventually consistent system. You register a domain, and it may take a few days to propagate to all DNS servers across the Internet. But at no time is any particular DNS server unavailable (assuming you can connect to it, that is).

A CAP Adventure, Part II: Eventual Consistency

Let's rewind two years, back to 2009. You've been on the island for three years at this point, and you spot a bottle in the sand—precious contact with the outside world. You uncork it and rejoice! You've just received an integral piece of knowledge...

The number of studio albums Beyoncé has is of utmost importance to the world's aggregate knowledge. It's so important, in fact, that every time she releases a new album, someone writes the current date and the number on a piece of paper. They place that paper in a bottle and throw it out to sea. If someone, like yourself, is partitioned from the rest of the world on a desert island, they can *eventually* have the correct answer.

Skip forward to the present. When the ship captain asks, "How many studio albums does Beyoncé have?" you remain *available* and answer "three." You may be *inconsistent* with the rest of the world, but you are reasonably certain of your answer, having not yet received another bottle.

The story ends with the captain rescuing you, and you return home to find her new album and live happily ever after. As long as you remain on land, you needn't be partition tolerant and can remain consistent and available until the end of your days.

CAP in the Wild

The databases in this book largely occupy one corner or another of the CAP trade-off triangle. Redis, PostgreSQL, and Neo4J are consistent and available (CA); they don't distribute data and so partitioning is not an issue (though arguably, CAP doesn't make much sense in non-distributed systems). MongoDB and HBase are generally consistent and partition tolerant (CP). In the event of a network partition, they can become unable to respond to certain types of queries (for example, in a Mongo replica set you flag slaveok to false for reads). In practice, hardware failure is handled gracefully—other still-networked nodes can cover for the downed server—but strictly speaking, in the CAP theorem sense, they are unavailable. Finally, CouchDB is available and partition tolerant (AP). Even though two or more CouchDB servers can replicate data between them, CouchDB doesn't guarantee consistency between any two servers.

It's worth noting that most of these databases can be configured to change CAP type (Mongo can be CA, CouchDB can be CP), but here we've noted their default or common behaviors.

The Latency Trade-Off

There is more to distributed database system design than CAP, however. For example, low latency (speed) is a chief concern for many architects. If you read the Amazon Dynamo[1] paper, you'll notice a lot of talk about availability but also Amazon's latency requirements. For a certain class of applications, even a small latency change can translate to a large costs. Yahoo's PNUTS database famously gives up both availability on normal operation and consistency on partitions in order to squeeze a lower latency out of its design.[2] It's important to consider CAP when dealing with distributed databases, but it's equally important to be aware that distributed database theory does not stop there.

1.   http://allthingsdistributed.com/files/amazon-dynamo-sosp2007.pdf
2.   http://dbmsmusings.blogspot.com/2010/04/problems-with-cap-and-yahoos-little.html

Bibliography

[Tat10]   Bruce A. Tate. *Seven Languages in Seven Weeks*. The Pragmatic Bookshelf, Raleigh, NC, 2010.

Index

Thank you!

How did you enjoy this book? Please let us know. Take a moment and email us at support@pragprog.com with your feedback. Tell us your story and you could win free ebooks. Please use the subject line "Book Feedback."

Ready for your next great Pragmatic Bookshelf book? Come on over to https://pragprog.com and use the coupon code BUYANOTHER2018 to save 30% on your next ebook.

Void where prohibited, restricted, or otherwise unwelcome. Do not use ebooks near water. If rash persists, see a doctor. Doesn't apply to *The Pragmatic Programmer* ebook because it's older than the Pragmatic Bookshelf itself. Side effects may include increased knowledge and skill, increased marketability, and deep satisfaction. Increase dosage regularly.

And thank you for your continued support,

Andy Hunt, Publisher

More Seven in Seven

From Web Frameworks to Concurrency Models, see what the rest of the world is doing with this introduction to seven different approaches.

Seven Web Frameworks in Seven Weeks

Whether you need a new tool or just inspiration, *Seven Web Frameworks in Seven Weeks* explores modern options, giving you a taste of each with ideas that will help you create better apps. You'll see frameworks that leverage modern programming languages, employ unique architectures, live client-side instead of server-side, or embrace type systems. You'll see everything from familiar Ruby and JavaScript to the more exotic Erlang, Haskell, and Clojure.

Jack Moffitt, Fred Daoud
(302 pages) ISBN: 9781937785635. $38
https://pragprog.com/book/7web

Seven Concurrency Models in Seven Weeks

Your software needs to leverage multiple cores, handle thousands of users and terabytes of data, and continue working in the face of both hardware and software failure. Concurrency and parallelism are the keys, and *Seven Concurrency Models in Seven Weeks* equips you for this new world. See how emerging technologies such as actors and functional programming address issues with traditional threads and locks development. Learn how to exploit the parallelism in your computer's GPU and leverage clusters of machines with MapReduce and Stream Processing. And do it all with the confidence that comes from using tools that help you write crystal clear, high-quality code.

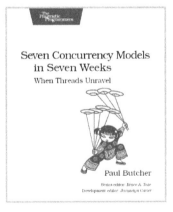

Paul Butcher
(296 pages) ISBN: 9781937785659. $38
https://pragprog.com/book/pb7con

Learn Why, Then Learn How

Get started on your Elixir journey today.

Adopting Elixir

Adoption is more than programming. Elixir is an exciting new language, but to successfully get your application from start to finish, you're going to need to know more than just the language. You need the case studies and strategies in this book. Learn the best practices for the whole life of your application, from design and team-building, to managing stakeholders, to deployment and monitoring. Go beyond the syntax and the tools to learn the techniques you need to develop your Elixir application from concept to production.

Ben Marx, José Valim, Bruce Tate
(242 pages) ISBN: 9781680502527. $42.95
https://pragprog.com/book/tvmelixir

Programming Elixir ≥ 1.6

This book is *the* introduction to Elixir for experienced programmers, completely updated for Elixir 1.6 and beyond. Explore functional programming without the academic overtones (tell me about monads just one more time). Create concurrent applications, but get them right without all the locking and consistency headaches. Meet Elixir, a modern, functional, concurrent language built on the rock-solid Erlang VM. Elixir's pragmatic syntax and built-in support for metaprogramming will make you productive and keep you interested for the long haul. Maybe the time is right for the Next Big Thing. Maybe it's Elixir.

Dave Thomas
(398 pages) ISBN: 9781680502992. $47.95
https://pragprog.com/book/elixir16

A Better Web with Phoenix and Elm

Elixir and Phoenix on the server side with Elm on the front end gets you the best of both worlds in both worlds!

Programming Phoenix ≥ 1.4

Don't accept the compromise between fast and beautiful: you can have it all. Phoenix creator Chris McCord, Elixir creator José Valim, and award-winning author Bruce Tate walk you through building an application that's fast and reliable. At every step, you'll learn from the Phoenix creators not just what to do, but why. Packed with insider insights and completely updated for Phoenix 1.4, this definitive guide will be your constant companion in your journey from Phoenix novice to expert, as you build the next generation of web applications.

Chris McCord, Bruce Tate and José Valim
(325 pages) ISBN: 9781680502268. $45.95
https://pragprog.com/book/phoenix14

Programming Elm

Elm brings the safety and stability of functional programing to front-end development, making it one of the most popular new languages. Elm's functional nature and static typing means that run-time errors are nearly impossible, and it compiles to JavaScript for easy web deployment. This book helps you take advantage of this new language in your web site development. Learn how the Elm Architecture will help you create fast applications. Discover how to integrate Elm with JavaScript so you can update legacy applications. See how Elm tooling makes deployment quicker and easier.

Jeremy Fairbank
(250 pages) ISBN: 9781680502855. $40.95
https://pragprog.com/book/jfelm

Better by Design

From architecture and design to deployment in the harsh realities of the real world, make your software better by design.

Design It!

Don't engineer by coincidence—design it like you mean it! Grounded by fundamentals and filled with practical design methods, this is the perfect introduction to software architecture for programmers who are ready to grow their design skills. Ask the right stakeholders the right questions, explore design options, share your design decisions, and facilitate collaborative workshops that are fast, effective, and fun. Become a better programmer, leader, and designer. Use your new skills to lead your team in implementing software with the right capabilities—and develop awesome software!

Michael Keeling
(358 pages) ISBN: 9781680502091. $41.95
https://pragprog.com/book/mkdsa

Release It! Second Edition

A single dramatic software failure can cost a company millions of dollars—but can be avoided with simple changes to design and architecture. This new edition of the best-selling industry standard shows you how to create systems that run longer, with fewer failures, and recover better when bad things happen. New coverage includes DevOps, microservices, and cloud-native architecture. Stability antipatterns have grown to include systemic problems in large-scale systems. This is a must-have pragmatic guide to engineering for production systems.

Michael Nygard
(376 pages) ISBN: 9781680502398. $47.95
https://pragprog.com/book/mnee2

Java in Depth

Get up to date on the latest Java 8 features, and take an in-depth look at concurrency options.

Functional Programming in Java

Get ready to program in a whole new way. *Functional Programming in Java* will help you quickly get on top of the new, essential Java 8 language features and the functional style that will change and improve your code. This short, targeted book will help you make the paradigm shift from the old imperative way to a less error-prone, more elegant, and concise coding style that's also a breeze to parallelize. You'll explore the syntax and semantics of lambda expressions, method and constructor references, and functional interfaces. You'll design and write applications better using the new standards in Java 8 and the JDK.

Venkat Subramaniam
(196 pages) ISBN: 9781937785468. $33
https://pragprog.com/book/vsjava8

Programming Concurrency on the JVM

Stop dreading concurrency hassles and start reaping the pure power of modern multicore hardware. Learn how to avoid shared mutable state and how to write safe, elegant, explicit synchronization-free programs in Java or other JVM languages including Clojure, JRuby, Groovy, or Scala.

Venkat Subramaniam
(280 pages) ISBN: 9781934356760. $35
https://pragprog.com/book/vspcon

Python and Data Science

For data science and basic science, for you and anyone else on your team.

Data Science Essentials in Python

Go from messy, unstructured artifacts stored in SQL and NoSQL databases to a neat, well-organized dataset with this quick reference for the busy data scientist. Understand text mining, machine learning, and network analysis; process numeric data with the NumPy and Pandas modules; describe and analyze data using statistical and network-theoretical methods; and see actual examples of data analysis at work. This one-stop solution covers the essential data science you need in Python.

Dmitry Zinoviev
(224 pages) ISBN: 9781680501841. $29
https://pragprog.com/book/dzpyds

Practical Programming, Third Edition

Classroom-tested by tens of thousands of students, this new edition of the best-selling intro to programming book is for anyone who wants to understand computer science. Learn about design, algorithms, testing, and debugging. Discover the fundamentals of programming with Python 3.6—a language that's used in millions of devices. Write programs to solve real-world problems, and come away with everything you need to produce quality code. This edition has been updated to use the new language features in Python 3.6.

Paul Gries, Jennifer Campbell, Jason Montojo
(410 pages) ISBN: 9781680502688. $49.95
https://pragprog.com/book/gwpy3

The Pragmatic Bookshelf

The Pragmatic Bookshelf features books written by developers for developers. The titles continue the well-known Pragmatic Programmer style and continue to garner awards and rave reviews. As development gets more and more difficult, the Pragmatic Programmers will be there with more titles and products to help you stay on top of your game.

Visit Us Online

This Book's Home Page
https://pragprog.com/book/pwrdata
Source code from this book, errata, and other resources. Come give us feedback, too!

Register for Updates
https://pragprog.com/updates
Be notified when updates and new books become available.

Join the Community
https://pragprog.com/community
Read our weblogs, join our online discussions, participate in our mailing list, interact with our wiki, and benefit from the experience of other Pragmatic Programmers.

New and Noteworthy
https://pragprog.com/news
Check out the latest pragmatic developments, new titles and other offerings.

Save on the eBook

Save on the eBook versions of this title. Owning the paper version of this book entitles you to purchase the electronic versions at a terrific discount.

PDFs are great for carrying around on your laptop—they are hyperlinked, have color, and are fully searchable. Most titles are also available for the iPhone and iPod touch, Amazon Kindle, and other popular e-book readers.

Buy now at *https://pragprog.com/coupon*

Contact Us

Online Orders:	*https://pragprog.com/catalog*
Customer Service:	*support@pragprog.com*
International Rights:	*translations@pragprog.com*
Academic Use:	*academic@pragprog.com*
Write for Us:	*http://write-for-us.pragprog.com*
Or Call:	+1 800-699-7764

CPSIA information can be obtained
at www.ICGtesting.com
Printed in the USA
BVHW070708180620
581663BV00007B/393